National and Regional Tourism Planning

7

The importance of effective tourism planning in ensuring economic benefit and sustainability is now widely recognized. This volume introduces concepts of national and regional tourism planning and looks at the basic approaches, techniques and principles applied at this level.

Divided into two sections, the book first explains basic planning concepts and describes planning and marketing methodologies. The discussion takes into account economic, environmental and socio-cultural factors in achieving sustainable development. Emphasis is placed on practical techniques and applications in implementing plans.

The second section offers a range of carefully selected international case studies drawn from WTO experience which illustrate the different elements of planning in practice and the issues involved.

Covering the essential principles and techniques of tourism planning, this volume is an important contribution to the understanding of tourism development and sustainability.

National and Regional Tourism Planning was developed with the assistance of WTO consultant **Edward Inskeep**, a California-based consultant who has wide experience in planning, research and training, and has worked on projects for the World Bank, the UNDP and the WTO. He has written extensively for both academic and professional audiences including the textbook *Tourism Planning: An integrated and sustainable development approach* (VNR).

National and Regional Tourism Planning

Methodologies and case studies

INTERNATIONAL THOMSON BUSINESS PRESS

I ⓉP® An International Thomson Publishing Company

London • Bonn • Boston • Johannesburg • Madrid • Melbourne • Mexico City • New York • Paris
Singapore • Tokyo • Toronto • Albany, NY • Belmont, CA • Cincinnati, OH • Detroit, MI

National and Regional Tourism Planning

Copyright ©1994 World Tourism Organisation

 A division of International Thomson Publishing Inc.
The ITP logo is a trademark under licence

British Library Cataloguing-in-Publication Data
A catalogue record for this book is available from the British Library

First edition 1994
Reprinted by Routledge 1995
Reprinted by International Thomson Business Press 1997

Typeset by J & L Composition Ltd., Filey, North Yorkshire
Printed in the UK by TJ International, Padstow, Cornwall

ISBN 0-415-10990-6

International Thomson Business Press
Berkshire House
168–173 High Holborn
London WC1V 7AA
UK

International Thomson Business Press
20 Park Plaza
13th Floor
Boston MA 02116
USA

http://www.itbp.com

Contents

Figures and table

FIGURES

TABLE

Introduction

It is now recognized that tourism must be developed and managed in a controlled, integrated and sustainable manner, based on sound planning. With this approach, tourism can generate substantial economic benefits to an area, without creating any serious environmental or social problems. Tourism's resources will be conserved for continuous use in the future.

There are numerous examples in the world where tourism has not been well planned and managed. These uncontrolled developments may have brought some short-term economic benefits. Over the longer term, however, they have resulted in environmental and social problems and poor quality tourist destinations. This has been detrimental to the area's residents, and tourist markets have been lost to better planned destinations elsewhere. Many of these places are now undergoing redevelopment. It is obviously better to plan for controlled development initially, and prevent problems from arising in the first place.

Tourism planning is carried out at all levels of development – international, national, regional and for specific areas and sites. This publication introduces concepts of national and regional planning, and the basic approaches, techniques and principles applied to this level. It is designed to be complementary to the recent WTO publication, *Sustainable Tourism Development: Guide for Local Planners*. That guide covers the issues, approaches, techniques and principles for tourism planning at the local level of planning. It encompasses planning for urban and community tourism, resorts, various special forms of tourism, tourist attractions, and management of tourism at the local level. In order to make each publication self-contained, there is necessarily some overlap between the contents of each document.

This national and regional tourism planning publication also complements two other recent WTO publications – *An Integrated Approach to Resort Development: Six Case Studies* and *Guidelines: Development of National Parks and Protected Areas for Tourism* (published in cooperation with UNEP). As is emphasized in those documents, resorts and parks must be planned and developed within their national and regional contexts.

National and regional planning lays the foundation for tourism development of a country and its regions. It establishes the policies, physical and institutional structures and standards for development to proceed in a logical manner. It also provides the basis for the continuous and effective management of tourism which is so essential for the long-term success of tourism.

This publication is divided into two parts. The first part briefly explains planning concepts and describes planning and marketing methodologies. Emphasis is placed on the integrated approach, balancing economic, environmental and socio-cultural factors, and achieving sustainable development. Importance is also given to techniques that need to be used in implementing plans. Without adopting and applying these techniques, tourism plans cannot be realized.

The second part presents case studies of tourism policies and plans which have actually been prepared and, for the most part, are being implemented. The case studies have been selected to represent the several different elements of plans that must be considered in integrated development. Most of the case studies are ones that have been prepared by the WTO for several countries and regions during the past decade.

One of the important functions of the WTO is its technical cooperation activities. The organization has assisted many countries throughout the world in preparing planning, marketing, economic and other types of tourism studies, advising on all aspects of tourism development, and training local tourism-related personnel. Both Parts I and II of this publication reflect the WTO's basic approach to planning for the integrated and sustainable development of tourism in its global technical cooperation activities.

The WTO hopes that this publication will provide tourism officials, planners and others involved in tourism with an understanding of national and regional tourism planning. Their application of sound planning practice can then provide the basis for their countries to achieve successful tourism development.

Part I

Tourism planning methodologies

Chapter 1

The importance of planning tourism

Planning tourism at all levels is essential for achieving successful tourism development and management. The experience of many tourism areas in the world has demonstrated that, on a long-term basis, the planned approach to developing tourism can bring benefits without significant problems, and maintain satisfied tourist markets. Places that have allowed tourism to develop without the benefit of planning are often suffering from environmental and social problems. These are detrimental to residents and unpleasant for many tourists, resulting in marketing difficulties and decreasing economic benefits. These uncontrolled tourism areas cannot effectively compete with planned tourist destinations elsewhere. They usually can be redeveloped, based on a planned approach, but that requires much time and financial investment.

Tourism is a rather complicated activity that overlaps several different sectors of the society and economy. Without planning, it may create unexpected and unwanted impacts. Tourism is also still a relatively new type of activity in many countries. Some governments and often the private sector have little or no experience in how to develop tourism properly. For countries that do not yet have much tourism, planning can provide the necessary guidance for its development. For those places that already have some tourism, planning is often needed to revitalize this sector and maintain its future viability.

First, tourism should be planned at the national and regional levels. At these levels, planning is concerned with tourism development policies, structure plans, facility standards, institutional factors and all the other elements necessary to develop and manage tourism. Then, within the framework of national and regional planning, more detailed plans for tourist attractions, resorts, urban, rural and other forms of tourism development can be prepared.

There are several important specific benefits of undertaking national and regional tourism planning. These advantages include:

- Establishing the overall tourism development objectives and policies – what is tourism aiming to accomplish and how can these aims be achieved.

- Developing tourism so that its natural and cultural resources are indefinitely maintained and conserved for future, as well as present, use.
- Integrating tourism into the overall development policies and patterns of the country or region, and establishing close linkages between tourism and other economic sectors.
- Providing a rational basis for decision-making by both the public and private sectors on tourism development.
- Making possible the coordinated development of all the many elements of the tourism sector. This includes inter-relating the tourist attractions, activities, facilities and services and the various and increasingly fragmented tourist markets.
- Optimizing and balancing the economic, environmental and social benefits of tourism, with equitable distribution of these benefits to the society, while minimizing possible problems of tourism.
- Providing a physical structure which guides the location, types and extent of tourism development of attractions, facilities, services and infrastructure.
- Establishing the guidelines and standards for preparing detailed plans of specific tourism development areas that are consistent with, and reinforce, one another, and for the appropriate design of tourist facilities.
- Laying the foundation for effective implementation of the tourism development policy and plan and continuous management of the tourism sector, by providing the necessary organizational and other institutional framework.
- Providing the framework for effective coordination of the public and private sector efforts and investment in developing tourism.
- Offering a baseline for the continuous monitoring of the progress of tourism development and keeping it on track.

The planned approach to developing tourism at the national and regional levels is now widely adopted as a principle, although implementation of the policies and plans is still weak in some places. Many countries and regions of countries have had tourism plans prepared. Other places do not yet have plans, but should consider undertaking planning in the near future. In some countries, plans had previously been prepared but these are now outdated. They need to be revised based on present day circumstances and likely future trends. Founded on accumulated experience, the approaches and techniques of tourism planning are now reasonably well understood. There is considerable assurance that, if implemented, planning will bring substantial benefits to an area.

Chapter 2

Approaches to tourism planning

It is important to understand the basic approaches to planning and managing tourism development. These are described in the following sections.

PLANNING TOURISM AS AN INTEGRATED SYSTEM

An underlying concept in planning tourism is that tourism should be viewed as an inter-related system of demand and supply factors. The tourism system is illustrated in Figure 2.1. The demand factors are international and domestic tourist markets and local residents who use the tourist attractions, facilities and services. The supply factors comprise tourist attractions and activities, accommodation and other tourist facilities and services. Attractions include natural, cultural and special types of features – such as theme parks, zoos, botanic gardens and aquariums – and the activities related to these attractions. Accommodation includes hotels, motels, guest houses and other types of places where tourists stay overnight. The category of other tourist facilities and services includes tour and travel operations, restaurants, shopping, banking and money exchange, and medical and postal facilities and services. These supply factors are called the tourism product.

Other elements also relate to supply factors. In order to make the facilities and services usable, infrastructure is required. Tourism infrastructure particularly includes transportation (air, road, rail, water, etc.), water supply, electric power, sewage and solid waste disposal, and telecommunications.

DEMAND FACTORS

- International tourist markets
- Domestic tourist markets
- Residents' use of tourist attractions, facilities and services

SUPPLY FACTORS

- Attractions and activities
- Accommodation
- Other tourist facilities and services
- Transportation
- Other infrastructure
- Institutional elements

Figure 2.1 The tourism system

Provision of adequate infrastructure is also important to protect the environment. It helps maintain a high level of environmental quality that is so necessary for successful tourism and desirable for residents.

The effective development, operation and management of tourism requires certain institutional elements. These elements include:

- Organizational structures, especially government tourism offices and private sector tourism associations such as hotel associations.
- Tourism-related legislation and regulations, such as standards and licensing requirements for hotels and tour and travel agencies.
- Education and training programmes, and training institutions to prepare persons to work effectively in tourism.
- Availability of financial capital to develop tourist attractions, facilities, services and infrastructure, and mechanisms to attract capital investment.
- Marketing strategies and promotion programmes to inform tourists about the country or region, and induce them to visit it, and tourist information facilities and services in the destination areas.
- Travel facilitation of immigration (including visa arrangements), customs and other facilities and services at the entry and exit points of tourists.

The institutional elements also include consideration of how to enhance and distribute the economic benefits of tourism, environmental protection measures, reducing adverse social impacts, and conservation of the cultural heritage of people living in the tourism areas.

As an inter-related system, it is important that tourism planning aim for integrated development of all these parts of the system, both the demand and supply factors and the physical and institutional elements. The system will function much more effectively and bring the desired benefits if it is planned in an integrated manner, with coordinated development of all the components of the system. Sometimes, this integrated system approach is also called the comprehensive approach to tourism planning because all the elements of tourism are considered in the planning and development process.

Just as important as planning for integration within the tourism system is planning for integration of tourism into the overall development policies, plans and patterns of a country or region. Planning for this overall integration will, for example, resolve any potential conflicts over use of certain resources or locations for various types of development. It also provides for the multi-use of expensive infrastructure to serve general community needs as well as tourism.

Emphasis is given to formulating and adopting tourism development policies and plans for an area in order to guide decision-making on development actions. The planning of tourism, however, should also be recognized as a continuous and flexible process. Within the framework of the policy and plan recommendations, there must be flexibility to allow for adapting to changing circumstances. Planning that is too rigid may not allow development to be responsive to changes. There may be advancements in transportation technology, evolution of new forms of tourism and changes in market trends. Even though allowed to be flexible, the basic objectives of the plan should not be abrogated although the specific development patterns may be changed. Sustainable development must still be maintained.

Planning for tourism development should make recommendations that are imaginative and innovative, but they must also be feasible to implement. The various techniques of implementation should be considered throughout the planning process. This approach ensures that the recommendations can be accomplished, and provides the basis for specifying the implementation techniques that should be applied. Implementation techniques can also be imaginative and not only rely on established approaches. It is common practice for a tourism plan to include specification of implementation techniques, and sometimes a separate manual on how to achieve the plan recommendations.

PLANNING FOR SUSTAINABLE DEVELOPMENT

The underlying approach now applied to tourism planning, as well as to other types of development, is that of achieving sustainable development. The sustainable development approach implies that the natural, cultural and other resources of tourism are conserved for continuous use in the future, while still bringing benefits to the present society. The concept of sustainable development has received much emphasis internationally since the early 1980s, although tourism plans prepared even before that period often were concerned with conservation of tourism resources.

The sustainable development approach to planning tourism is acutely important because most tourism development depends on attractions and activities related to the natural environment, historic heritage and cultural patterns of areas. If these resources are degraded or destroyed, then the tourism areas cannot attract tourists and tourism will not be successful. More generally, most tourists seek destinations that have a high level of environmental quality – they like to visit places that are attractive, clean and neither polluted nor congested. It is also essential that residents of the tourism area should not have to suffer from a deteriorated environment and social problems.

One of the important benefits of tourism is that, if it is properly developed based on the concept of sustainability, tourism can greatly help justify and pay for conservation of an area's natural and cultural resources. Thus, tourism can be an important means of achieving conservation in areas that otherwise have limited capability to accomplish environmental protection and conservation objectives.

A basic technique in achieving sustainable development is the environmental planning approach. Environmental planning requires that all elements of the environment be carefully surveyed, analyzed and considered in determining the most appropriate type and location of development. This approach would not allow, for example, intensive development in flood plain and steep hillside areas.

An important aspect of sustainable development is emphasizing community-based tourism. This approach to tourism focuses on community involvement in the planning and development process, and developing the types of tourism which generate benefits to local communities. It applies techniques to ensure that most of the benefits of tourism development accrue to local residents and not to outsiders. Maximizing benefits to local residents typically results in tourism being better accepted by them and their actively supporting conservation of local tourism resources. The community-based tourism approach is applied at the local or more detailed levels of planning, but it can be set forth as a policy approach at the national and regional levels. The benefits accruing to local communities are also beneficial to the country, through the income and foreign exchange earned, employment generated and support that local communities give to national tourism development and conservation policies.

Also related to sustainable development is the concept of quality tourism. This approach is being increasingly adopted for two fundamental reasons – it can achieve successful tourism from the marketing standpoint and it brings benefits to local residents and their environment. Quality tourism does not necessarily mean expensive tourism. Rather, it refers to tourist attractions, facilities and services that offer 'good value for money', protect tourism resources, and attract the kinds of tourists who will respect the local environment and society. Quality tourism development can compete more effectively in attracting discriminating tourists. It is also more environmentally and socially self-sustaining. Achieving quality tourism is the responsibility of both the public and private sectors. This concept should be built into the tourism planning, development and management process.

LONG-RANGE AND STRATEGIC PLANNING

Long-range comprehensive planning is concerned with specifying goals and objectives and determining preferred future development patterns. Tourism development policies and plans should be prepared for relatively long-term periods – usually for 10 to 15 and sometimes 20 years – depending on the predictability of future events in the country or region. These may seem to be long planning periods, but it commonly requires this length of time to implement basic policy and structure plans. Even development of specific projects, such as major resorts or national park-based tourism, can require a long time.

A planning approach which has received considerable attention in recent years, and is applicable to some tourism areas, is strategic planning. While the

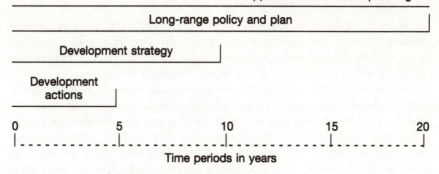

Figure 2.2 Long-range and strategic planning

outcomes of strategic and long-range comprehensive planning may be very similar, strategic planning is somewhat different. It focuses more on identification and resolution of immediate issues. Strategic planning typically is more oriented to rapidly changing future situations and how to cope with changes organizationally. It is more action oriented and concerned with handling unexpected events.

Applied only by itself, strategic planning can be less comprehensive in its approach. By focusing on immediate issues, it may deviate from achieving such long-term objectives as sustainable development. But if used within the framework of integrated long-range policy and planning, the strategic planning approach can be very appropriate. The relationship between long-range and strategic planning is illustrated, in a simple manner, in Figure 2.2.

PUBLIC INVOLVEMENT IN PLANNING

Planning is for the benefit of people, and they should be involved in the planning and development of tourism in their areas. Through this involvement, tourism development will reflect a consensus of what the people want. Also, if residents are involved in planning and development decisions – and if they understand the benefits the tourism can bring – they will more likely support it. At the national and regional levels of preparing tourism plans, the common approach to obtaining public involvement is to appoint a steering committee. This committee offers guidance to the planning team and reviews its work, especially the draft reports and policy and planning recommendations that are made. A planning study steering committee is typically composed of representatives of the relevant government agencies involved in tourism, the private sector, and community, religious and other relevant organizations.

Also, open public hearings can be held on the plan. These hearings provide the opportunity for anybody to learn about the plan and express their opinions. Another common approach, when the plan is completed, is to organize a national or regional tourism seminar. This meeting informs participants and the general public about the importance of controlled tourism development and the recommendations of the plan. Such seminars often receive wide publicity in the communications media.

In a large country or region, the usual procedure is for the tourism plan to be prepared by the central authority with public involvement as described above. This can be termed the 'top-down' approach. Another procedure sometimes used is the 'bottom-up' approach. This involves holding meetings with local districts or communities to determine what type of development they would like to have. These local objectives and ideas are then fitted together into a national or regional plan. This approach achieves greater local public involvement in the planning process. But it is more time consuming and may lead to conflicting objectives, policies and development recommendations among the local areas. These conflicts need to be reconciled at the national and regional levels in order to form a consistent plan. It is important that the development patterns of the local areas complement and reinforce one another, but also reflect the needs and desires of local communities. Often a combination of the 'top-down' and 'bottom-up' approaches achieves the best results.

Chapter 3

The tourism planning process

The process for preparing tourism plans at the national and regional levels – based on the sustainable, integrated and implementable approaches described in Chapter 2 – can be described as a step-by-step procedure. This procedure, which is applicable to any national and regional planning situation, is illustrated in Figure 3.1 and explained in the following sections.

STUDY PREPARATION

The first step in the planning process is careful preparation of the study so that it provides the type of development guidance that is needed. Study preparation involves formulating the project terms of reference, selecting the technical team to carry out the study, appointing a steering committee, and organizing the study activities.

The terms of reference (TOR) for the planning study should be carefully formulated so that the study achieves its desired results and outputs. The TOR for a national or regional plan indicates the outputs and activities that are necessary to prepare the development policy and plan. The special considerations to be made in planning – such as economic, environmental or social issues and the critical institutional elements – should be specified in the TOR. Identification of implementation techniques are also specified. The TOR format typically follows the planning process explained here, but it is tailored to the specific characteristics and needs of the planning area.

Many places already have some limited tourism development, and these existing patterns must be considered in formulating the TOR. Other countries or regions will have considerable existing tourism development, but it may be declining or not be in a form that generates optimum benefits. The TOR will therefore emphasize how to rejuvenate and improve existing development, along with how to provide guidance on the future expansion of tourism.

It is common for a single study to include various levels of tourism planning, such as national and regional plans along with detailed planning for priority development areas and projects. The planning for all these levels will need to be specified in the TOR. An advantage of including various levels of

| Study preparation→ | Determination of objectives → | Survey of all elements → | Analysis and synthesis → |

| Policy and plan formulation → | Formulation of other recommendations → | Implementation and monitoring |

Figure 3.1 Tourism planning process

planning in one study is that there is greater continuity and consistency of the recommended development patterns. However, for detailed planning, only those areas and projects to be developed in the near future should be included in the overall study. The longer-term development areas and projects should be planned in detail later, based on circumstances prevailing at that time.

The TOR should indicate a horizon year when the plan and its targets and recommendations are to be realized. As indicated in Chapter 2, planning horizon years are typically for 10, 15 to 20 years. Development phasing or staging – usually for five-year periods – should be specified. Establishing a horizon year and staging periods provides a time framework for making projections, setting targets and phasing development.

Appendix 1 explains other aspects of preparation and organization that are essential to carry out a successful planning study.

DETERMINATION OF OBJECTIVES

Early in the planning process, the objectives of developing tourism should be determined. Deciding on objectives is very important because they state the desired results of developing tourism in the country or region. Objectives usually relate to various types of socio-economic benefits. They also specify the special considerations that must be made in tourism development, such as minimizing negative environmental and socio-cultural impacts. Objectives should be determined in close consultation with the government (or steering committee) because they are basic determinants of the tourism development policies and plan.

Objectives are first established in a preliminary manner. They are later refined based on the results of the surveys and analyses and the plan formulation. Certain preliminary objectives may be found to be in conflict with one another, and they cannot all realistically be achieved. For example, one objective may state that the economic benefits of tourism should be maximized, and another objective may stipulate that environmental and socio-cultural impacts must be minimized and sustainable development maintained. It may not be possible to prepare a policy and plan that simultaneously achieves both of these objectives, at least over the long-term period. The objectives must balance economic, environmental and socio-cultural considerations.

Tourism development objectives should also reflect and reinforce any general development objectives already adopted for the country or region. This is important so that tourism is well integrated into overall development patterns. In some cases, however, it may be decided to modify the general objectives in order to achieve those tourism objectives that seem to be reasonable, and contribute to overall national and regional development.

SURVEY OF ALL ELEMENTS

The survey stage of the planning process involves collecting data, both quantitative and qualitative, on all relevant aspects of tourism. These include the components of the tourism system and other factors as follows:

- Global and regional tourism patterns and trends. Regional here refers to several geographically related countries such as Africa, East and South Asia, Pacific Islands, North and South America, Western Europe, etc. This information can be obtained from the World Tourism Organization.
- Characteristics of existing or potential competing tourist destinations that offer similar tourism products and attract much the same tourist markets.
- Tourist arrival trends in the planning study country or region. These include the number and characteristics of tourist arrivals.
- Existing and potential tourist attractions and activities.
- Existing and already planned tourist accommodation and other tourist facilities and services.
- Existing and already planned transportation facilities and services, including both access to the country or region and the internal transportation system.
- Other types of infrastructure which are existing or already planned.
- Existing natural resource, land use and land tenure patterns. Land tenure refers to land ownership or leasing patterns.
- Existing economic and employment patterns, including employment in tourism, and economic and manpower development plans.
- Physical and social development plans – these are sometimes combined with the economic and manpower development plans listed above.
- Environmental characteristics and environmental quality. Environmental characteristics include such factors as climatic patterns and topography. Environmental quality includes the extent of air, water, noise and visual pollution, congestion, architectural interest and other factors.
- Socio-cultural patterns, especially as they relate to the effects of tourism development on the local societies and cultural patterns.
- Existing and already planned education and training programmes and training institutions designed to prepare persons to work in tourism.
- Existing government and private sector organizations in tourism, and their organizational structures and staffing.

- Present investment policies and availability of capital for investment in tourist facilities, services and infrastructure.
- Present tourism legislation and regulations.

One of the most important elements of the survey is that of tourist attractions and activities. These are what induce tourists to visit the country or region. Tourist attractions and related activities are categorized by type, and evaluated with respect to accessibility, feasibility of development, market trends of what tourists want to see and do, and other factors. They are also identified as primary attractions – those which basically attract tourists to visit the place (if the attractions are properly conserved and developed with facilities), or as secondary ones – those attractions which are less important but complement the primary attractions and increase touristic interest and length of stay.

For many of these elements – such as tourist attractions and activities, accommodation, other tourist facilities and services and some types of infrastructure – field surveys are required. These surveys should include evaluation of the elements along with noting their characteristics. Evaluation of tourist attractions was described above. Tourist facilities and services must also be evaluated as to their suitability, quality and efficiency to serve tourists properly. Infrastructure must be assessed as to how adequately it serves tourism development. Often market surveys are conducted, with visits made to interview tour operators in the market source countries.

Other types of surveys require document research and discussion meetings with local persons. Some of the types of surveys – such as for infrastructure, natural resources, land use and land tenure patterns and environmental characteristics – are carried out generally at the national and regional levels. They are conducted more specifically in the detailed planning for tourism development areas such as resorts.

ANALYSIS AND SYNTHESIS

Both quantitative and qualitative analysis and synthesis of the survey information must be carefully carried out. Synthesis refers to combining and integrating the various components of the analysis, in order to obtain a more comprehensive understanding of the situation. Major aspects of the analysis and synthesis are described as follows:

- The market analysis is derived from several sources. The survey of global, national and regional tourism patterns and market trends is essential input. The survey and evaluation of the tourist attractions, facilities and services in the study area is also very important. The tourism development objectives must be considered. Accessibility to the country or region from the major tourist markets areas, including cost, distance and convenience of travel, is a very important factor too. However, accessibility can often be improved if it is presently a problem. The market analysis includes establishing market targets of the number and types of tourists that potentially can be attracted, but only if the development and marketing recommendations are implemented. Market targets are usually established by five-year periods, up to the horizon year of the plan.

- Several calculations can be made from the market analysis. The number and types of accommodation required are projected, and other tourist facilities and services needed are identified. Analysis of the economic impact of tourism is derived from the market targets and tourist characteristics. This includes the projection of the number and type of employees needed to work in tourism. Appendix 2 explains how accommodation needs are projected.
- Based on the projection of tourist facilities and services needed and the movement patterns of tourists, the transportation and other infrastructure facilities and services required can be determined.
- From several of the surveyed elements, the integrated analysis or synthesis of physical, economic and social factors is prepared. This synthesis provides much of the basis for formulating the structure plan. It includes establishing carrying capacities, an essential consideration in achieving sustainable tourism development. The carrying capacity of an area is the maximum level of development or use that the area can absorb without resulting in serious environmental damage, socio-economic problems, or decline in the quality of visitor experience. Appendix 3 explains how carrying capacity is calculated.
- All the institutional elements are evaluated and analysed as a basis for formulating policy and recommendations about each of them.

An important type of synthesis is identification of major opportunities and problems or constraints for developing tourism. This provides a focus for formulating recommendations, and how to take advantage of opportunities and overcome constraints, all leading to better development of tourism.

The offerings of possible competing destinations that have similar tourism products and markets should be evaluated. There may be sufficient growth in the tourist markets to satisfy the needs for tourists in both the country or region being planned and competing destinations. But there may not be that much market growth. If the planning study area can offer some comparative advantages over competing destinations in its development of attractions, facilities and services, it will be better positioned to attract the desired numbers and types of tourists.

POLICY AND PLAN FORMULATION

This step in the planning process involves formulating policy on tourism development and preparing the physical structure plan. The best approach to policy and plan formulation is first to prepare and evaluate alternative development scenarios. There is seldom a single ideal set of policies and plans, but rather optimum ones that balance costs and benefits. Alternative policies and plans are evaluated according to several factors – meeting the development objectives; optimizing economic benefits; reinforcing positive and minimizing negative environmental and socio-cultural impacts; and effectively competing with other tourist destinations. Based on this evaluation, the final policies and plans are selected and refined.

Policy and plan formulation should be carried out in close consultation with the steering committee and other interested parties, in order to ensure that they reflect a consensus about the most appropriate future tourism development patterns.

FORMULATION OF THE INSTITUTIONAL RECOMMENDATIONS

Based on the survey, analysis and evaluation of the institutional elements, conclusions and recommendations can be made. For many types of recommendations, alternatives must be evaluated before the most suitable ones can be determined. There may be no need for changes in some of these elements, but this fact should be stated. In certain cases, alternative recommendations, all of which are acceptable, can be made. The government or private sector can later decide on which course of action to pursue, depending on future circumstances. It is also essential to involve the steering committee and other interested parties in formulating the institutional recommendations.

IMPLEMENTATION AND MONITORING

The final step in the planning process is specifying implementation techniques. As referred to in Chapter 2, the means of implementation should be considered throughout the planning process, and especially during the formulation of the policy, plan and other recommendations. This is important so that the final plan and recommendations are realistic to achieve and implementable. During and after implementation, tourism development must be monitored to ensure that it is accomplishing the objectives and achieving the recommended policies. Monitoring will detect any problems that arise so that remedial measures can be taken before the problems become serious.

ELEMENTS OF A COMPREHENSIVE TOURISM PLAN

An integrated and comprehensive national or regional tourism plan contains many different elements. Appendix 4 presents a checklist of the elements that should be included in a typical tourism plan. This can serve as a guide for ensuring that all the necessary elements are considered in preparing the plan.

Chapter 4

Forms of tourism development

In formulating the tourism policy and plan, it is important to understand the different forms of tourism development and types of tourism related to specific travel motivations that can be considered for the country or region. The forms of tourism described in the following sections are mostly those which represent the planned development approach. Some of them have also developed spontaneously, but often with problems resulting from lack of planning and development controls, and they require planned rejuvenation.

RESORTS

One of the most common forms of modern holiday tourism is some type of resort-based development. A tourist resort can be defined as a destination area that is relatively self-contained. It typically provides a wide range of tourist facilities and services including those designed for recreation and relaxation. Because of the present trend of more tourists wanting to participate in recreation, sports, cultural and other activities, resorts are now emphasizing the provision of a wide variety of facilities and services. These often include major commercial and conference/meeting facilities.

Some resorts, located where there are seasonal differences in climate (summer and winter or dry and rainy), have traditionally experienced wide seasonal variations in guest arrivals. The current trend is for these resorts to offer facilities and services for year-round use, often catering to different types of guests during the different seasons. In addition to containing their own facilities for tourist use, many resorts also serve as a base for tourists to take sightseeing trips to points of interest in the nearby area.

Resorts have their primary orientation to several types of attractions and activities – beach relaxation and recreation; marine sports in both lake and ocean coastal areas; water recreation and sports on rivers; mountain winter skiing and summer hiking and horse riding; golf and tennis sports; health facilities related to mineral springs (spas) or dry sunny climate; important archaeological and historic sites and national parks; or a combination of features. Some resorts are very large with a variety of types of accommodation, including self-catering units, and many recreation and commercial facilities. Other resorts may be composed of only one hotel but still offer a range of facilities, services and activities. 'Retreat' type resorts may be small and isolated, but they provide a high quality level of facilities and services. They cater to guests who want a quiet remote environment. Holiday villages are a type of resort.

Integrated resorts are ones which have been carefully planned as single entities, even though larger integrated resorts are usually constructed in phases over a long period of time. Most new resort areas are carefully planned to function efficiently and provide an interesting environment for tourists while not generating any serious environmental and social problems. Many unplanned resorts also exist in various parts of the world, but some of these are experiencing environmental and social problems and require redevelopment.

Town resorts combine the usual land uses and activities of a town community, but are economically focused on resort activities. They include hotels, other types of accommodation and a variety of tourist facilities and services. They contain or are located near major attraction features, such as beaches or ski facilities. Town resorts were often not initially planned as integrated developments. Many of these places are now undergoing redevelopment and applying controls in order to improve their environmental quality and economic viability. Some recently developed planned resorts include new towns where the resort support population lives. These then function as viable resort towns.

URBAN TOURISM

Tourism in towns and cities is very widespread. These urban places often offer a broad range of historic and cultural attractions, shopping, restaurants and the appeal of urban vitality. Many urban attractions and amenities are primarily developed to serve residents, but their use by tourists can greatly help to support them. Additionally, urban areas may function as points of arrival and departure of tourists to the country or region, and serve as a base for tourists to take excursions to nearby areas. Hotels and other tourist facilities are an integral part of the urban fabric and serve both business and holiday travellers.

Urban tourism must also be carefully planned. Determination must be made of the location of hotels and other tourist facilities, location and development of attraction features, the additional infrastructure required for them, and perhaps institutional improvements. It is now common practice to develop or redevelop certain urban areas – such as historic districts and waterfront sites – which are oriented particularly to tourism and residents' leisure use. Major convention and sports facilities are often developed to attract more tourists.

SPECIAL INTEREST AND ADVENTURE TOURISM

One of the rapidly expanding types of tourism is special interest and adventure tourism. This type of tourism reflects the increasing fragmentation of tourist markets. Special interest tourism refers to tourists, usually in small groups, who are travelling to learn about and experience particular features of an area. These special interest themes are often associated with the tourists' long-term avocational or professional/vocational interests.

Special interest tourism can focus on a wide range of features. Cultural themes include dance, music, drama, fine arts, handicrafts, architecture, archaeology, history and historic routes, traditional life styles, and unusual economic activities. Nature themes relate to flora, fauna, geology, scenic beauty, national parks and marine environments. Professional interests involve visits to meet people of similar professions and exchange ideas. Educational tours are a type of special interest tourism. Participatory activities are common, such as tourists working under supervision at an archaeological site excavation.

Adventure tourism involves the tourists engaging in physically and personally challenging and sometimes dangerous activities. These include safaris and trekking in remote areas, hiking, mountain climbing, river rafting and white water boating through river rapids. Hunting and fishing may be considered as an aspect of special interest and adventure tourism.

Related to special interest tourism is a form that has been variously termed alternative, responsible, appropriate and even sustainable tourism. (However, the tourism development approach used in this publication is that all forms of tourism should be planned to be responsible, appropriate and sustainable.) This form of tourism refers to small-scale, non-conventional types of development, including the following:

- Village tourism – small groups of tourists staying in or near traditional, often remote, villages, and learning about village life and the local environment. Facilities are owned and managed by the villagers.
- Rural, farm or agrotourism – tourists staying with farm families and learning about farming activities, or staying on tropical plantations and learning about plantation life and activities, or staying in fishing villages with fishermen's families and going on fishing trips.
- Walking and cycling tours – tourists travelling by walking or bicycling and staying in inns, hostels, private homes or bed and breakfast houses, meeting local people and learning about the culture and environment.
- Ecotourism (a controlled form of nature tourism) – tourists hiking or boating in natural areas, with local guides to explain about the flora, fauna and ecology. Ecotourism may also include visits to local villages and farms. This type of tourism is currently receiving much attention because of its emphasis on environmental conservation and learning about nature.
- Community assistance programmes – small groups of tourists, often

community organizations in their home countries, visiting an area and assisting local people with a particular development project such as building low-cost housing or constructing a village water supply.

OTHER FORMS OF TOURISM

There are several other forms of tourism that are suitable in many places. These include:

- Water transport tourism – cruise ship travel, boating on rivers and canals and yachting, all of which are very popular in certain regions of the world. Shore-based facilities of piers, docks and marinas and related facilities and services are required for this type of tourism.
- Residential tourism – development of various types of housing, and related community facilities and services, for use as vacation or retirement homes. This is a very common form of tourism.
- Camping and caravan tourism – development of camping facilities, usually near an important attraction or recreation feature, and caravan or parks for recreational vehicles located along highways or near attractions.
- Transportation-oriented tourism – hotels and other tourist facilities and services located near major transportation centres, especially airports for transit passengers. Airport-related tourism development is now providing meeting facilities for business travellers. Associated with road travel is the development of motels along major highways, especially in the peripheral areas of towns and cities and at major highway intersections.
- Youth tourism – travel by young people and students for education, sports and recreation has long been an established form of tourism and is currently being encouraged in many countries. Youth tourism requires development of inexpensive accommodation, often hostels or dormitories. 'Elderhostel' programmes for older people undertaking educational travel and staying in hostel-type accommodation are also popular.

Not related to any particular form of tourism, but based on specialized travel motivations, are the following important types of tourism:

- Religious tourism – travel by pilgrims to places of religious significance, such as the Hajj to Mecca and visits to the Vatican in Rome and Varanasi in India, is very important in some countries. Religious pilgrims often require tourist-type facilities and services.
- Ethnic tourism – as used here, refers to persons who are visiting their own original homelands or places of their ancestral origin. Some countries are encouraging persons who have migrated overseas to visit their homelands as an important type of tourist market.
- Nostalgic tourism – persons visiting places where they previously had been involved in some activity. Visits by Americans and Japanese to places

where they were assigned and fought in World War II is an example of nostalgic tourism. Nostalgic tourism may be important in an area for only a limited period of time.

As can be seen, many of these forms of tourism, especially those related to special interest and sightseeing activities, depend heavily on the natural and cultural resources of a tourism area. Consequently, environmental and cultural heritage conservation and interpretation is one of the major themes of contemporary tourism development. Many of the techniques that have been developed for interpretation of heritage sites are quite imaginative in educating visitors in an interesting and entertaining manner.

Chapter 5

Policy considerations and structure planning

Tourism development policy establishes the basis for developing and managing tourism and is an essential element of national or regional tourism planning. The structure plan provides the physical framework for the type and location of development. This chapter describes how the policy and structure plan are formulated.

FORMULATING TOURISM DEVELOPMENT POLICY

Tourism development policy consists of a set of statements related to various aspects of tourism development. Policy is determined based on several considerations, of which the most important is achieving the objectives of developing tourism. More generally, tourism policy should reflect the overall development policy of the country or region so that tourism is well integrated. Policy also evolves from the survey and analysis of present tourism development patterns and infrastructure, tourist attractions and activities and the tourist markets. Socio-economic and environmental factors are very important to consider.

The government should assume the lead role in deciding tourism policy. Policy affects the entire country or region and their communities and it must balance economic, environmental and social concerns. National and regional objectives should prevail over individual, group or sector interests. However, the policy should provide a framework within which the private sector and other special interests groups can effectively function.

Tourism policy can take many forms. Some of the basic issues that need to be addressed in policy formulation are as follows:

- The reasons for developing tourism should be stated in the policy. These reasons often include a combination of the following:
  - economic reasons of increasing income, providing employment, earning foreign exchange, increasing government revenues and using tourism as a catalyst for expansion of other sectors;

- social reasons of encouraging cross-cultural exchange and introducing the country to foreigners (for international tourism) and educating persons about their own country and providing recreation opportunities (for domestic tourism);
- using tourism to help achieve environmental and cultural conservation objectives for which resources are not otherwise available.

- The forms of tourism to be developed and related types of international and domestic tourist markets to be attracted are a basic policy consideration. The various forms of tourism were described in Chapter 4. Usually several forms of tourism are suitable for development within a single country or region, but in different areas and sometimes in different time periods. The general quality level of tourism also needs to be set forth in policy. Many destinations are now, by policy, opting for what they term quality tourism.

- Another consideration is whether tourism should be 'market-led' – developing forms of tourism that will attract a broad market regardless of the impact of the development, or 'product-led' – developing forms of tourism that are most compatible with the environment and society, and targeting only those markets that are consistent with the product even though this may result in fewer economic benefits. Usually the attempt is to balance these two approaches.

- A policy consideration is the extent of development to be allowed – should tourism be limited, maintained at a medium level, or encouraged to become a major sector of the economy. A large country or region may decide to develop different levels of tourism in different areas and at different times based on environmental, socio-cultural and infrastructure development considerations.

- The growth rate of tourism to be aimed for – slow, medium or fast – is often a policy consideration. Even though the potential exists for fast growth, for example, it may be desirable to control the growth rate for several reasons:
  - social reasons of allowing residents adequate time to adjust to tourism and learn to participate in it;
  - development reasons of balancing development of tourist facilities with development of infrastructure;
  - manpower planning reasons of allowing sufficient time to train persons to work effectively in tourism;
  - economic reasons of integrating the development of tourism with other economic sectors, and not creating distortions in the economy.

- The respective roles of the government and private sector in developing and managing tourism can be an important type of policy. The various roles of the government and private sector are reviewed in detail in Chapter 7.

- Achieving environmental protection, cultural conservation and sustainable development are all important policy considerations.
- The general location and staging of development may be stated in the policy, and then further refined in the structure plan.

Other types of policy may, for example, relate to multi-use of tourism infrastructure, the inter-relationships between domestic and international tourism, education and training programmes, social integration of tourism, and investment and employment considerations.

FORMULATING THE STRUCTURE PLAN

The national or regional structure plan is composed of several elements – the primary and often secondary tourist attractions; the tourism development regions (in the national plan) and tourism development areas such as resorts (in the regional plan); the access points to the country or region; and the internal transportation linkages. Tourist excursion routes and staging of development are also often shown on the structure plan. Preparing the structure plan is based on several considerations, including the following:

- Development objectives and policies – these are basic inputs to the structure plan, for example, the recommended forms of development.
- Type and location of the major tourist attraction features.
- Type and location of existing accommodation, and the projected accommodation and other tourist facility needs.
- Location of existing and already planned transportation facilities, and other critical infrastructure such as water supply.
- Overall environmental, land use, tenure, resource, social and economic analysis and synthesis. This indicates various important influencing factors – suitable climatic zones for tourism; location of developable and available land for tourism development; the carrying capacities of potential tourism development areas; location of resource areas that may be more important for other types of development; areas where labour supply will be available to work in tourism; and location of economically depressed areas where development is needed.

Each country and region must be planned according to its particular characteristics and development policies. However, there are certain basic concepts and principles which are generally applicable. These are based on what has proven to be functional and successful in already developed tourism areas. As is always the case in the planning process, imaginative new ideas should also be considered.

Suitable international access to a country and good regional access are essential for tourism. These access points are often termed the national and regional gateways. International airports are often the access points to countries, especially for long-haul tourists. Land border crossings and seaports also function as gateways for international travellers to some countries. Regional access may be by air, land or sea. These gateways usually have already been established before tourism was considered, and thus become a given factor around which tourism is planned. In a small country or region, a single major gateway is usually sufficient. Larger countries and regions may have more than one gateway. Multiple gateways offer the advantage of tourists entering at one point, making their tour, and exiting at another point, thus saving backtracking to the entry point. Tourists are encouraged to see more of the area and there is greater flexibility in organizing itineraries.

Related to the gateway concept is the principle of establishing a staging area at or near each of the gateways. Staging areas provide tourist facilities and services for overnight stays of tourists waiting for transportation to other parts of the country or region, or waiting for departure from their tour. They often contain various attraction features or can be developed with some features, including shopping facilities, which tourists can enjoy while waiting for onward transportation. These staging areas provide tourism employment and income for local residents. When the national or regional gateway is located in or near a major city, the city becomes the staging area.

Clustering of tourist attractions and activities is an important planning principle. Many attractions – such as good beaches, national parks, ski slopes and major archaeological and historic sites – have specific locations which determine much of the planning of tourism. Other types of attractions, such as cultural performances, are more mobile. Special types of attractions, such as theme parks, can be located in many places. Clustering of attractions in particular areas can attract more tourists to each area, and induce them to stay longer. Grouping of attractions also typically makes it less expensive to provide infrastructure and more convenient for organizing tours.

A clustering approach often used is to develop several secondary attractions near to a primary attraction. These secondary features may already exist in the area and only need development, or they may be mobile or special types which can be newly developed. For example, a secondary attraction of a cultural centre – for local dance and music performances, and demonstration and sale of handicrafts – can be developed near a national park or in a historic town.

Designation of tourism development regions at the national level and development areas, such as resorts, at the regional level is an important principle. This applies especially where a substantial amount of tourism development is envisaged. These development regions or areas are often termed tourism zones. Concentration of tourism development, as opposed to dispersed development, offers several advantages:

- Better opportunity for the planning of integrated development and application of development, design and environmental controls.

- More efficient provision of transportation access and other infrastructure.
- Convenience to tourists of facilities and services being in proximity.
- Capability of concentrated development to support a greater variety and more specialized facilities and services.
- Containment of any negative environmental and socio-cultural impacts in specific areas.

Tourism regions are logical geographic and planning entities. They are selected based on several considerations – containing significant tourist attractions and related activities; existing good access or potential for developing a regional gateway; an existing integrated internal transportation network, or potential for developing such a network; and suitable areas for developing integrated tourist facilities. Within the development region, it is often desirable to establish a tourism centre – this may also be the staging area for the region. A tourism centre should have good access from outside the region, transportation connections to other places within the region, and offer a range of tourist facilities and services. The centre may be an existing city or town or a new resort.

Within each of the tourism development regions or areas, the general type and extent of tourism should be specified. This is expressed in terms of the type and number of accommodation units. These are determined based on several factors – the development policy; the types of attractions in the region; ease of accessibility; carrying capacity; environmental and socio-cultural factors; and other considerations. Specification of accommodation provides a guide for later detailed planning of the region or area, and for decision-making on proposed development projects.

An efficient and interesting transportation facilities network and services system, whether by air, road, rail or water, is important. Transportation should provide efficient access from the national gateway to the regional gateways, and to attractions and facility development areas within the regions. The transportation network, or portions of it, also often serves as excursion routes for sightseeing tourists. An important principle of planning for development of transportation and other infrastructure is that they be as multi-purpose as possible, serving general use as well as tourism needs. In this way, overall infrastructure costs can be reduced, and tourism can help support infrastructure improvements that bring benefits to the entire economy and society.

It is common practice to designate tourist excursion routes – sometimes called tourist circuits – on the plan. These are selected to pass through scenic areas with stopovers at particularly interesting places. The stopovers, which can also be shown on the plan, should be developed with visitor facilities – restaurants, shopping and toilets. They may include such activities as local walking tours, visits to specific attraction features and cultural performances. Tour routes should be designed, to the extent possible, to form loops in order to avoid backtracking over the same route on the return journey.

The tourism plan should be formulated so that it is easy to stage tourism development over a long period of time. Effective staging requires that the various tourism regions and development areas are selected so that each one can be developed economically and efficiently as separate units when needed. Development stages are indicated for the various tourism regions and areas, usually as first, second and third stages. The stages are typically for five-year periods but can be longer. Determination of staging is based on several considerations – accessibility; when the basic infrastructure can be developed; market demands; feasibility of undertaking development of the tourist attractions and facilities; relative economic needs of the areas; and social acceptance of the people living in the tourism zones.

SELECTING DEVELOPMENT SITES

Specific tourism development sites such as for integrated resorts should be carefully selected according to certain criteria, including the following:

- Location at or near a tourist attraction feature (or features) such as a beach, marine area, lake, ski slope, and major archaeological or historic site. The development, however, should not impinge upon the immediate setting of the features, but be set away from them.
- Desirable micro-climatic conditions as related to the type of development. Local climatic conditions can vary greatly from one place to another and must be carefully investigated in selecting development sites.
- Attractive physical environment of the site and nearby area.
- Sufficient amount of available and developable land, which is economically feasible to acquire and develop and does not have a more important economic, conservation or other resource use.
- Good existing or potential access from the tourist gateway to the area and from the area to other attraction features in the region.
- Existing availability of, or feasibility of, developing infrastructure of adequate water supply, electric power, sewage and solid waste disposal and telecommunications at an acceptable cost. After transportation access, provision of an adequate water supply is often the most critical type of infrastructure.
- Suitable general area for the resort with compatible nearby land uses, with no excessive air, water or noise pollution of the site environment.
- No possibility of the resort generating problems related to the local natural environment, if the development is environmentally well planned and managed.
- Positive attitude of any nearby residents to developing tourism and their desire to work in tourism. There should be no likelihood of the tourism development generating any serious socio-cultural or economic problems for residents of the general area, if appropriate measures are applied.

- Availability of a nearby labour supply to work in tourism. If there is no nearby source of employees, there should be the possibility of attracting employees from elsewhere. If employees come from outside the area, it should be feasible to provide adequate housing and community facilities and services for them.

There may be additional criteria depending on the local circumstances and type of resort being planned. A single site may not perfectly meet all the criteria, and it may be necessary to balance site advantages and disadvantages. In the later detailed planning of the site, it is important that the nearby areas also be planned, with development controls applied to those areas. This will help avoid land use and infrastructure problems developing near to site – a common problem in many resort areas.

REDUCING SEASONALITY

It is common for the country, region or development area to experience seasonal differences in tourist arrivals. This situation leads to underuse of tourist facilities and services during certain periods of the year, and often excessive demand at other times. The seasonality factor can result from either the types of tourist attractions or the characteristics of the tourist markets (or both). Therefore, the national or regional plan should incorporate ways to reduce seasonality, although it is often impossible to eliminate this factor.

Various techniques can be applied to reduce seasonality. Types of tourist attractions can be selected or developed which will attract visitors at different times of the year, and especially during the typical low season. Tourism areas can usually develop some low-season activities – such as festivals and special events, conferences, and special types of recreation facilities and activities. It is now common practice for beach resorts to develop conference tourism during the historic low season. Ski resorts often develop mountain hiking, horse riding and other recreational activities, as well as conferences and special events, during the summer season.

Marketing and pricing techniques can be used to attract tourists during the low season. These may be combined with the product development approaches described above. Discounted transportation and accommodation rates can be offered during the low period which, if well marketed, can attract tourists. A low season is often the result of the market source countries' traditional vacation periods being at certain times of the year. In this situation, marketing can be targeted to older tourists who are free to travel anytime. These tourists also often prefer the less congested destination environments that are available during the low season. Domestic tourist use of international resorts and urban tourist facilities can also be encouraged during the low season.

Chapter 6

Economic, environmental and socio-cultural considerations

Economic, environmental and socio-cultural considerations must be well understood in order to plan, develop and manage tourism successfully. The primary reason for developing tourism in most countries and regions is for its economic benefits, although there are often other reasons, as well. In keeping with the concept of sustainable development, environmental and socio-cultural considerations are also of the utmost importance. Economic, environmental and socio-cultural costs and benefits must all be weighed together to achieve balanced development. Particular emphasis in this chapter is given to the types of impacts generated and the policies and impact control measures which should be pursued. Even though many of the control measures presented are applicable at the local level, they need to be adopted as standards, regulations and guidelines at the national and regional levels.

MEASURING ECONOMIC IMPACTS

Several standard types of economic measurements are made in tourism. Tourism is still not usually listed as a separate sector in national economic tables but is included in the service sector. (The WTO has developed the Standard International Classification of Tourism Activities (SICTA) which has been provisionally approved by the United Nations Statistical Commission.) Therefore, it is more difficult to measure the economic contribution of tourism. But, by drawing on various information sources, tourism economists can make calculations sufficient to indicate the general extent of tourism's economic impact. The standard economic measurements are as follows:

- Income generated and contribution to Gross National or Domestic Product. This indicates the relative importance of tourism in the total economy.
- Foreign exchange earned from international tourism. This includes calculation of both the gross foreign exchange earnings – the total

expenditures of foreign tourists, and net foreign exchange earnings – the foreign exchange remaining in the country after deducting the foreign exchange leakage factor. This leakage is the foreign exchange spent for imported goods and services used in tourism – food items and hotel equipment and supplies; expatriation of salaries of foreign workers and of profits of foreign-owned facilities; payments made to foreign hotel management companies; and other leakages. At the regional level, the gross and net money earned from outside the region can be calculated.

- Local employment generated by tourism. Employment is calculated by type:
  - direct employment – the persons who work in tourism enterprises such as hotels, restaurants, tourist shops and tour and travel agencies;
  - indirect employment – jobs generated in the supplying sectors such as agriculture, fisheries and manufacturing;
  - induced employment – additional persons supported by the spending of income made by the direct and indirect employees;
  - construction employment – jobs generated in the construction of tourist facilities and infrastructure (this is usually temporary but may be long-lasting in places with continuing development of tourism).
- The multiplier effect. This refers to the stimulus that an external source of income has on an economy. It is the number of rounds of spending in the local economy of the initial tourist spending. This effect measures the way in which tourist expenditures filter through the economy and generate other economic activities.
- Contribution to government revenues. This includes hotel and other types of tourist user taxes, airport departure taxes, customs duties on imported goods used in tourism, income taxes on tourism enterprises and employees, and property taxes on tourism establishments.

Although not as quantifiable, a benefit of tourism is that it helps justify and pay for transportation facilities and services and other infrastructure that are used by the entire community. Also an important general benefit is that tourism can serve as a catalyst for expansion of other economic sectors.

If not carefully controlled, tourism can generate some economic problems. Loss of economic benefits can occur if there is a high import content of goods and services used in tourism, and if many tourist facilities are owned and managed by outsiders. This situation reduces the net income and foreign exchange earned from tourism, and may lead to resentment by residents of the tourism area. For certain types of tourism development, however, there may be few alternatives to outside ownership and management. This can be the case especially during the initial stages of development when local capital and managerial capabilities are limited. In small island economies with little local production of goods, it may be difficult to greatly reduce the import content of tourism. But the employment and income generated is still usually considered worth the investment in tourism.

Economic distortions can take place geographically if tourism is concentrated in only one or a few areas of a country or region, without corresponding development in the other places. Employment distortions may be created if tourism attracts too many employees from other economic sectors, because of its higher wages and better working conditions. Inflation of local prices of land and certain goods and services may take place in rapidly developing tourism areas. This places a financial burden on residents.

ENHANCING ECONOMIC BENEFITS

There are several techniques that can be applied to enhance the economic benefits of tourism. These should be incorporated into the planning process so that possible problems are prevented or reduced before they occur.

Strengthening the linkages between tourism and other economic sectors is a very important technique. This reduces the import content of tourism and provides more local employment – the indirect and induced employment – and income from tourism. Opportunities often exist, for example, to increase the locally produced food items used in tourism. Also, the tourism industry should be encouraged (or required) to utilize more local items, including building materials and interior decoration, in its development and operation of hotels and other facilities.

Encouraging in-country, in-region and local ownership of tourist facilities and services is also important so that more of the profits from tourism are retained. This can be done in various ways – providing investment incentives; organizing stock companies with sale of shares to the general public; and requiring joint ventures of local and foreign companies. Certain forms of tourism can be encouraged which will provide opportunities for local small business enterprises. If local capital is very limited, then a policy can be taken of initially allowing foreign ownership, but requiring purchase by local owners when capital is available.

Foreign hotel management by transnational hotel companies of large hotel properties results in a loss of some income to countries. However, it also offers the advantages of professional management and international marketing and reservation services. Whether to allow transnational management must be decided based on the circumstances of each particular country. It is also important that local tour operators be given the opportunity to handle foreign tour groups, and that local ground handling operations are not pre-empted by foreign tour operators.

Maximizing local employment in tourism can be encouraged by proper training of persons to work in tourism. In some places, there may be some social resistance to service employment. It will be necessary to educate local people to understand that employment in tourism is a respected and worthwhile type of occupation. Training should be extended to the supervisory and management levels, so that these higher level positions can also eventually be filled by local staff. When a trained pool of employees exists, then tourist facility and service establishments can be required to employ local persons. For the higher level positions, replacement of foreign employees by local ones can be phased in over a period of time.

Tourist expenditures can be increased in various ways. More shopping opportunities, especially of local arts and crafts, can be provided in many places. Tourist activities can be expanded, for example by organizing more attractions and tours, which will induce tourists to stay longer. Tourism product enrichment and diversification is becoming an important aspect of expanding and upgrading tourism in many already developed tourism areas.

By developing tourism in a gradual manner, the problems of inflated prices for land and goods can often be reduced because the economy has more time to adjust to new development. This also provides local residents with more opportunity to adapt to and be trained to participate in the benefits of tourism.

ENVIRONMENTAL IMPACTS

Tourism and the environment are inter-dependent. The physical (natural and man-made) environment provides many of the attractions for tourists, and the development of tourism can generate both positive and negative environmental impacts. Developing and managing tourism so that it is compatible with the environment, and does not degrade it, is a major factor in achieving sustainable development. In order to plan tourism environmentally, it is first important to understand the possible impacts of tourism on the environment.

If tourism is well planned, developed and managed, it can generate important positive environmental impacts. These include the following:

- Helps justify and pay for conservation of important natural areas and wildlife, including marine environments, and development of national and regional parks and reserves, because these are major attractions for tourists. This is an especially significant benefit in countries with limited resources for undertaking environmental conservation.
- Helps justify and pay for the conservation of archaeological and historic sites as attractions for tourists. Otherwise many of these sites would be allowed to deteriorate or disappear. Even entire historic districts in towns and cities are being conserved and developed for tourism.
- Helps improve the environmental quality of areas because tourists like to visit places that are attractive, clean and not polluted. Tourism provides the incentive to clean up environments through controlling air, water, noise and visual pollution, reducing congestion and upgrading overall

appearance with suitable landscaping and building design. Also, well sited and designed tourist facilities themselves can contribute to the attractive appearance of both urban and rural environments. Improvement of infrastructure, especially of water supply and sewage and solid waste disposal, also contributes to improved environmental quality.

- Increases local environmental awareness when residents, and especially young people, observe tourists' interest in conservation. They then begin to realize the importance of conservation in their areas.

If tourism is not well planned, developed and managed, it can generate several types of negative environmental impacts. These include the following:

- Water pollution resulting from improper development of sewage and solid waste disposal systems for hotels and other facilities. There can be pollution of river, lake and coastal waters from sewage outfall lines, and of groundwater by seepage of waste material.
- Air pollution resulting from excessive use of internal combustion vehicles (cars, taxis, buses, motorcycles, etc.) in tourism areas. Airplanes, used by many tourists for longer-distance travel and for local air tours generate some air (and noise) pollution.
- Noise pollution generated by a concentration of tourists and tourist vehicles.
- Visual pollution resulting from several factors – poorly designed hotels and other tourist facilities; badly planned layout of facilities; inadequate landscaping of facilities; use of large and ugly advertising signs; and obstruction of scenic views by tourism development.
- Waste disposal problems of littering the landscape by tourists, and improper disposal of waste generated by tourist facilities.
- Ecological disruption of natural areas by overuse and misuse by tourists and inappropriate tourism development. Coastal, marine, mountain and desert environments, all important types of tourism areas, are particularly vulnerable to ecological damage.
- Damage to archaeological and historic sites by overuse or misuse by tourists and inappropriate tourism development.
- Environmental hazards and land use problems resulting from poor planning, siting and engineering of tourist attractions and facilities.

ENVIRONMENTAL PROTECTION MEASURES

Concern with environmental protection should be an integral part of the planning process. Application of the environmental planning and sustainable development approach is essential, including establishing and staying within the carrying capacities of tourism areas. Selecting the forms of tourism development that are most suitable for the environment also greatly help limit negative environmental impacts. Application of sound principles, such as concentration of facilities in certain zones with provision of adequate infrastructure, is very important in maintaining environmental protection. More generally, development of tourism on a gradual basis allows for sufficient time to monitor its environmental impacts, and make changes in the development approach if any problems have arisen.

Adopting techniques of reducing the seasonality of tourism, especially peak season use of tourism areas, is another very useful technique. Environmental problems often occur only during the peak season when overloading of the infrastructure and overuse of attractions, facilities and services take place. Reducing seasonality was reviewed in Chapter 5.

In addition to these general approaches, specific environmental impact control measures should be applied. These include the following:

- Install properly designed utility systems of water supply, electric power, sewage and solid waste disposal and drainage for tourist facilities. Conservation techniques should be applied – such as treatment and recycling of waste water and use of solar heating devices. Often these systems can be extended to serve general development in the tourism area, thus benefiting local communities.
- Develop adequate road and other transportation systems, with emphasis on development of public transit and non-polluting forms of transportation of tourists. Electric shuttle buses, for example, can be used in resorts. Proper maintenance of tourist vehicles is important.
- Provide open space, parks and suitable landscaping in tourism areas.
- Apply environmentally suitable land use and site planning principles, zoning regulations, development standards and architectural design in tourism areas. Control of advertising signs is also important.
- Carefully manage visitor flows at tourist attraction features. At fragile sites, the number of visitors may need to be limited or completely prohibited at certain times, or even year-round. For some important sites, the technique of modelling can be used – building a replica of the feature for tourists to visit, with prohibition of tourists at the original site.
- Prohibit tourists to cut trees in camping and trekking areas, to collect rare plant and animal species, and to disturb the natural behavioural patterns of wild animals. Hunting and fishing should be allowed only under carefully controlled conditions.
- In marine areas, several types of controls are necessary – operations related to ship bilge cleaning and ballast dumping; use of motorized boats in environmentally sensitive areas; collection of live sea shells, coral and endangered sea life; spear fishing; disturbance of nesting turtles; use of boat anchors in coral-bottom bays; and mining of beach sand and coral for

construction purposes. Boat piers should be properly designed so that they do not lead to erosion or other problems.

- Maintain environmental health and safety standards for the benefit of both tourists and residents.

There may be other control measures which should be applied in particular tourism areas depending on their characteristics. With respect to visitor use controls, it is important to inform tourists about the controls and why they must be applied. If tourists understand why the controls are necessary, they will more likely abide by them.

SOCIO-CULTURAL IMPACTS

Tourism can bring both benefits and problems to the local society and its cultural patterns. Although more difficult to measure than economic or environmental impacts, socio-cultural impacts are major considerations in developing tourism in any place. These impacts can be especially critical in countries that still have strongly traditional societies and economies. Although tourism can generate socio-cultural impacts, it should be kept in mind that any type of new development brings changes. Tourism is only one source of change in a society.

If tourism is well planned, developed and managed in a socially responsible manner, it can bring several types of socio-cultural benefits. These include the following:

- Improves the living standards of people and helps pay for improvements to community facilities and services, if the economic benefits of tourism are well distributed.
- Conserves the cultural heritage of an area which otherwise might be lost as a result of general development taking place. Conservation of archaeological and historic sites was referred to under environmental impacts. Cultural patterns of music, dance, drama, dress, arts and crafts, customs, ceremonies, life styles, traditional economic activities and architectural styles are also important attractions for tourists. If these are lost, cultural tourism will not be successful in the area. Tourism helps justify their conservation. In some places, tourism can be the impetus for revitalizing cultural patterns which might be disappearing.
- Helps develop and maintain museums, theatres and other cultural facilities. These are, in part, supported by tourism but are also enjoyed by residents. Many major museums and theatres in the world receive much financial support from the admission fees paid by tourists.
- Reinforces or even renews a sense of pride by residents in their culture, when they observe tourists appreciating it. This is especially true of some traditional societies which are undergoing rapid change and losing their sense of cultural self-confidence.

- Provides the opportunity for cross-cultural exchange between tourists and residents who learn about, and come to respect, one another's cultures. This exchange can best be achieved through certain forms of tourism – educational and other types of special interest tours; village tourism; and home visit programmes whereby tourists can arrange to visit local families.

Tourism can generate some socio-cultural problems if not well planned, developed and managed. A common problem is overcrowding by tourists and loss of convenience for residents, which leads to their resentment and sense of hostility toward tourism. If there are too many tourists in an area – which can happen particularly at peak season periods – attraction and amenity features, and restaurant, shopping and transportation facilities can become so overcrowded by tourists that residents cannot easily use them. If residents are completely prohibited from access to amenity features such as hotel beaches, they may become even more resentful. Large numbers of tourists can be especially disruptive in small rural communities. Resentment can particularly arise if residents perceive that they are not receiving many economic benefits from tourism, and that tourism development is controlled by outside interests.

Some problems can lead to cultural degradation and lessening of a sense of cultural identity. Deterioration of important archaeological and historic sites can result from overuse by tourists. There can be excessive commercialization and loss of authenticity of local customs, ceremonies, music, dance, crafts and other cultural patterns when these are inappropriately presented as tourist attractions. There can be a 'demonstration effect' of residents, especially young people, imitating the behavioural patterns and dress of tourists. This is done without understanding the different cultural backgrounds and socio-economic status of the tourists. Also, misunderstandings and conflicts may arise between tourists and residents because of different languages and customs.

Social problems of drug abuse, alcoholism, crime and prostitution may be worsened by tourism. The research conducted on these problems indicates that tourism is seldom their basic cause, but it may provide the opportunity to expand them.

PREVENTING SOCIO-CULTURAL PROBLEMS

Some of the general policies that are applicable to economic and environmental considerations are also appropriate for socio-cultural reasons. An important general policy is to develop tourism on a gradual basis so that the society has time to adapt to it, be educated about it, and learn how to participate in its benefits. This approach also gives the government sufficient time to monitor the socio-cultural impacts of tourism, and remedy any problems before they become serious. As has been emphasized, residents should be involved in the planning and development process of tourism so that they can influence its decision-making and feel that they are part of tourism. Suitable forms of tourism must be selected that are compatible with the local societies. Also, selective marketing can attract the types of tourists who will respect the local social customs and cultural traditions.

As a policy, deliberate use of tourism as a technique of cultural conservation can greatly help in reducing its negative impacts on the culture. At the same time, many societies want to experience some positive change and participate in the benefits of modern development. The approach that they often wish to take is to be culturally selective. They want to keep the best of their traditions that give them a distinctive cultural character, but adopt the best of the changes that will make their lives more comfortable and interesting. Each society must decide on what approach is most suitable for their people when making choices about their tourism development patterns.

Several more specific socio-cultural impact control measures can be applied in tourism areas. These include the following:

- Maintain the authenticity of local dance, music, drama, arts, crafts and dress, even though they are somewhat adapted for presentation to tourists. This may require special training programmes being organized and quality controls being applied. However, certain types of ceremonies and rituals such as religious ones should not be modified for tourism, and tourist viewing of them must be carefully controlled.
- Preserve existing distinctive local architectural styles and encourage new development, including tourist facilities, to use local architectural motifs.
- Make certain that residents have convenient access to tourist attractions, amenity features and other facilities, and apply visitor control measures to prevent overcrowding.
- If residents cannot afford to use existing commercial tourist facilities, provide inexpensive or subsidized facilities for them to use. It is also common practice to allow residents to pay lower admission fees to attraction features than those paid by foreign tourists.
- Educate residents about tourism – its concepts, benefits and problems, the local tourism development policy and programme, how they can personally participate in tourism, and the social patterns of tourists visiting the area. Public awareness programmes about tourism can be organized, utilizing radio, television, newspapers, magazines and public meetings. Education about tourism should be included in the public and private school system.
- Inform tourists about the local society – its customs, dress codes, acceptable behaviour in religious and other places, courtesies to observe in taking photographs, tipping policies, and any local problems such as

crime. If tourists understand these matters, they will be more likely to respect them.

- Train employees to work in tourism effectively, including language and social sensitivity training where needed. In addition to providing better services, this will reduce any possible misunderstandings between tourists and employees.
- Apply strict controls on drugs, crime and prostitution if these are considered to be problems in the tourism areas.

Other types of controls may be appropriate in particular tourism areas.

ENVIRONMENTAL IMPACT ASSESSMENT

Application of the environmental planning approach and incorporation of environmental protection measures into the planning process will prevent many environmental problems from arising. However, it is still important that an environmental impact assessment (EIA) be carried out for each specific tourism development project (as well as for all types of major projects). This procedure ensures that specific projects will not generate any serious environmental problems. If it appears that a proposed project will cause problems, then it should not be approved unless it is modified to be made acceptable. The EIA procedure is established at the national and regional levels. Many countries have adopted environmental protection legislation and the EIA procedure, but others have not yet done so.

The EIA should include all types of impacts – environmental, economic and socio-cultural. Even though a project may generate substantial economic benefits, for example, it may result in unacceptable environmental or social problems. It should not, therefore, be approved without modification.

Chapter 7

Planning the institutional elements

Achieving successful integrated tourism development and management depends as much on effective institutional factors as it does on development policy, physical planning and impact controls. This chapter examines the major institutional elements of tourism – organizational structures, manpower planning and training, tourism legislation and regulations, and attracting investment in tourism development.

ORGANIZATIONAL STRUCTURES FOR TOURISM

The most appropriate types of public and private organizational structures for tourism must be adapted to the particular circumstances in each country or region. The types of structures may also be changed through time as situations change. Before deciding on organizational structures, a basic decision to be made is determining the respective roles of government and the private sector in the development and management of tourism.

The government or a statutory board typically has several responsibilities – policy, planning and development coordination; statistics and research; industry standards and regulations; investment incentives; some marketing services; tourism manpower planning and training, including establishing education and training standards; and provision of basic infrastructure and major public-type attractions. The private sector is responsible for the commercial development and operation of accommodation and most other tourist facilities and services, along with marketing of these. In newly developing tourism areas, however, the government may need to be initially involved in some commercial development in order to get tourism started.

In order to handle its functions, the national government must establish a National Tourism Administration (NTA) – a Department or Ministry of Tourism. This ministry may be single portfolio only for tourism, if this sector is currently or expected to become a major activity in the country. Or the ministry may be a mixed portfolio, combining tourism with some other related functions. If the ministry is single portfolio, this gives tourism more

Ministry or department of tourism

Marketing services
- Market planning and promotion
- Operation of overseas tourism offices
- Operation of local tourist information offices

Planning and development
- Development policy and planning
- Coordination of development implementation
- Establishment and administration of facility and service standards

Statistics and research
- Statistical collection, compilation and reporting
- Operation of the tourism information system·
- Conducting research studies

Education and training
- Manpower planning and programming
- Establishment and administration of training standards
- Operation of training programmes and institutions

Figure 7.1 Model NTA structure

priority and importance in the government structure. Regional governments also often establish their own tourism organizations.

The NTA is organized into various divisions and sections, often similar to that shown in Figure 7.1. Separate sections are typically organized for planning and development, statistics and research, education and training and marketing services.

Many countries have established a separate autonomous entity for marketing services, and sometimes other management functions. Assigning marketing to an autonomous body, such as a national promotion board, offers the advantage of its being able to apply flexible internal management that is more responsive to changes in market trends. Also, it allows for the possibility of coordinating with the private sector (if that is relatively well developed in the country) on joint promotion activities. However, close liaison must be maintained between the board and the NTA in order to ensure that a consistent development policy is carried out. The board must be held accountable for effective use of its funds, usually through an annual review of its programme and expenditures by the NTA.

Because tourism is a multi-sectoral activity, it is essential that maximum coordination be maintained between the NTA and other relevant government agencies and between the public and private sectors. This can best be achieved by establishing a Tourism Advisory Committee to the NTA, with representation from government agencies, the private sector and other relevant organizations.

Adequate funding and staffing are essential for effective operation of the NTA. Funding is from the government, although there may be joint public and private sector funding of some marketing activities. If there is some type of tourism tax, such as a hotel or tourist expenditure tax in the country, that can be a logical source of funding for part or all of the NTA budget. In this manner, tourism can help support its own management.

If the government needs to become involved in development of resorts or other types of tourist attractions or facilities, a commonly used approach is to organize a public development corporation. This entity is funded by the government, but functions as an independent company subject to government review. When the private sector becomes more mature in the area, the public corporation may sell its assets to private investors.

Tourism private sector organizations serve several important functions: providing a forum for discussing and resolving common problems of tourism enterprises; making coordinated recommendations to the NTA for improvements in the tourism sector; providing representation on tourism boards and committees; conducting research and training for their member enterprises; establishing and maintaining adequate facility and service standards of their members; and sponsoring special events. The private sector can be organized in various ways. There can be separate hotel, restaurant, tour and travel, and other special purpose associations, some combination of these or, in a small tourism area, perhaps a single tourism enterprises' association. Private sector associations are funded by membership dues.

TOURISM MANPOWER PLANNING

Manpower planning is applying a systematic approach to ensure that the right people are in the right place at the right time. This is especially important in tourism, which is a service activity depending in large part for its success on the quality of personnel working in tourism. Manpower planning involves the four steps of:

- Surveying and evaluating the present utilization of manpower in tourism and identifying any existing problems and needs.
- Projecting the future manpower needed. Projections are made for the number of personnel required in each category of employment. Then the qualifications for each category of job are determined.
- Evaluating the total human resources that will be available in the future.
- Determining training needs and formulating the education and training programme required to provide the qualified manpower.

All types of tourism employees must be considered in manpower planning. These include both public sector employees in the NTA and employees needed in private sector – hotel, catering and tour and travel operations including tour guides. Also, some training of tourism-related personnel may be required. Immigration and customs officials often need to be sensitized in how to handle tourists properly. There may be need for specialized training of persons working in tourism-oriented retail shops, handicraft producers, entertainers, and others. It is important that the need for upgrading the knowledge and skills of present employees be identified. Often these persons have not been properly trained. Satisfying this need for upgrading must be incorporated into the training programme.

Evaluation of human resources refers to review of the total manpower which will be available in the country or region, and allocation of this manpower to the different economic activities including tourism. Future tourism manpower needs are projected based on application of formulas to the types and amount of expected future tourism development.

Many kinds of education and training programmes are applicable to tourism – on-the-job training; correspondence (distant learning) courses; short upgrading and specialized courses; study tours; and one-, two-, three- or four-programmes at the vocational school and university levels. In countries where tourism is being developed into a substantial sector, tourism education institutes are established. The manpower planning programme needs to be periodically reviewed and updated to meet current and projected future needs.

TOURISM-RELATED LEGISLATION

Tourism legislation includes the basic tourism law. This law typically sets forth the policy for developing tourism and establishes the functions, structure and sources of funding of the NTA (or regional tourism office). Various specific regulations are necessary. These relate to the standards, licensing requirements and inspection procedures for hotels, tourist restaurants, tour and travel agencies, tour guides and other tourism enterprises. In some countries, a hotel classification system has been established and requires administration. These regulations are carefully prepared based on understanding the needs of the country or region. The necessary mechanisms and staff capabilities must be available to apply the regulations on a continuing basis. Procedures for administering the industry standards should be set forth in the regulations.

Certain related laws and regulations are also important for the development and management of tourism. There is need for zoning regulations to designate the regional tourism zones, and control land uses and apply development standards in specific tourism development areas. If zoning regulations already exist, it may be necessary to modify them to include tourism-type land uses such as hotel zones. Environmental protection legislation, including the EIA requirements, will be necessary if these do not already exist. Public health, sanitation, safety and fire codes, building codes, facility operating regulations, liability laws relating to guests and their belongings, labour and taxation legislation are all important for the development and operation of tourist facilities. Regulations on transportation facilities and services – control of fares, licensing of carriers, safety requirements and travel routes – also affect tourism operations.

In many countries, tourism development is based on scenic areas, nature parks and archaeological and historic places. Legislation on parks and conservation is very important to protect these resources. Conservation areas need to be legally designated and planned, with land and visitor uses carefully controlled.

Tourist consumer protection legislation is being adopted in many countries. This legislation is designed to protect tourists from being taken advantage of by unscrupulous or mismanaged tourism enterprises.

TOURISM INVESTMENT POLICIES AND INCENTIVES

As indicated previously, the government typically must finance major infrastructure projects and public-type tourist attractions. Some or all of this investment – such as for electric power, water supply, sewage and solid waste disposal, and even attraction features – can eventually be recovered through payment of user fees. Financing of on-site infrastructure such as for hotel or resort sites is typically the responsibility of the private developer, or a public corporation if one is involved.

For private investment in hotels and other commercial facilities and services, the investment policy will depend on the local situation. If sufficient private capital resources are available, there is no problem. If capital is limited and tourism must compete with other sectors for its use, then international capital must be sought. International capital can be allowed for total financing, or there can be joint ventures organized between international and local companies. Joint ventures are obviously preferable, in order for the country to receive some of the investment profits.

Often investment incentives offered by the government are needed to attract private sector investment. Some of the common types of incentives, which can be offered singly or in combination, are as follows:

- Provision of development land, and assembly of the required amount of land, at moderate or no cost at suitable sites.
- Provision of off-site infrastructure (which is usually provided in any case), or provision of on-site infrastructure at no cost to the investor.
- Complete or partial exemption from customs duties on imported items used in the development and operation of tourist facilities and services. These may include building materials, machinery, equipment and supplies, and transportation vehicles such as tour buses.
- Complete or partial exemption from company income or property taxes for a specified number of years, and offering favourable depreciation allowances which reduce taxes.
- Provision of financial assistance – loans at regular or low interest rates;

extended periods of repayments of loans; subsidies for payments made on interest of private loans; or guarantee by the government of private loans made. Outright grants of money can also be provided.

- Unrestricted repatriation of all or part of foreign capital, profits, dividends and interest, after taxes have been paid.
- Guarantees against nationalization or appropriation of the investment.

It is important that the incentives be provided only for approved projects that conform to the development plan and programme and are suitably designed. Incentives may also be restricted to certain types of development that the government wants to encourage, for example, certain quality levels of hotels, certain types of services such as tour operations, and tourism development in remote areas. The types of incentives offered should be reviewed periodically and adjusted to current investment needs. Incentives offered during the initial stages of development may no longer be needed at a later time or should be modified to suit current needs.

In many places investment incentives are not required and the profitability of tourism development is assured. In such cases, the government may require that developers make payments, perhaps through an association, for their proportionate share of the costs of infrastructure development. Even other costs, such as for any environmental or social problems resulting from the development, can be required to be paid by the developer. These costs, for example, may include buying land and planting forest cover elsewhere to replace that which was removed from the development site, and resettlement costs of families dislocated from the site.

Chapter 8

Tourism market planning

Marketing of tourism for a country or region is essential. Marketing informs prospective tourists about what the area has to offer, and tries to induce them to visit it. Market planning needs to be understood as part of the overall tourism planning process, and as it relates to development of the tourism product. Marketing involves several activities – establishing the marketing objectives; formulating the marketing strategy; preparing and implementing the promotion programme; and providing tourist information services. Market planning can be done for both international and domestic tourists or a combination of these.

ESTABLISHING THE MARKETING OBJECTIVES

In the comprehensive and integrated planning approach, the marketing objectives are represented by the market targets of the types and numbers of tourists to be attracted. As was explained in Chapter 3, market targets are set based on the markets that can likely be attracted only if the development and marketing plans are being properly implemented.

Market targets are usually established by five-year periods. The targets are expressed in terms of the approximate numbers of tourist arrivals by type, average length of stay, countries or country regions of origin, and other characteristics. The tourist groups aimed for should be closely related to the tourism product and the kinds of tourists and tourism desired. They may include, for example, general interest sightseeing or beach resort oriented tourists, various types of special interest, nature, cultural and adventure tourists, ethnic tourists and cruise ship stopover passengers. Some tourist markets may be multi-destination oriented. These tourists visit the country as part of a tour of several countries. Other markets will be single destination oriented.

In already developed tourist destinations, the marketing objectives may also relate to changing the types of markets, such as aiming for higher quality or special interest markets. Such objectives must, of course, be coordinated with corresponding changes made in the tourism product of attractions, facilities and services.

FORMULATING THE MARKETING STRATEGY

The marketing strategy sets forth the most effective approach to be applied to achieve the marketing objectives. The strategy may include, for example:

- Whether the marketing will be general, aimed at general interest tourists, or be selective and directed to specific types of tourist markets. Primary, secondary and opportunity markets are identified.
- The general types of promotional techniques to be used and where they should be directed – to tour operators, the tourist consumer or a combination of these.
- The timing or priority scheduling of promotional efforts to certain types of markets or countries. Timing may depend on the scheduling of tourism development projects.
- The image and reality of the area to be conveyed. A newly developing tourist destination may need to create a desirable image of itself first before engaging in specific promotion.
- Any particular obstacles to overcome such as recent political instability or a natural disaster.
- Whether promotion offices should be established in the major market source countries, or local marketing representation contracted in those countries, or promotion handled directly from the home office.
- Consideration of any contingencies which may arise such as the opening of previously closed market sources.

The marketing strategy should be related to both the longer- and shorter-term objectives. By doing this, the foundation is laid to achieve the longer-term objectives but with the shorter-term ones planned more specifically. The marketing strategy should be reviewed fairly often. It can be modified, if necessary, depending on market trends and any changes in development of the tourism product.

PREPARING THE PROMOTION PROGRAMME

The promotion programme is prepared based on several considerations: the marketing strategy; knowledge of marketing distribution channels; the promotion techniques available; and the amount of the budget. This programme is usually designed for a three- to five-year period. It specifies by year the types of promotion to be undertaken and their estimated costs. Continuing costs, such as for maintenance of offices in the market source countries and local tourist information offices, are usually included in the promotion budget. The most commonly used promotional techniques are as follows:

- Preparing printed material such as brochures, posters, maps, postcards and travel agent manuals, and distributing these to travel agents, tour operators and the tourist consumers.
- Preparing audio-visual material – slide, film and video shows – for use in travel seminars and other types of presentations.
- Advertising in newspapers, magazines, radio and television aimed at the tourist consumers, and in travel trade publications aimed at tour operators.
- Attending travel trade fairs, of which there are now many held annually in Europe, North America and East Asia.
- Undertaking special promotional trips to the market countries in order to contact travel agents and tour operators.
- Inviting and hosting visits by tour operators and travel writers and photographers.
- Preparing and publishing guide and general information books about the area, if these are not available commercially. These books can be sold to recover the costs involved.

Marketing of specialized forms of tourism, such as convention and cruise ship tourism, requires specific knowledge and promotional techniques.

Promotion of an area and its attractions and facilities should be accurate and honest. If promotion misrepresents the area and tourists are attracted by inaccurate statements made in the promotion, they may well be dissatisfied. This can lead to tourists advising their friends not to visit the area, and to unfavourable publicity in the public media of the market source countries. Under present tourist consumer protection legislation, now adopted in many countries, it can also result in legal action being taken against tour and travel operators.

Promotion should be closely coordinated between the public and private sectors. A common practice is to establish a joint promotion board for coordinating and carrying out promotional activities. This board is jointly funded by the public and private sectors. The private sector will still undertake promotional activities for their own enterprises. The government must provide an adequate budget for its share of marketing, if tourism is to be successful. At the same time, marketing should be carefully programmed so as to maximize effective use of the funds that are available. Often national air carriers can greatly assist in promotion activities, including promotion through their overseas offices, if government funding for promotion is limited.

PROVIDING TOURIST INFORMATION SERVICES

An important function of marketing is providing information to tourists before and after they arrive at their destinations. Various types of information should be available – the general geographical, historical and cultural background of the area; the attractions, facilities and services (and their costs) that are available; transportation schedules; location of shopping, medical and postal facilities, consulates, embassies and religious institutions; and other specific information. As was emphasized in Chapter 6, it is also very important to inform tourists about local customs, dress and behavioural codes, tipping policy, and any security problems they should be aware of.

Tourist information offices should be established in convenient locations, and be staffed by knowledgeable personnel. Information officers should have foreign language capabilities where needed. Often, a successful approach is to develop visitor information centres. In addition to information material, visitor centres contain exhibits, offer audio-visual shows and have literature, slides and other material for sale.

Chapter 9

Implementing and monitoring the plan

Specifying how to carry out the plan's policy and recommendations is an essential aspect of the planning process. As has already been emphasized, techniques of implementation should be considered throughout formulation of the plan. This gives greater assurance that recommendations are implementable. Specific techniques of implementation should be set forth. An increasingly common practice is to prepare an implementation manual which the government can use as a guide on implementation techniques and procedures. The major elements of implementation are explained in the following sections.

PLAN ADOPTION AND ALLOCATION OF RESPONSIBILITIES

After careful review and agreement, the tourism plan should be adopted by the government as its official guide for developing tourism. Through adoption of the plan, the legal basis for its implementation is established. It then becomes more difficult to deviate greatly from the policy and plan, although some adjustments will inevitably need to be made. Also essential for effective implementation is political commitment to developing tourism on a planned basis, and strong leadership exercised in both the public and private sectors of tourism.

In the implementation approach, the first step is to decide on the respective roles of government, the private sector and special bodies such as public corporations. These roles were examined in Chapter 7. Whichever respective roles are decided on, close cooperation and coordination between the government and private sectors on implementation must be maintained.

STAGING AND PROGRAMMING DEVELOPMENT

To achieve the physical development recommendations systematically, the first step is to determine the general staging of development. Staging is usually indicated as part of the structure plan, as was explained in Chapter 5.

Within the framework of the recommended staging, specific projects are identified for development, and then organized into an integrated development programme. This programme should include all types of development – government infrastructure, attractions and facilities, and private sector development of commercial facilities and services. It is preferable also to specify other actions that are needed for implementation – establishing certain tourism organizations; adopting tourism laws and regulations; or carrying out socio-cultural and environmental programmes. Appendix 5 presents a model tourism action programme that demonstrates the approach used to prepare such a programme.

The projects and actions are shown by year, usually for a five-year period. For long-term projects, continuation of the projects over two or more years is indicated. Pre-development activities, such as detailed planning, design and feasibility analysis for future projects, should be included in the programme. General cost estimates of development projects are shown, and the responsible parties for carrying out the projects or actions are specified. The responsible parties involved may include, for example, the relevant government agency, the private sector or a public corporation.

The tourism programme should be carefully coordinated with the programmes of related agencies, such as the transportation, parks and cultural departments. In order to give greater assurance of programme coordination, the tourism programme may even include a listing of projects that are the responsibility of those agencies, such as national park or museum projects. The programme must also be carefully coordinated with the overall development programme of the country or region. In fact, tourism is typically incorporated into the overall development programme.

The first stage action programme is often prepared as part of the initial tourism planning study so that it is well integrated with the planning recommendations. Alternatively, it can be prepared later after the plan has been adopted. Action programmes for the subsequent stages of development are prepared at a later time near the completion of the previous stage programme. These later stage programmes can incorporate any minor adjustments made to the plan, as well as actions and projects which could not be accomplished in the previous programme. Thus these programmes become 'rolling plans' that are always relatively up-to-date.

A common technique for achieving efficient development programming, especially at the project development level, is critical path analysis. This involves preparing a special type of chart – a network – consisting of arrows and circles. These depict the entire development process, with an event, such as developing a hotel in a resort, being represented by a circle, and an activity, such as constructing the hotel foundation, by an arrow. The circles are connected by the arrows. Logically, an event cannot take place until all activities leading up to it have been completed. Estimated 'time to completion' values are then placed on each activity. The critical path of the network is determined by considering each event in turn, and calculating the earliest possible time in which it can occur. If an event is dependent on two or more activities, the earliest time for completion is determined by the longest activity.

The critical path is the resultant sequence of inter-connected events and activities which will require the longest time to accomplish. Adding together all the times on the critical path will give the shortest time for the project to be completed. Critical path analysis for major programmes or projects can be complicated. However, computer technology can be used to simplify preparation of the chart and for evaluating different development implementation scenarios to arrive at the most effective one.

APPLYING ZONING AND OTHER REGULATIONS

At the national and regional planning levels, zoning should be applied to designate tourism development regions or areas – the tourism zones. These zones may include other types of land uses but their zoning for tourism indicates that they are places where tourism is to be developed. The appropriate types of tourism development are also often shown for each of the tourism zones. Within the designated zones, the government can develop infrastructure suitable for tourism – tourist attractions and other public-type tourist facilities and services. Designation of the tourism zones also informs the private sector where and what type of tourism is desired, and will more likely be approved. If necessary, the government can offer incentives for private sector development in the tourism zones.

At the local level of planning, tourism zoning regulations demarcate specific areas for different types of land uses, and the standards to be applied within each of the land uses. In a resort area, for example, the zoning will designate the accommodation, commercial, recreation and conservation zones.

Other tourism related laws and regulations were described in Chapter 7. These need to be adopted as soon as possible, in order to provide the basis for managing tourism and applying facility standards.

As a tourism area develops, it is often desirable to apply a hotel classification system, usually based on star classification levels. The advantages of a hotel classification system are that they inform tour operators, travel agents and tourists about the general quality level of the facilities so that they can better select the ones they want to use. The application of a classification system also gives incentives to the private hotel enterprises to upgrade hotels to a higher star level, where that is desirable, and provides a guide for development of new hotels. For the same reasons, classification systems can also be applied to restaurants. If needed, other types of regulations, such as those on hygiene, sanitation and building construction, should be adopted. In areas prone to earthquakes and high winds, special construction standards should be incorporated into the building code.

The government procedures for reviewing and taking action on tourism development project proposals – such as hotels, and their licensing and inspection procedures – should be clearly set forth. These procedures should be efficient and fair to enterprises making the proposals but also ensure that proper standards are met.

APPLYING DEVELOPMENT STANDARDS

Application of suitable development standards and design guidelines for tourist facilities helps ensure that tourism development is environmentally appropriate, and meets tourists' and residents' expectations. These may be applied at the national, regional or local levels of government, depending on the particular governmental situation. However, it is the central or regional government's responsibility to make certain that appropriate standards are applied at the local level. Therefore, development standards and design guidelines are usually included in national and regional plans, and are adopted as part of the plan. The types of development standards to be considered are as follows:

- Density of development – usually expressed in terms of number of accommodation units such as hotel rooms per acre or hectare. The density of development greatly determines its overall character.
- Heights of buildings – also very important in setting the character of development and environmentally integrating it. For example, in many rural resorts, buildings are not allowed to exceed the heights of trees so that they blend well into the natural environment.
- Setbacks of buildings – from amenity features, shorelines, roads, site boundaries and other buildings. Setbacks are important for various reasons. For example, adequate setbacks from beaches and shorelines prevent damage to buildings resulting from possible shoreline erosion, preserve the natural appearance of the shoreline, and allow sufficient space for landscaping, recreation and public access to the shoreline.
- Floor area ratio (FAR) – the ratio, expressed in percentage, of the total area of all the floors of the building to the total site area. FARs also help determine the development character and sense of openness.
- Coverage of the site by buildings and other structures – expressed as a percentage of the site covered by buildings and structures. Establishing maximum site coverage ratios particularly determines the amount of open space and landscaping in the development.
- Vehicular parking spaces and other requirements – the amount of landscaping and open space, public access to amenity features, sign controls and under-grounding of utility lines, all of which are important in making a development more attractive and functional.

These development standards are usually set forth in zoning regulations, or may be adopted separately for particular tourism development areas. The actual standards applied will, of course, vary among different types of tourism areas, depending on the desired type and character of development. It is also very important to adopt suitable engineering standards to be applied in the development of infrastructure.

Guidelines for site planning and architectural and landscaping design should be adopted. They also affect how well the development is integrated into the natural and cultural environment. These are usually prepared as guidelines, and not regulated standards, because they need to be flexible and allow for the creative imagination of the designer. Site planning refers to the exact location of buildings on the development site. Site planning guidelines should consider several factors – preventing environmental hazards of erosion, landslides and flooding; achieving proper relationships among buildings; and maintaining views from buildings and vista points. Architectural guidelines should be related to use of local traditional building styles and materials, as well as overall design attractiveness. Landscaping guidelines should consider various factors – use of local indigenous plants; appropriately designed outdoor furniture; suitable night lighting; low-cost landscape maintenance; and conservation of water in dry areas.

Site planning, architectural and landscaping guidelines are typically administered by a design review committee composed of professional persons. This committee reviews all development proposals and makes any recommendations for improvements needed to their design. The guidelines should be made available to the designers before they do their work, so that they will know what the design parameters are.

IMPLEMENTING OTHER PROGRAMMES

Other programmes recommended by the tourism plan need to be implemented. These may include, for example, the training programme for employees in tourism, public awareness programme on tourism, and an economic programme to produce more local food items used in tourism. The promotion programme will require implementation. Environmental awareness and protection programmes often must be pursued. Park, historic conservation and cultural programmes must be carried out.

Certain critical aspects of tourism may need to be resolved. The government and private sector should be conscious of maintaining tourist health. Any special health problems, such as endemic malaria or AIDS, should be addressed and tourists informed. Travel facilitation requirements and procedures, especially immigration and customs, should be made as efficient and 'user-friendly' as possible, while still enforcing the regulations.

MONITORING AND MANAGEMENT

Monitoring should be considered an integral part of plan implementation and management. Monitoring will detect problems in their early stages, so that remedial measures can be taken. The progress of implementation, especially of the action programme, should be continuously monitored. The number and characteristics of tourist arrivals should be monitored to see if the market targets are being maintained. Determining tourist satisfaction levels through special surveys of them is especially important. Monitoring the economic, environmental and socio-cultural impacts of tourism generally, and for specific projects, is essential. Appendix 6 presents a checklist of factors that should be monitored to determine if the plan and programme are being implemented properly and on schedule.

Even though time-based targets are established, they should be considered flexible based on changing circumstances. There are many unpredictable influences on meeting targets. The overall recommendations are not necessarily invalid just because certain targets are not met exactly on schedule. During the shorter term, it is more important to maintain a balance between the development of tourist facilities, services and infrastructure and actual market demand. By maintaining a balance, resources are not wasted. Over the long term, efforts can be made to catch up on and achieve the various market and development targets.

One of the necessary tools for research, monitoring and the overall management of tourism is establishment of a tourism information system. This needs to be an integrated system, using computer technology. Various data are placed into the system – tourists' arrivals and their characteristics; accommodation and other tourist facilities and services; economic, environmental and social data; the results of special surveys; and any other relevant data. By building up information in the system, comparisons can be made over a period of time. Any significant problems and trends can be determined, and actions taken accordingly. It is essential that data fed into the information system be reliable and accurate, or the research results will not be usable.

Review should be made periodically of whether the overall tourism development policy, plan and programme are the most effective ones to achieve the development objectives. Each country or region is unique and development approaches must be adapted to each specific place. If, through experience in applying them, certain approaches and recommendations are seen to be deficient, then different ones should be considered. Through experimentation, the most effective approaches can be determined.

Emphasis must be given to the continuous management of tourism. Tourism management relates to many considerations – adapting to changing market and product trends; maintaining and improving the quality of facilities and services; continuously expanding the benefits of tourism socially and geographically; solving problems as they arise; and other matters. Both effective implementation of the plan and efficient management are required for the long-term success of tourism and its sustainable development.

Chapter 10

Tourism development funding

The financing of tourism development is an essential consideration in implementation. The type of funding needs and possible sources of financing must be understood, and an investment strategy formulated. The funding needs and approach must be specifically identified for each particular country or region. However, there are certain basic considerations that should be made, as explained in the following sections.

FUNDING NEEDS

There are three types of funding needs that should be considered in developing tourism. Funding is needed for preparation of tourism plans – the general national or regional plan; more detailed planning of tourism development areas; and planning and feasibility analyses of specific development projects. Funding the general level of planning is typically the responsibility of the government. Financing the more detailed plans and projects can be either by the government or private sector, depending on the local situation. However, the more detailed planning must still be carried out according to government planning standards, and reviewed and approved by the government. If financing is not available locally for planning, then international assistance must be sought.

Funding is required for development of the infrastructure necessary for tourism. The importance of developing adequate infrastructure has been emphasized in previous chapters. Major infrastructure is typically the responsibility of the government to finance. However, at least some of this investment, such as for utility services, can be recovered through payment of user fees. As has been emphasized, much of the infrastructure can be developed to serve general community and economic needs, as well as tourism, and thus bring substantial overall benefits to the country. Infrastructure is expensive and many countries need international assistance in financing it, especially for the foreign exchange component of the cost. Infrastructure costs within commercial development sites are usually paid by the private developers of the sites. Private developers may also be required to pay for some of the off-site infrastructure costs that benefit their sites.

Many types of major attraction features, such as national parks and museums, typically are financed by the government. However, user fees can help recover the initial investment, or at least pay for the operational and maintenance costs of these features. These attractions also serve residents of the area, as well as tourists, and their costs can be justified as providing an important public recreational or educational facility.

Human resources development, such as establishment of a hotel and tourism education centre, must also be funded, usually by the government but often with private sector involvement. A training levy may be applied as a tax on tourists' hotel and restaurant expenditures to help pay for operation of a tourism education centre.

Major funding is needed for development of the commercial revenue producing tourist facilities and services including accommodation, restaurants, tour and travel agencies and shopping facilities. These are typically funded by the private sector but, in newly developing tourism areas, the government may need to be a pioneer developer until the private sector has developed the confidence to make its own investments. Development incentives may also need to be offered to induce the private sector to make investments. These incentives were reviewed in Chapter 7. National tourism development banks are often organized, sometimes with some international financial support, to make loans to the private sector for investment in tourist facilities. Development corporations are also organized for implementation and operation of specific projects and enterprises. Joint venture international and local financing is a common approach to tourism project investment.

Finally, funding is required for the public management of tourism by the NTA office, including for the overall national or regional marketing of tourism. The NTA budget is typically provided by the government. However, if there is a tourism tax such as a hotel and restaurant expenditure tax, some or all of this can be allocated to the NTA budget. Thus tourism can directly pay for its own management.

A funding mechanism sometimes used by the government is to establish a Tourism Development Fund supported by the hotel tax or other sources such as duty-free shopping facilities. This fund can be used for development, marketing, training and other purposes.

INTERNATIONAL SOURCE OF FUNDS

There are several types of international funding sources available for financing tourism development, as follows:

- World Bank Group – The IBRD (International Bank for Reconstruction and Development), although not now directly involved in tourism projects, provides major funding for infrastructure, environmental and conservation projects which benefit tourism as well as serve general needs.

This funding is provided in the form of long-term loans at commercial rates of interest. The IDA (International Development Association), makes loans to low-income countries at no interest rates, with ten-year grace periods and very long-term repayment schemes. The IFC (International Finance Corporation) makes loans directly to the private sector for development of revenue-producing projects, including hotels and other tourism projects. IDA loans are usually for not more than 25 per cent of the project cost, and thus serve more as a catalyst to development.

- UNDP (United Nations Development Programme) – The UNDP is mainly a technical assistance agency. It is an important source agency for the funding of tourism planning and other tourism-related projects, through the WTO as the executing agency. Many of these projects include provision of equipment as well as technical assistance. The UNCDF (United Nations Capital Development Fund) provides small-scale capital assistance in the form of grants or long-term loans for social facilities and services and economic activities.

- European Union – The EU is becoming quite involved in supporting tourism projects in the many countries which constitute the ACP group under the Lome IV Convention. These projects are both technical assistance (including planning, marketing and training) and investment oriented.

- Bilateral sources – Bilateral funding sources usually operate on a government-to-government basis, and several of these programmes include technical assistance and investment oriented tourism projects. Many countries offer bilateral assistance, including countries in Europe, North America and the East Asia and Pacific region. Each bilateral programme has its own particular assistance policy.

- Regional development banks – The Asian Development Bank (ADB), African Development Bank (ADB), Inter-American Development Bank (IDB) and other regional development banks offer some assistance on aspects of developing tourism in their member countries. The European Development Fund has been established to provide assistance to countries in Eastern Europe.

- Private international capital sources – Many private sector companies, including those involved in tourism, are seeking to invest outside of their home countries. This type of investment often brings with it competent management resources, marketing connections and desirable international images which can benefit tourism in the countries seeking outside investment. It is important for countries to understand the nature of these corporations and how to negotiate with them. The United Nations Centre on Transnational Corporations can offer countries technical assistance on dealing with international hotel and other tourism-related corporations, for example, on negotiating hotel management contracts.

These various funding sources are, of course, not mutually exclusive. They can be used in various combinations to meet the particular investment requirements of a country.

TOURISM INVESTMENT STRATEGY

Each country should devise a strategy for tourism investment which best suits its circumstances and needs. Such a strategy should involve the following considerations:

- Specific tourism development projects, whether public or private investment oriented, should, wherever possible, be identified based on their being part of a tourism development plan and programme.
- The projects should additionally be identified on the basis of a thorough feasibility analysis (which may have been conducted as part of the overall development planning and programme process).
- Projects should be carefully evaluated to minimize the foreign exchange costs wherever possible.
- Domestic funding should be explored as a priority source of financing, before seeking international funding sources. The next priority should be joint domestic–international funding.
- Fiscal, legislative and administrative structures should be supportive of the project. Project development procedures should be streamlined as much as possible, while still maintaining the integrity of project review.
- When a package of investment incentives is to be offered for private sector projects, this should be selective, monitored and adjusted periodically based on current investment needs.
- Care should be taken to ensure that project management is monitored, but not to the extent where initiative is stifled.

Countries must carefully determine their priorities for the tourism sector and within the sector. Investment strategies should be realistic and targeted to achieve their stated objectives.

Appendices

APPENDIX 1: HOW TO ORGANIZE A TOURISM PLANNING PROJECT

The first step in organizing a tourism project is to conduct a tourism assessment of the country or region. This assessment reviews the resources for tourism, its potential tourist markets, and the major development opportunities and constraints. Based on the assessment, the terms of reference (TOR) of the study can be written specifically to suit area's planning needs.

As was emphasized in Chapter 2, the TOR should be carefully formulated so that the study considers all the relevant factors and achieves the intended results. If the local understanding of tourism planning is limited, an outside specialist should be brought in to conduct the assessment and write the TOR.

Preparation of a comprehensive national or regional tourism plan requires a team of various specialists. The exact composition of the team will depend on the specific TOR of the study, and the extent to which some team members can perform more than one function. The core team members are typically as follows:

- Tourism development planner
- Tourism marketing specialist
- Tourism economist
- Tourism transportation/infrastructure planner

The additional specialists who are often required include:

- Tourism development ecologist or environmental planner
- Tourism development sociologist or anthropologist
- Air transportation planner
- Tourism manpower planning specialist
- Tourism organization specialist
- Tourist legislation and regulations specialist

- Hotel and tourist facility specialist
- Tourist facility architect/development standards specialist

If some detailed planning, project feasibility analysis or special studies are included in the project, additional types of team members will be required. These may include, for example, specialists on land use planning, project feasibility analysis, cultural heritage planning and ecotourism.

In organizing the planning team, it is important that a team leader be appointed for coordination of project activities, and with the government and project steering committee. Usually this position is filled by the tourism development planner who assumes both administrative and technical functions. Typically, an international team is contracted to carry out the project because of the specialized knowledge needed. To the extent possible, the team should include local experts from the country so that they can provide their specific knowledge of the area, as well as technical capabilities. Counterparts from the tourism office and other agencies should be appointed to work with the team, so that team members can transfer their knowledge to local staff. Also, if local officials understand how and why the plan recommendations were made, they will be better able to help implement them.

A detailed project work programme should be prepared. This programme specifies when each work activity should take place, and shows the inter-relationships and sequence of the activities. It also indicates when each project report should be completed. By following the work programme, the work activities are well coordinated and the study remains on schedule.

Several types of planning reports are necessary, as follows:

- Inception report – After assessment of field conditions, the project team leader prepares the inception report. This report includes the detailed work programme and schedule, when the various team members should commence and complete their work, and any other pertinent information.
- Interim report – This report presents the preliminary objectives and results of the survey and analysis steps of the planning process along with any particular conclusions, opportunities and constraints which have been identified. The interim report is useful to prepare for a large project but can often be combined with the draft report for smaller studies.
- Draft report – This report presents the objectives, results of the survey and analysis, conclusions and preliminary tourism development policy, structure plan and other types of recommendations.
- Draft final report – This report presents the final policy, structure plan and other recommendations and implementation programme as prepared by the planning team, along with all the background survey and analysis.
- Final report – The final report presents all the final recommendations and implementation programme agreed to between the planning team and

steering committee, along with all the background material. It includes the final plan maps and other graphic information.

When each of the first four reports referred to above is ready, it is presented to and reviewed by the project steering committee and other interested parties, in order to obtain their feedback. Any differences are reconciled and agreement reached on the conclusions and recommendations. These are incorporated into, progressively, the draft, the draft final and final reports.

APPENDIX 2: PROJECTING ACCOMMODATION NEEDS

The formula for projecting accommodation needs, and an example for determining average annual and high season demand, are set forth below. This example is only for one type of tourist market and accommodation. The formula should be applied to each of the tourist markets and related type of accommodation to determine the total accommodation for the country or region. Calculating high season demand is important because that season determines the maximum needs.

Demand for beds

The formula is:

$$\frac{\text{No. of tourists (per time period)} \times \text{average length of stay (in nights)}}{\text{No. of nights (per time period)} \times \text{accommodation occupancy factor}}$$

For example, to calculate annual beds demand:

$$\frac{150{,}000 \text{ tourists per year} \times 10 \text{ nights}}{365 \text{ nights} \times 75\% \text{ occupancy}} = \frac{1{,}500{,}000}{274} = 5{,}475 \text{ beds}$$

For example, to calculate high season beds demand:

$$\frac{75{,}000 \text{ tourists per 4 months} \times 10 \text{ nights}}{120 \text{ nights} \times 95\% \text{ occupancy}} = \frac{750{,}000}{114} = 6{,}580 \text{ beds}$$

Demand for rooms

The formula is:

$$\frac{\text{No. of beds demand}}{\text{Average room occupancy (persons per rooms)}}$$

For example, to calculate annual rooms demand:

$$\frac{5{,}475 \text{ beds}}{1.7 \text{ persons per room}} = 3{,}220 \text{ rooms}$$

For example, to calculate high season rooms demand:

$$\frac{6,580 \text{ beds}}{1.7 \text{ persons per room}} = 3,870 \text{ rooms}$$

Allowance should be made for the percentage of tourists who stay in non-commercial accommodation such as with friends and relatives. If this factor is, for example, 5 per cent, that percentage should be deducted from the calculated bed and room demand.

APPENDIX 3: ESTABLISHING CARRYING CAPACITIES

Establishing tourism carrying capacities is based on the concept of maintaining a level of development and use that will not result in serious environmental deterioration, socio-cultural or economic problems, or be perceived by tourists as depreciating their enjoyment and appreciation of the area. Any development engenders some changes. Carrying capacity analysis typically is based on not exceeding the levels of acceptable change. It is now a basic technique being widely applied in tourism and recreation planning to systematically determine the upper limits of development and visitor use, and optimum utilization of tourism resources. Numerous tourism areas in the world show evidence of having exceeded their carrying capacities. This has resulted in environmental, social and sometimes economic problems, with a decrease in visitor satisfaction and consequent marketing problems.

In practice, determining carrying capacities is often not easy or precise. It depends considerably on the assumptions that are made. Carrying capacities may also change through time. However, it remains a very useful technique in guiding planning for a sustainable level of development.

Carrying capacities can be established for both undeveloped tourism areas and those that are already developed, and perhaps even reaching or exceeding their saturation levels. It is often the developed destinations, which are experiencing some problems of overdevelopment, which have become concerned about their capacity levels. Carrying capacities can best be calculated for specific development regions or areas based on environmental and socio-economic analysis. At the national and regional levels, they must be considered more generally. At these levels, carrying capacities are often based on the total of capacities calculated for specific major attractions, such as national parks and archaeological sites, and development areas such as resorts.

The measurement criteria presented here are for establishing carrying capacities primarily for tourist destinations. The capacities of the transportation facilities and services used by tourists travelling to their destinations are also important to analyse. Each area and its type of tourism is unique and must be specifically defined for the area, but some common criteria exist for virtually all places. Some criteria are quantifiable while others must be evaluated qualitatively. In determining capacities, the two major factors to be considered are described as follows:

The indigenous physical and socio-economic environment

This refers to the capacity of development and visitor use that can be achieved without resulting in damage to the physical (natural and man-made) environment and generating socio-cultural and economic problems to the local community, while still benefiting the community and maintaining a proper balance between development and conservation. Exceeding saturation levels will lead to permanent damage of the physical environment or socio-economic problems, or both. The criteria for determining optimum capacities include:

Physical

- acceptable levels of visual impact and congestion
- point at which ecological systems are maintained before damage occurs
- conservation of wildlife and natural vegetation of both the land and marine environments
- acceptable levels of air, water and noise pollution

Economic

- extent of tourism that provides optimum overall economic benefits without economic distortions or inflation
- level of tourism employment suited to the local community

Socio-cultural

- extent of tourism development that can be absorbed without detriment to the life styles and activities of the local community
- level of tourism that will help maintain historic and cultural monuments, arts, crafts, belief systems, customs and traditions without detrimental effects

Infrastructure

- adequate availability of transportation facilities and services
- adequate availability of utility facilities and services of water supply, electric power, sewage and solid waste disposal and telecommunications
- adequate availability of other community facilities and services such as those related to health and safety, and of housing for employees in tourism

The tourism image and product

This refers to the levels of development and numbers of tourists that are compatible with the image of the tourism product, and the types of environmental and cultural experiences that the visitors are seeking. If the area exceeds saturation levels, the development environment and attractions which visitors come to experience will be destroyed or degraded, tourist satisfaction will decrease, and the destination will decline in quality and popularity. The criteria for determining optimum capacities include:

Physical

- overall cleanliness and lack of pollution of the destination
- lack of undue congestion of the destination including attractions
- attractiveness of the landscape or townscape including quality and character of architectural design
- Maintenance of the ecological systems and flora and fauna of natural attraction features

Economic

- cost of the holiday and 'value for money'

Socio-cultural

- intrinsic interest of the indigenous community and culture
- quality of local arts, crafts, cultural performances and cuisine
- maintenance of archaeological, historic and cultural monuments
- friendliness of residents

Infrastructure

- acceptable standards of transportation facilities and services
- acceptable standards of utility services
- acceptable standards of other facilities and services

For each of the factors, measurement standards must be decided for each particular area. For example, a measurement standard for the amount of sandy beach area and frontage for each tourist coming to a beach resort can be established based on various assumptions of what is acceptable environmentally and necessary to maintain visitor satisfaction.

Seasonality is a major consideration in the concept of carrying capacity. The saturation level of visitor use of a destination is often reached during the peak periods of use, and not during the low season or on an average annual basis. Therefore, carrying capacity must be calculated for the peak period of use. As was discussed in the text, various approaches can be applied to reduce the peak period use and even out seasonality during the year. This achieves more optimum use of attractions, facilities, services and infrastructure. For some types of natural attraction features, visitor use may need to be controlled or prohibited during an ecologically critical period, such as the bird or turtle breeding season.

APPENDIX 4: CHECKLIST OF THE MAJOR ELEMENTS OF A NATIONAL OR REGIONAL TOURISM PLAN

This list specifies the elements that typically should be included in a comprehensive national or regional plan. These are listed according to their general sequence in the tourism planning process, but feedback takes place among the various elements as explained in Chapter 3.

Tourism development objectives

● Economic, environmental, socio-cultural and other objectives.

General background analysis

● Brief historical background of the country or region, especially as related to possible tourist attractions.
● Brief geographical description of geology, land forms and hydrography of rivers, lakes and coastal areas, with identification of areas geographically suitable for tourism development. Any susceptibility to natural disasters, such as volcanic eruptions and earthquakes or other problems such as coastal erosion, should be noted.
● Climatic patterns, with identification of climatically suitable areas for tourism development and activities. Any susceptibility to high winds, rainfall and flooding should be noted.
● Natural resource areas, and existing land use and land tenure patterns, with identification of areas that should not or cannot be developed with tourism.
● Environmental quality generally and especially in existing and potential tourism areas, with identification of any particular problems of pollution or environmental damage taking place.
● Existing national and regional development policies, plans and programmes, with evaluation of their influence on tourism development.
● Demographic patterns of the number and distribution of the population, age-sex profiles, population growth rates and trends, migration patterns and any other relevant characteristics.
● Economic patterns of the existing economic sectors and growth trends, Gross National/Domestic Product (GNP and GDP), per capita income,

employment/unemployment patterns, and other economic characteristics, with identification of any particular problems such as location of economically depressed areas.

- Cultural patterns of traditions, religious and social values and other relevant characteristics, and the effects of development on cultural traditions and values.

Infrastructure analysis and recommendations

- Analysis of access to the country or region by air, land and water related transportation, including capacities and convenience of facilities and services for tourists.
- Analysis of the internal transportation system of facilities and services as related to tourism use.
- Analysis of other infrastructure of water supply, electric power, sewage and solid waste disposal and telecommunications, as related to present and potential tourism areas.
- Review of any already approved plans and programmes for improvements to infrastructure.
- Identification of any particular infrastructure constraints on developing tourism, and recommendations on improvements required to the infrastructure for tourism development.

Tourist attractions and activities, and their improvements

- Survey and inventory of existing and potential attractions and activities, with categorization into a logical system such as natural, cultural and special types of attractions.
- Evaluation of the tourist attractions, with identification of primary and secondary attractions and any particular problems of existing attractions such as overuse or misuse.
- Recommended improvements (and conservation) required of the attractions.
- Identification of any particular positive or negative influences on attracting tourists such as strong or weak image in the market countries, recent political instability or natural disasters, extent of crime in the area and travel time, distance and cost from the major market countries.

Tourist facilities and services, and their improvements

- Survey of existing and already planned accommodation by number, type, location and quality level.
- Survey of existing and already planned other tourist facilities, including tour and travel operations, restaurants, banking and money exchange,

handicraft, speciality and convenience shopping, medical and postal facilities and services, public safety and tourist information services.
- Evaluation of tourist facilities and services, with recommendations on improvements required.

Recommended extent and forms of tourism

- Determination of tourism carrying capacities of various potential tourism areas and the entire country or region, based on environmental, socio-cultural, infrastructure and tourist satisfaction considerations.
- Determination of the most appropriate forms of tourism, by location, based on the inventory and evaluation of tourist attractions and activities, carrying capacity and market analysis and other considerations.
- Determination of the most suitable amount or extent of tourism (by type of tourism), based on the carrying capacity and market analysis, importance of tourist attractions and other considerations.

Market analysis and projections

- Review of global and inter-country regional tourism patterns and trends.
- Analysis of tourist arrival patterns and trends in the country or region being planned, including both international and domestic tourists, and of the specific characteristics of tourists visiting the country or region; special tourist surveys may need to be conducted.
- Evaluation of the effect of existing or potential competing tourist destinations.
- Determination of the major influencing factors on the types and extent of future tourist arrivals, and determination of the primary and secondary markets.
- Establishment of market targets by number, type and country or region of origin, socio-economic group, touristic interest groupings, length of stay and other relevant characteristics.
- Consideration of local residents' use of tourist attractions, facilities and services.
- Projection of the number, type and quality level of accommodation, other tourist facilities and services and infrastructure required based on the market targets.

Recommended tourism development policy and structure plan

- Recommended policy statement including economic, environmental and socio-cultural factors.
- Recommended structure plan including type and location of tourist

attractions, designated tourism development regions or areas (tourism zones) and the transportation linkages.
- Recommended staging of development by time periods.
- Recommended tour patterns and programmes indicating tourist excursion routes or circuits.

Economic analysis and recommendations

- Determination of the present and projected tourist expenditures by amount and type.
- Calculation of the present and projected economic impact of tourism by the standard measurements of contribution to GNP or GDP (or contribution to the regional economy), gross and net foreign exchange earnings, extent and types of national or regional economic leakages, income generated, the multiplier effect, direct, indirect and induced employment generated and contribution to government revenues.
- Recommendations on ways to enhance the economic benefits of tourism at the community, regional and national levels.

Environmental considerations and recommendations

- Identification of any present environmental problems generated by tourism and recommendations on ways to lessen them.
- Recommendations on measures to prevent future negative environmental impacts and reinforce positive ones.
- Recommendations on ways to improve the overall environmental quality of tourism areas.
- Recommendations on environmental protection and conservation policies and programmes needed, and application of environmental impact assessment procedures to specific tourism projects.

Socio-cultural considerations and recommendations

- Evaluation of any existing and potential positive and negative socio-cultural impacts resulting from tourism.
- Recommendations on ways to lessen negative impacts and reinforce positive ones.
- Recommended public awareness programme on tourism and a tourist information brochure to inform tourists about local cultural traditions and expected tourist behaviour.
- Recommendations on ways to achieve community involvement in all aspects of tourism at the local level.

Institutional considerations and recommendations

- Review and evaluation of present public and private organizational structures for tourism, with recommendations on changes or new structures required for the effective management of tourism, including how to achieve close coordination on tourism among pubic agencies and between the public and private sectors.
- Review and evaluation of present legislation and regulations related to tourism, with recommendations on modifications or new regulations required.
- Review and evaluation of financial capital resources available for investment in tourism, with recommendations on ways to provide more financial resources if needed, including development incentives.
- Manpower planning analysis for tourism, with recommendations for education and training programmes required in the public and private sectors to provide the requisite manpower.
- Evaluation of present travel facilitation procedures, with recommendations for any improvements needed.

Marketing and promotion recommendations

- Specification of the marketing objectives and strategy.
- Recommended specific promotion programme with cost estimates and possible sources of funding.
- Recommendations on respective and joint roles of the public and private sectors in promotion.
- Recommendations on overseas promotion representation.
- Recommendations on provision of tourist information services.

Plan implementation and monitoring

- Recommended development or action programme, with cost estimates and identification of responsible parties.
- Specification of implementation procedures including the respective roles of government and other agencies and the private sector.
- Specification of tourist facility development and design standards, and how these should be applied.
- Specification of zoning and other land use regulations.
- Recommended use of incentives or disincentives to encourage development according to the plan.
- Recommendations on establishing a tourism information system, or improving an existing system.
- Preparation of detailed area plans and project feasibility studies for the first stage of development, including demonstration projects.

- Identification of possible sources of funding for project development.
- Specification of the techniques and procedures to monitor plan implementation and the progress of tourism generally.

APPENDIX 5: MODEL TOURISM ACTION PROGRAMME

This model tourism action programme presents a typical five-year programme for projects and other actions required to implement the first stage of a national or regional tourism development plan. It exemplifies the principles that should be applied in preparing such a programme.

Explanation of the model

The model programme is shown in Table A.1. It is for a hypothetical medium size country or region which has had a modest level of business tourism in the past, but now wants to embark on development of controlled holiday tourism. The model is assumed to be based on a comprehensive tourism planning study, including the institutional elements. The development plan is focused on a combination of beach and marine attractions, mountain and nature attractions and some archaeological, historic and cultural features. The plan applies the gateway and staging area concept, with designation of zones for coastal and mountain tourism development. The plan also shows excursion roads for general sightseeing and to provide access to the tourism zones and attraction features.

The action programme is organized for a five-year period, representing the first development stage of the plan. The programme is focused on further developing the gateway city as a staging area, one of the coastal tourism zones (a beach resort) and two of the mountain zones, each based on a national park. Although this model is only for the first five-year development period, preparatory activities are indicated for projects which will be undertaken or completed in the next five-year period, including the opening up of new tourism zones. This overlapping of activities reflects the need to have continuity from one programme to the next. The model represents an idealized situation in which there is rapid execution of projects. In reality, most countries or regions would take longer to accomplish the projects and actions.

The programme is organized based on project categories – tourist facilities; tourist attractions; major infrastructure; and other projects and actions. Although organized into categories, all components of the programme are scheduled for development in a coordinated manner. This coordination of projects and actions is the basic principle of successful development programming. For example, infrastructure improvements must be available at the appropriate time in order for tourist attractions, facilities

Table A.1 Model tourism action programme

Project/action	Year 1	Year 2	Year 3	Year 4	Year 5
Tourist facilities					
Gateway city					
Historic district with commercial tourist facilities	Prepare and adopt plan	Apply historic preservation regulations and tourist facility investment incentives on a continuous basis			
Historic urban hotel restoration	Design	Restore	Open		
Urban hotel expansion	Design	Construct	Open		
New urban hotel 1		Design	Construct	Open	
New urban hotel 2 (to be opened in second programme period)				Design	Construct
Tourist information centre	Design	Construct	Open		Expand
Tour and travel agency 1		Organize	Open		Expand
Tour and travel agency 2			Organize	Open	
Duty-free shop	Design	Construct	Open		Expand
Beach resort					
Overall resort plan	Prepare and adopt plan				
Infrastructure		Design	Construct		Expand
Recreation facilities		Design	Construct		Expand
Resort hotel 1		Design	Construct	Open	
Resort hotel 2			Design	Construct	Open
Resort hotel 3 (to be opened in second programme period)				Design	Construct
Employee community		Design	Construct	Open	Expand
Mountain tourism					
Mountain lodge 1 (near national park 1)		Design	Construct	Open	
Mountain lodge 2 (near national park 2)			Design	Construct	Open
Tourist stopover 1		Design	Construct	Open	
Tourist stopover 2			Design	Construct	Open
Village tourism project 1	Prepare programme	Organize community	Develop facilities	Open	
Village tourism project 2 (to be opened in second programme period)			Prepare programme	Organize community	Develop facilities
Tourist attractions					
National park 1	Prepare plan	Design facilities	Construct facilities	Open	
National park 2		Prepare plan	Design facilities	Construct facilities	Open

Table A.1 Continued

Project/action	Year 1	Year 2	Year 3	Year 4	Year 5
Marine park (near beach resort)	Prepare plan	Design facilities	Construct facilities	Open	
Archaeological site	Prepare plan	Design facilities	Construct facilities	Open	
Historic site		Prepare plan	Design facilities	Construct facilities	Open
Cultural centre (in gateway city)	Select site	Design facilities	Construct facilities	Open	
Museum expansion (in gateway city)			Design	Construct	Open

Infrastructure

Project/action	Year 1	Year 2	Year 3	Year 4	Year 5
Airport expansion	Design	Construct	Construct	Open	
Excursion road improvements	Design	Implement on phased basis during three-year period			
Electric power extensions	Design	Implement on phased basis during three-year period			
Urban water supply improvements	Design	Implement on phased basis during three-year period			
Urban waste disposal improvements	Design	Implement on phased basis during three-year period			
Telecommunications improvements	Design	Implement on phased basis during three-year period			

Other projects and actions

Project/action	Year 1	Year 2	Year 3	Year 4	Year 5
Tourism law and regulations	Review and adopt	Apply on a continuous basis			
Facility development and design standards	Review and adopt	Apply on a continuous basis			
Tourism office	Organize	Train staff	Train staff		Expand
Marketing	Request funding	Improve image	Implement annual promotion programmes		
Investment incentives	Review and adopt	Apply incentives and adjust as needed			
Tourism training school	Design facilities	Construct facilities	Implement training programme		Expand
Public awareness programme on tourism	Prepare programme	Implement programme on continuous basis			
Tourist education		Prepare brochure	Distribute brochure on continuous basis		
Detailed planning for new tourism areas (to be developed in second programme period)				Conduct planning	Adopt plans

and services to be developed and start functioning. Some tourist attractions need to be available by the time that accommodation and other facilities are developed.

The model programme shows tourist facilities and services being improved in the gateway city/staging area first because some facilities already exist and can easily be expanded. Thus a small amount of holiday tourism can be encouraged in the city even before the beach resort and mountain tourism facilities are opened. Also, the staging area will need to be reasonably well developed by the time other tourism areas are open. Within the tourism zones, development is shown to take place on a phased basis. This approach is important because capital resources and construction capability can be severely strained if too many facilities are developed at one time. Also, it is usually not possible for marketing to attract the sudden major increases of tourists required to occupy a large new supply of accommodation rooms.

As shown in the model, development is programmed so that complementary facilities are available in a balanced manner. Some accommodation is shown being opened in the gateway city, beach resort and mountain area in the same years. By the time this accommodation is open, the excursion roads (which also function as access roads), along with tourist stopovers and some attraction features, are scheduled to have been improved. This coordination of development will provide alternative destinations and rapidly broaden tourist markets, and allow for efficient organization of circuit touring with overnight stops.

The other major infrastructure improvements required are programmed to be available when needed. Airport expansion is scheduled to be completed by Year 4, when there is expected to be an increase in tourist arrivals using the new beach and mountain resorts. Electric power extensions to those places will have been completed by then. Urban infrastructure will have been improved for use by both tourism and general development. The national/regional telecommunications system, important for both tourism and general development, will also have been improved by Year 4.

As shown in the model, the institutional elements must be programmed along with physical development. The tourism law and regulations and any other necessary legislation should be adopted in Year 1, so that these can be applied to tourism development. The tourism office also must be organized – or perhaps reorganized if an office already exists – early on. Funding for marketing needs to be budgeted. Image-building of the destination is often the first step in marketing, and that can be commenced before many facilities are available. Then the specific promotion programme can be started, with its timing coordinated with the development of attractions and facilities. Investment incentives, if needed, should be adopted during the first year in order to attract the private investment required. The public awareness programme on tourism should also be commenced early so that people are informed about the anticipated tourism development and can prepare for it.

Having personnel trained to work effectively in tourism is essential. Training must be coordinated with the development of tourist facilities and services. The tourism training school or other type of training must be started early in the development programme, with phasing of training, so that trained personnel are available as the facilities are opened.

In addition to listing of projects and actions by year, a complete action programme will also include general cost estimates for projects, where relevant, and the agencies (or private sector) responsible for implementing the projects or actions. In some cases, project profiles including a calculation of costs and benefits will be attached to the programme. In order to maintain its viability, an action programme needs to be adjusted as it proceeds, taking into account unexpected delays or changing circumstances.

APPENDIX 6: CHECKLIST FOR MONITORING PLAN IMPLEMENTATION

This checklist identifies factors that should be periodically monitored to determine if the tourism plan and programme are being implemented properly and on schedule. Some different or additional factors might also be monitored, depending on the particular characteristics of the tourism area and its plan.

Development factors

- Improvement of existing and development of new tourist attractions and activities, including tour programmes.
- Upgrading of existing accommodation, by number and type of units.
- New accommodation development by number and type of units.
- Location of upgraded and new accommodation.
- Occupancy levels of accommodation by type and month.
- Upgrading and expansion of other tourist facilities and services including tour and travel agencies, tourist restaurants, shopping, banking and money exchange and medical and postal facilities and services.
- New development of other tourist facilities and services.
- Improvement of existing and development of new tourism-related infrastructure, including access to the country or region, the internal transportation system, water supply, electric power, sewage and solid waste disposal and telecommunications.
- Extent that location criteria and development and design standards of tourist facilities are being applied to new development.
- Tourism projects that have been planned and approved but are not yet developed.

Marketing factors

- Number of tourist arrivals, by month, and their characteristics – place of origin, socio-economic group, age-sex profile, etc.
- Average length of stay of tourists by type.
- Tourist satisfaction levels and attitudes toward attractions, facilities and services.
- Promotion activities by the public and private sectors.
- Effectiveness of the different types of promotion activities.
- Improvements in tourist information services.
- Number of visitors at the various tourist attraction features.

Economic impact

- Expenditure patterns of tourists.
- Economic impact of tourism by the various standard measurements, including direct and indirect employment.
- Type and extent of economic leakages from tourism, and reduction of leakages.
- Extent that economic benefits of tourism are being received by local communities, including local development of tourism enterprises and employment of local residents in tourism.

Environmental and socio-cultural impact

- Improvement of any environmental problems of existing tourism development, including air, water, noise and visual pollution and ecological disruption.
- Improvement in overall environmental quality of tourism areas.
- Application of environmental protection policies and programmes and impact assessment procedures to proposed tourism projects.
- Identification of any specific environmental problems such as congestion at tourist attraction features or degradation of these features.
- Maintenance of authenticity of traditional arts, crafts and dance and music performances.
- Involvement of local communities in tourism, and any complaints from residents about tourism.
- Progress of the public awareness programme on tourism, and informing tourists about the local environment and society.
- Extent of crime, drugs and other social problems being generated by tourism.

Institutional factors

- Extent of implementation of recommendations on organizational structures.
- Extent of adoption of tourism-related legislation and regulations.
- Application of the legislation and regulations, and their effectiveness in achieving the desired results.
- Application of development incentives, and their effectiveness in achieving the desired results.
- Extent of implementation of the education and training programme, and the actual output of trained personnel by type and number.
- Improvements made to travel facilitation.
- Any particular problems relative to coordination among public agencies and between the public and private sectors.

The results of this monitoring are compared to the tourism plan recommendations, and especially the development or action programme. An evaluation can then be made whether development is on track with a minimum of problems. If there are some problems, monitoring should detect these in their early stages and remedial actions can be taken. Some development delays may be inevitable and the programme will need to be adjusted accordingly.

Part II

Tourism planning case studies

Chapter 11

Tourism planning approach of Malta

Tourism planning for the Republic of Malta represents an approach applied to an already established tourist destination. Planning is to shift the direction of the country's tourism development and to guide its future expansion.

BACKGROUND

The Republic of Malta is an independent country located in the central Mediterranean Sea south of Sicily. The country is composed of the islands of Malta, Gozo and Comino and encompasses 316 square kilometres. The population is about 350,000, most of which is concentrated on the island of Malta. The country has a long history reflected in highly interesting archaeological sites, medieval villages, old town districts and buildings and extensive fortifications. The historic area around the Grand Harbour at the capital city of Valletta is particularly interesting. Malta is the home of the Knights of the Order of St. John. Some major historical battles were fought in Malta.

For tourism, Malta offers a mild Mediterranean climate combined with good beaches and scenic views. In addition to major archaeological and historic places, the traditional village and life styles are important cultural attractions. The country is conveniently located near to major tourist market countries in nearby Europe. Access for virtually all tourists is by air.

Malta already has considerable development of tourism. Tourism is mostly focused on Malta Island, but there is also some tourism on Gozo. The country received almost 900,000 tourist arrivals in 1990. Most accommodation is small scale, including many self-catering units, with only a few larger hotels developed. Tourist arrivals are heavily skewed toward the British market, and generally are low spending types of tourists. In the late 1980s, the tourism development issues were identified by the government as the need to increase income and employment from tourism. At the same time, it wished to improve the quality of tourism, including attracting higher spending tourists. The government also wanted to reduce the impact of high seasonality by expanding tourism during the shoulder and off-peak periods.

THE TOURISM PLANNING APPROACH

The Maltese Islands Tourism Development Plan was prepared in 1989 (UNDP and WTO. 1989. *The Maltese Islands Tourism Development Plan*. Madrid: WTO). Although a separate project, the tourism plan was designed to be incorporated into the overall development plan and programme of the country. The overall planning was scheduled to be carried out subsequent to the tourism planning.

The tourism planning approach is a comprehensive one. The tourism development objectives are specified, based on the government's general objectives indicated above. A detailed environmental analysis was conducted. This is an especially important procedure because of Malta's small size and limited remaining natural areas. The environmental analysis identifies environmentally sensitive areas which should be preserved, as follows:

- Agricultural – lands of good agricultural capability that should be retained for agricultural use.
- Ecological – lands that contain important flora and fauna that should be preserved.
- Geological – areas of important geological features that should be preserved.
- Entomological – areas important as insect habitats.
- Ornithological – areas important as bird habitats, including stopover points for migratory birds.

Also identified is the location of underground water aquifers where any development permitted should have strict controls applied, so that groundwater recharging capability is not impaired nor the groundwater polluted. Because of limited water supply in the islands, maintenance of groundwater resources is essential.

Existing land use is surveyed and mapped, using the categories of:

- Development zone boundaries – areas which are zoned and mostly already developed with urban uses. These areas generally would not be available for new tourism development (except urban tourism).
- Industrial areas – areas which have been industrially developed and therefore are not compatible with tourism development.
- Airport – the airport area is one where tourism development would be adversely affected because of aircraft movements and noise.

The tourist attractions are surveyed in detail and categorized, as follows:

- Places of major historic interest – these particularly include entire historic urban districts and archaeological sites.
- Towers, forts and palaces – these are specific historic features of touristic interest.

- Traditional village cores and clusters – these are village areas of traditional architectural character and lifestyles.
- Major panoramic views – the Maltese islands are small scale but hilly, and an interesting aspect of island tours are the many scenic views offered.
- Beaches – these are specifically located, named and classified into rocky or sandy types.

The approach to surveying tourist attractions includes identification and evaluation of the coastal bay resources for tourism. The existing areas of intensive tourism development were also surveyed and mapped in order to graphically show the relationships of existing development to the various attraction features. The location of existing tourism development is also, of course, a consideration in planning for expansion. This survey includes evaluation of the quality of existing tourism development, and its environmental integration as related to the beaches and coastal areas.

All types of transportation are surveyed and evaluated. First, the organization of the transport sector is reviewed. Then, the major issues of air transport access to Malta are identified, with consideration given to travel facilitation procedures. The sea links to and among the islands are examined. Internal surface means of transportation, including bus, taxi and rent-a-car services, are evaluated. The short cruise boat tours offered by tour operators among the islands are also reviewed. Recommendations on improvement to all aspects of transportation are made in the plan.

All tourist accommodation is inventoried. A market analysis is conducted and market targets established based on the development objectives, evaluation of tourist attractions and other factors. These targets reflect the greater mix of types of tourist markets which the country wishes to attract and are realistic to accomplish. Based on the market targets, the number and type of future accommodation are projected. The institutional elements of tourism – organizational approaches and structures, investment incentives, legislation requirements and manpower planning – were investigated, with recommendations made for any improvements required. Economic, environmental and socio-cultural impacts are evaluated and recommendations made on these factors.

In preparing the plan, the major consideration was the need to improve and diversify the tourism product. This is necessary in order to upgrade and diversify the tourist markets, one of the plan objectives. Based on another plan objective, market and product improvements must be accomplished within the framework of expanding tourism as a major economic sector of the country.

For planning purposes, the two main islands of Malta and Gozo were divided into 12 zones, 10 on Malta and two on Gozo. This division provides for the systematic analysis of relatively homogeneous areas for which recommendations can be made. Within each zone, many recommendations are made on the specific policies that should be adopted and the actions that are required in order to improve the areas (as related to tourism development). TPUs (tourism planning units) are designated as specific 'no go' areas – places where no new tourism development should be allowed until detailed plans have been prepared and adopted to guide future development. Two of the tourism zones are designated as priority areas for improvements.

As part of the planning project, detailed planning and some urban design improvements were prepared for the two priority areas. Detailed planning, design and development programming were also prepared for visitor facilities at selected major archaeological and historic sites. In the implementation programme, the plan recommends an effective institutional approach for reviewing and taking action on future tourism development projects, such as hotels and resorts, proposed by the private sector. This procedure is essential so that new development projects reflect the plan's recommendations, and do not generate any environmental or social problems. Also it allows for efficient processing of the project proposals. The implementation approach includes a specific action and project development programme.

A major element of the planning study is the marketing plan and related product improvement programme. The market planning approach reflects the close relationship between developing the tourism product and promoting tourist markets. The strategy recommended in the marketing plan comprises the three elements of: 1) market diversification; 2) quality improvement; and 3) lengthening the tourist season. Then, derived from the strategy, marketing policies are determined and the action plans set forth for 1990–94. The action plans recommend specific actions and activities, related to coordinated product development and promotion, that should be carried out.

The product development programme specifies various actions for the short- and medium-term periods. These include the following:

- Implementing the tourism area upgrading schemes.
- Promoting hotel and other facilities upgrading with an incentive package.
- Encouraging the development of high quality hotels and other facilities related to specific target markets.
- Promoting the development of leisure facilities, such as yacht marinas, sports complexes, entertainment facilities, an underwater national park, cultural heritage sites, more shopping, and a light and laser harbour show.

The plan states that sufficient time will be required to achieve the shifting of markets and the product improvement needed, and that progress can best be made on a step-by-step basis. But it anticipates that, if the policies and programme are followed on schedule, the desired changes will be well underway by 1995. Over the longer term, the plan envisages Malta as a quality 'good value-for-money' destination, appealing to diversified middle and higher income market groups.

CONCLUSIONS

The Malta plan is a good example of a substantially developed tourist destination that needs to expand tourism for economic reasons. At the same time, the country wishes to shift its tourist markets to more diversified and higher spending ones. Another objective is to have better seasonal distribution of tourists throughout the year. A principle here is that, in addition to the greater expenditures of more tourists in total, the higher spending tourists visiting throughout the year will generate more income per tourist. The desired income will be generated by a fewer number of higher spending tourists rather than a larger number of lower spending tourists. This reduces the negative environmental and social impacts of large-scale tourism.

To accomplish these objectives, the plan recognizes that the key issues are: 1) to improve and diversify (as well as expand) the tourism product of accommodation, other facilities and attraction features; and 2) to change the marketing strategy and promotion techniques. The plan rightfully emphasizes that tourism product improvements and market changes must proceed together, as a basic principle of tourism development. The plan also recognizes that these changes should take place within the framework of a comprehensive and specific physical plan, institutional improvements and development programming.

It is important to note that the planning includes a detailed environmental analysis which takes into account the scarce land and water resources of these small islands. This is an essential approach to achieve sustainable development. The land use patterns are also very important to understand in deciding on location of tourism areas. It is noteworthy that the tourism plan is intended to be integrated into the overall development plan of the islands. This should achieve better integration of tourism into the total development patterns of the country.

Dividing the country into tourism zones of relatively homogeneous areas represents an important planning principle. These zones provide a geographically rational basis for analysis and formulation of specific development policies, and for which to prepare detailed physical plans.

The marketing plan approach is a logical one that proceeds from general objectives to strategy, policies and action plans, with each policy and action plan specified in detail. Product development is carefully programmed and promotional techniques identified. In its statement that some time will be required to accomplish the desired changes, the plan presents a cautionary note to Malta that it needs to be patient but persistent in achieving its tourism objectives.

Chapter 12

Survey and evaluation of tourist attractions in the Oman tourism plan

A detailed survey and evaluation of tourist attractions were conducted as a major element of preparing the national tourism plan for Oman. These provided an important basis for formulating the development strategy and programme.

BACKGROUND

The Sultanate of Oman is located in the southeastern corner of the Arabian Peninsula. Its coastline of some 1,700 kilometres fronts on the Arabian Sea, an extension of the Indian Ocean, the Gulf of Oman and the Straits of Hormuz, which is the access to the Persian Gulf. The country encompasses a variety of geographical features of mountains, coastal plains and deserts. Summer temperatures can become very hot, including in the capital city of Muscat on the north coast. Summer temperatures are more moderate in the southern area, where the country's second major city of Salalah is located, because of a summer monsoon period. The average rainfall is light, but occasional heavy rains in the mountains can result in sudden flash floods that may cause considerable property damage. Oman contains about 1.5 million inhabitants, virtually all of whom are Ibadhi Moslems.

The country has a long and interesting history which provides many of its tourist attractions. There are numerous examples of settlements dating from the third millennium BC. Formerly known as Magan, the northern region has produced and exported copper, starting in about 2000 BC and continuing to the present. Frankincense has been produced and exported from the southern region since the first century AD. The Persians probably introduced the underground irrigation technique, known as the falaj system, in Oman in the fourth century BC. This system is still widely used in the country. Oman had a reputation of being a seafaring nation. There is evidence of trips being made to the Indian subcontinent from 1000 BC. During the seventeenth to nineteenth centuries, Oman became a colonial power and controlled Mombasa and Zanzibar – important trading centres in East Africa. During the twentieth century, the country's economy was based only on agriculture and fishing until oil was discovered in 1967. Oil production has significantly changed the economy and provided the resources for rapid economic development and rise of the people's income levels.

Until recently, international tourism was non-existent in Oman. Foreign visitors were allowed into the country only for business and related purposes. In 1987, the regulations were eased to permit holiday tourism to commence on a limited scale. Also, in that year, holiday visitors were allowed in without visas from the other GCC (Gulf Cooperation Council) countries. By 1990, 149,000 tourists of all types came to Oman, but the proportion of holiday tourists, excluding those from the GCC countries, is still quite small. The Gulf Coast tourists particularly like to visit the south during its relatively cool summer season. Oman has some excellent business-traveller oriented hotels in Muscat and Salalah, but tourist accommodation is limited elsewhere. Several tour operators and travel agents are established in the country. The national infrastructure is well developed and still being improved in the remote areas. Medical, educational and other services are being rapidly improved.

In order to diversify the economy and reduce the dependence on oil exports, Oman has decided to develop tourism on a very controlled basis. The focus of tourism should be on the country's inherent environmental and cultural attractions. The attitude toward developing tourism is a cautious one. Although the potential economic benefits of tourism are recognized, it is strongly felt by the government, and Omanis generally, that its growth must take place within a planned framework which seeks to safeguard the environment and protect cultural values. Mass tourism of the winter sun, sand and sea type is to be completely avoided. Tourism development that does take place will be carefully monitored to determine its environmental and socio-cultural effects.

TOURISM PLANNING APPROACH

The tourism plan for Oman is a comprehensive one (UNDP and WTO. 1991. *National Plan for Tourism – Sultanate of Oman*. Madrid: WTO). It is based on specific objectives, stated in the plan as follows:

- Develop a strategy for tourism which reflects the singular attractions of the Sultanate in relation to domestic and international markets.
- Base the strategy primarily on attractions of a cultural, environmental or scenic nature rather than on climatic or littoral (coastal) geography.
- Maximize the potential economic benefits of tourism within limits imposed by the need to protect cultural values and the environment.
- Provide opportunities for diversifying the economy and reducing regional economic disparities.

The plan examines all the components of tourism including the institutional elements. The market analysis includes tourist arrival targets established by five-year periods to 2005. These targets are broken down by holiday tourists of various types – international, Gulf expatriates and GCC citizens vacationing in Oman. The targets also specify various types of business travellers – international, Gulf expatriates, Gulf Arabs, and Omani business. It is anticipated that business travellers will still greatly outnumber holiday tourists by 2005. Based on the market targets, accommodation needs are projected. Development opportunities and constraints are identified and alternative development scenarios are evaluated. The plan sets forth guidelines for formulating the preferred development strategy.

The tourism development concept is based on providing opportunities for informed tourists to experience the special cultural and environmental features of Oman. Six tourism zones are designated – three primary zones of attraction and three secondary zones. The major types of attractions are indicated for each zone. The plan also identifies several special interest themes based on flora, fauna and the country's history.

The plan recommends various tourist itineraries, circuits and excursions. A national itinerary refers to movement of tourists about the Sultanate as a whole. A typical national itinerary would consist of six to seven days in the north and three days in the south. A tourist circuit is defined as a circular route with a number of attractions along it. A circuit may take several days to cover and involve overnight stays at different places. Two such circuits are recommended. An excursion is a visit of a few hours or a full day to a place of interest, going out from and returning to an established base.

The plan makes recommendations on developing domestic tourism. These relate to the principal activities of domestic tourists and the supporting facilities required, and include beach park and recreation development.

A marketing strategy is proposed. This strategy emphasizes image-building based on the country's cultural, historic and environmental attributes. Selective promotion would be directed toward the holiday target markets, and focus on both general interest and special interest themes. Assessments and recommendations are made in the plan on social, environmental and economic impacts.

Plan implementation considers several elements – organization for tourism; procedural controls including licensing of suitable tour operators; manpower planning and training for tourism; promotional measures; planning actions including establishing a tourism information system; a detailed development programme; planning and pre-feasibility analysis of three demonstration projects; and outline local plans for two tourism areas.

SURVEY AND EVALUATION OF TOURIST ATTRACTIONS

Because of the importance given to developing tourism based on the inherent environmental and cultural attractions of Oman, the survey and evaluation of tourist attractions are particularly detailed and specific. They are organized based on three categories of attractions – scenic beauty and environmental features; social and cultural attributes; and historic monuments.

A geographical analysis is made of the country's landscapes, including the mountains, coastal plains, deserts and the geographically transitional Muscat area. Within this context, areas of special scenic interest are identified, organized into the categories and evaluated as follows:

- Upper wadis – These are unique desert features of (mostly dry) streambeds, often within high rock walls, which can be travelled by footpath or road. The wadis are evaluated with respect to several factors – sense of enclosure; variation of views; frequency and variety of features of interest; interest of settlements; natural vegetation; water interest; and significance of end destination. Eleven wadis are designated as first grade attractions. The plan notes that some other remote wadis are likely to be at the same quality level.
- Mountain areas – Due to their accessibility and potential for providing recreational opportunities as well as outstanding views, three mountain areas are identified as having special touristic interest.
- Scenic routes – Scenic routes are defined as surfaced roads that offer visual enjoyment of the landscape. Scenic routes are evaluated based on several factors – dramatic scenery visible from the road; variety of interest; settlement character; special landscape features; density of vegetation; water interest; and length of scenic section. Based on this evaluation, eleven scenic routes are identified.
- Beaches – Tourist beaches are evaluated according to several criteria: fine light-coloured sand; a shallow gradient above the waterline; a regular gradient beneath the water permitting swimming within 15 metres of the shore; no off-shore current, undertow or fierce waves; sufficient length and depth to carry several groups in an uncrowded way; an attractive setting, preferably in a bay with a backdrop of hills; no incompatible development; a south/southwest orientation to maximize the number of hours of sunshine; and no conflict with sensitive environmental issues. The plan identifies eight first grade beaches and four second grade.

The plan examines the natural flora and fauna of Oman, and draws several conclusions. There is great diversity of birdlife, including migratory species stopping over in Oman on flights between Africa and India. Oman is internationally known as a breeding ground for marine turtles including four different species. The coastal waters support one of the best fisheries in the Indian Ocean. Major coral reefs lie offshore in several places. The plan indicates that Oman has been a leader in nature conservation, and that several nature reserves have been established. The plan evaluates and identifies the major environmental attractions related to flora and fauna which could form the basis of tourist itineraries and excursions, but under controlled conditions in order to protect the flora and fauna.

The plan indicates that the cultural roots of Oman lie in its historic towns and villages, and that these settlements are the focus for experiencing the culture and life styles of Omani people. Settlements are broadly classified into the three geographic groups – the communities of the coast, the mountains and inland desert plains. Each of these is examined in some detail. An inventory of these settlements was conducted and they are evaluated with respect to several factors – homogeneity of style or period; urban character; built form; setting; condition; general level of activity; special activities (such as festivals); and presence of exceptional buildings. Each of these criteria for evaluating settlements is assessed and assigned a one to five star rating. Based on the evaluation, the most culturally important settlements are identified, as follows:

- Settlements of the first order of attraction – 10 places.
- Settlements of a high order of attraction – 8 places.
- Other interesting settlements – 10 places.
- High order attractions in ruinous condition – 5 places.
- Settlements containing exceptional individual or groups of buildings – 8 places.

The third major type of attraction examined in the plan is historic monuments. Archaeological and historic sites are reviewed with respect to their historic period – prehistoric (about 10000 to 3000 BC); Bronze Age (about 3000 to 1000 BC); Iron Age (about 1000 BC to AD 650); early Islamic (about AD 650 to 1650); and Imperial (about AD 1650 to 1850). The plan points out that some archaeological excavations and inventorying of sites have been carried out, but these are far from complete. In the plan, these sites are listed by area, described and classified as attractions according to three grades, as follows:

- Grade A – Major site suitable for a visit of an hour or more.
- Grade B – Major site for less than an hour's visit.
- Grade C – Less important site with potential appeal.

There are many watch towers, forts, fortified houses and fortifications around towns, villages and entire palm tree plantations in Oman. Some 13 of these have been restored, and others are programmed for restoration. These are examined in the plan as a separate category, with the more important places specifically described. Other historic buildings and complexes of buildings are reviewed, including souks (traditional market places), mosques, falaj irrigation systems and aqueducts.

The survey and evaluation of tourist attractions are used as important input into formulating the tourism development strategy and programme. In addition, under the planning actions and policies section of the plan, general recommendations are made on the importance of conserving the urban fabric. Three categories of conservation of historic settlements are set forth in the plan – category 1 for restoration; category 2 for conservation; and category 3 for preservation. Policies are also recommended for managing the environment and inducing social and cultural harmony between tourists and the Omani host community. Detailed planning for demonstration projects include visitor and interpretation facilities at some priority attraction places.

CONCLUSIONS

The survey and evaluation of existing and potential tourist attraction features are given particular emphasis in the process of preparing the Oman tourism plan. This is because an important development objective is to base tourism on the inherent natural and cultural environment of the country, and to attract the types of general and special interest tourists who appreciate these features. Unless the attractions are thoroughly understood through survey and evaluation, it would not be possible to achieve the objective and prepare an appropriate plan. Also, the fact that there are a large number and diversity of both natural and cultural/historic attractions required that considerable attention be given to their survey and evaluation.

Because tourism is to be based on the inherent features of Oman, special types of attractions such as theme parks and casinos are not considered, as they might have been in some other tourist destinations. The approach used also reflects the development objective of not encouraging coastal tourism (the sun, sea and sand type of mass tourism). The survey and evaluation of beaches are related to development of recreation for domestic and Gulf Coast tourists, not for intensive use by international tourists.

The approach to survey and evaluation used in the plan is a thorough and systematic one. The attraction features are first categorized and then evaluated according to consistent grading systems. This grading provides an essential basis for deciding which attractions are the more important ones to recommend in the plan for conservation and development. Although the grading systems are obviously somewhat subjective, they do provide a meaningful basis for comparison when applied by experienced tourism planners.

An important approach used in this plan is to survey and evaluate the attractions within the context of researching and describing the overall geography of Oman and its cultural and historic development. This results in the planners (and users of the plan report) having a better understanding of the attraction features and being able to evaluate them more effectively. Serious tourists to the country will also have done some research and be knowledgeable about the geography, history and culture of the country. They will want to visit attractions that reflect this overall understanding.

Based on this survey and evaluation of attractions, the next step in the planning process was to select those attractions that will be integrated into the tourism development plan and programme. This involved other considerations such as access and location relative to tour itineraries and accommodation centres. Also conservation needs will be a consideration. For example, with respect to the attraction of marine turtles, utmost control of visitor viewing will be necessary during the season when they come ashore to lay eggs. When major attractions have been selected, they will require detailed planning for their conservation, development of visitor facilities and regulation of visitor use.

It is noteworthy that the government of Oman has established a highly progressive environmental conservation programme, with several nature reserves already designated. Coastal conservation management is also a major programme in Oman. Some restoration of historic monuments has already been carried out. This survey and evaluation of natural and cultural attractions, and the important role that these attractions play in tourism, may provide the impetus for continued and expanded conservation efforts.

Chapter 13

Tourism carrying capacity study of Goa

The tourism carrying capacity study of Goa, India, demonstrates application of carrying capacity analysis to several critical factors. This type of study provides important basic input to preparation of a tourism plan that is based on the concept of sustainable development.

BACKGROUND

The state of Goa is located on the west-central coast of India, facing the Indian Ocean. Goa has a coastline of 106 kilometres of which about 65 kilometres consist of sandy beaches. The state contains a population of some 1.1 million inhabitants. Regional access is primarily via road and air from Bombay in the north. The local airport also handles international air traffic including charter flights organized for international tour groups. The state already has substantial tourism development, and attracted more than 900,000 tourists in 1988. The majority of these are domestic visitors but there are also many international tourists. Domestic tourists visit Goa throughout the year, with some decrease of arrivals during the monsoon (rainy) season. However, there is a definite seasonality of foreign tourist arrivals, with the low period during the monsoon season.

Most of the existing tourist accommodation is beach oriented and concentrated in the central part of the region. Some substantial new beach resort development has recently opened in the southern area.

The important tourism resources of Goa are the tropical climate, extensive beaches and a scenic natural environment of lush vegetation along the coast and forested inland hills and mountains. These inland areas also offer the opportunity for wildlife viewing. Significant attractions are associated with the region's distinctive cultural patterns of arts, crafts, music, dance, cuisine and highly interesting religious and historic places. Goa was a Portuguese colony for several centuries which left a cultural heritage that is unique in India. Old Goa with its sixteenth-century European style buildings and ruins is a major feature. More generally, the Goan architectural style of churches, houses and other buildings is of considerable interest to tourists.

THE CARRYING CAPACITY STUDY

The tourism carrying capacity study for Goa was conducted in 1989 (UNDP and WTO. 1989. *Tourism Carrying Capacity Study – Goa, India.* Madrid: WTO). This study also included an assessment of the social and environmental impacts of tourism and guidelines for the planning, development and control of tourism. The study was designed to provide input into preparation of a comprehensive regional tourism plan, to be undertaken in the early 1990s.

In formulating the carrying capacity study, it was first determined that the major attraction of Goa for holiday tourists is the quality and extent of beaches combined with the warm climate. This is reflected in the fact that, except for a few mountain lodges and facilities for religious pilgrims, virtually all existing and new accommodation development is located along the coast. Although tourists visit the natural, historic and cultural attractions located in the inland areas, they stay in beach accommodation and take day tours to the inland features. Therefore, the carrying capacities of beaches – along with labour supply capabilities, social impact evaluation and infrastructure capacities – are the primary considerations in the analysis.

The study estimates that an average density of 40 square metres of beach area per tourist bed would be an appropriate standard in assessing beach carrying capacity. This standard is, in part, based on the considerations of seasonality of tourist arrivals and the fact that domestic tourists do not make as intensive use of beaches as do foreign tourists. Domestic tourists spend much of their time shopping and visiting places. Assuming an average width of sandy beach of 40 metres, application of this density standard means that not more than one tourist bed per 1 metre of beach frontage should be developed.

Additionally, the study determines that not more than 70 per cent of the beach – or 46 out of the 65 kilometres of total beach length – should be developed. This factor is applied in order to:

- Protect the general landscape character of the area, with particular reference to the vegetation of coconut trees, as well as other aspects of distinguished coastal configuration.
- Protect the coastal villages, including several fishing villages, and their surrounding areas, so that villagers can continue their customary daily activities without disturbances.
- Avoid ribbon or continuous development along the coastline, but instead encourage development to take place in groupings with adequate open space and natural vegetation between these development groupings.
- Avoid disfigurement of the coastal character resulting from extensive building development.
- Cater also for the recreational and other needs of local inhabitants through

development of public beach parks. These parks can be used by tourists as well as residents.

The standard of 1 metre of beach frontage per tourist bed is applied to the 46 kilometres of available beach. This results in an overall regional maximum development level of 46,000 tourist beds, or about 23,000 rooms.

Based on the existing configuration of accommodation development, the study estimates that about 30 per cent of beds of lower room rate level will be situated in places not directly facing the beach and sea, although they mostly will be within walking distance of the beach. Consequently, not more than 35 kilometres of beach frontage are expected to be actually utilized for development. This pattern will result in a density of about 57 square metres of beach area per tourist bed in accommodation fronting the beach. The study recognizes, however, that some tourists staying in the nearby non-beach fronting hotels will also use the beach.

The study indicates that, because many domestic tourists do not use the beach intensively, it is unlikely that the number of people on particular beaches on any given day will exceed the established density levels. Even when a concentration of users occurs at the popular beaches on peak use days, the density will not likely drop below 10 square metres per beach user. This level is considered acceptable, both in this region and internationally.

Based on the 46,000 tourist bed figure, the study projects that some 4.1 million annual tourist arrivals could be received at the optimum development level. This is more than four and one-half times the 1988 level of tourists visiting the region. This estimate was determined based on three factors – reasonable assumptions of the ratio of domestic to international tourists; the average length of stay of each of these groups; and average accommodation occupancy rates.

The implications of the optimum level of development are calculated in the study. Based on assumptions of direct employee requirements of one employee per bed (two per room) in the higher quality hotels and 0.4 employees per bed (slightly less than one per room) in the lower quality units, there would be an accommodation employment demand for 28,000 persons. With the addition of employment required in other tourist facilities and services, 60,000 persons would be needed in direct tourism employment. Additionally, there would be generation of a substantial number of jobs indirectly related to tourism – in the tourism supplying sectors and the tourism induced economic activities.

Based on the present level of underemployment and unemployment and projected growth of the economy and population, the study determines that an adequate labour supply will exist to serve the projected level of tourism development, as well as other economic sectors. In fact, an important reason for expanding tourism is to provide more employment in the region.

The study evaluates the social impact of the projected level of tourism development. The approach used is to calculate the ratio of the peak daily number of tourists to the resident population within the tourism coastal development areas. This ratio was found to be well within the range of major tourism regions elsewhere in the world. Another important consideration is that the great majority of tourists to Goa are currently, and will continue to be, domestic visitors. These are people with similar cultural backgrounds and customs to Goans. Therefore, the ratio of foreigners to residents is much less than the overall ratio.

The future demand for water supply to serve the projected level of tourism is also reviewed. This is considered to be the most critical component of the infrastructure required for development in the region. Water demand is based on an assumed average consumption of 0.8 cubic metres per day per tourist bed, for a total of 36,800 cubic metres maximum demand generated by tourism. The study investigates the existing and proposed water development schemes, and determines that an adequate water supply would be available in the state to serve both tourism and general community needs. It recommends that water conservation techniques still be applied, including recycling of sewage effluent for use as irrigation water.

The study examines the other infrastructure requirements of the transportation system, electricity, sewage and solid waste disposal, and telecommunications. It determines that these will be adequate for the future level of tourism development, if infrastructure improvement programmes are undertaken as needed. The report notes current deficiencies that should be corrected in the near future.

The overall conclusion of the study report is that the main factor in deciding the optimum level of tourism development is the environmental carrying capacity of the coastal area of the region. All the other factors are more than capable of meeting the demands established by the environmental carrying capacity. However, substantial improvements will be required in infrastructure in order to both remedy present deficiencies and meet future demands. It recommends, therefore, that future development of tourism in Goa should not exceed 46,000 beds, including those in existing accommodation.

CONCLUSIONS

The Goa study represents a systematic approach to determining tourism carrying capacity. Several of the important types of measurement criteria are considered – environmental capacity for development and use without overcrowding; infrastructure; availability of sufficient labour supply; and social impact. Environmental capacity standards are established based on evaluation of the local physical environment, and the expectations of the types of tourists who now and will in the future be visiting the region. These are then compared to the standards which are applied in similar situations elsewhere in the world, to·make certain that they are reasonable. The environmental capacity is focused on the capacity of the beaches to handle visitors. Although not specifically referred to in the report, the capacity of the adjacent lands for development of facilities was also considered and is, in fact, adequate for the proposed development.

An interesting and useful approach in establishing the coastal environmental capacity is first to remove from consideration those beach areas that should be preserved for non-tourism types of development. This helps give greater assurance that those places will actually be preserved for other uses. If an adequate amount of beach area has been designated for tourism based on the capacity study, there will not then be the pressure for expansion of tourism development into those places that should be preserved for non-tourism uses.

Infrastructure is considered with respect to its adequacy in serving the existing development, and also how well it will serve future development based on the proposed improvement programmes. This evaluation reveals that there is no problem in terms of basic infrastructure resources. The study, however, justifiably emphasizes the need to remedy existing deficiencies and pursue expansion programmes as tourism grows.

The social impact evaluation rightfully takes into account that the majority of tourists are, and will continue to be, domestic ones with similar cultural backgrounds to residents. Based on that factor, and the projected low ratio of tourists to residents, the study concludes that there is not expected to be any serious negative socio-cultural impacts. The limiting of visitor density on the beaches and provision of public beach parks are important techniques to reduce any possible resentment by residents, due to a sense of overcrowding and loss of amenities because of tourism.

In preparing the regional tourism plan for Goa, the optimum regional level of development that is determined in the carrying capacity study will need to be properly distributed among the proposed tourism development areas. The carrying capacities of each specific development area should be calculated to ensure that the recommended types and extent of development do not exceed these local capacities. In addition to designating the tourism development areas according to logical criteria, the regional plan will need to take an integrated approach. Consideration will need to be given to the preservation of existing coastal village areas, expansion of coastal urban areas, location of public beach parks, and other types of non-tourism land uses.

There are not expected to be any serious adverse environmental and socio-cultural impacts from the expansion of tourism. However, the final plan will still need to consider application of specific environmental and socio-cultural control measures. This will give additional assurance that no problems will result from future development.

Chapter 14

Tourism development policy of Zanzibar

The tourism development policy of Zanzibar reflects a comprehensive approach to developing tourism, and it provides much of the basis for preparing the regional tourism plan. Related to the policy are the criteria established to select the tourism development areas designated in the plan.

BACKGROUND

Zanzibar comprises the islands of Zanzibar and Pemba, situated off the coast of Tanzania in East Africa. The islands have a population of about half a million and constitute a semi-autonomous entity of Tanzania. The islands are well known for their production and export of cloves, which provide the major source of cash income. However, the government wishes to diversify the cash economy with the development of tourism.

Historically, Zanzibar was an important Arab trading centre for East Africa. It was a sultanate for many years prior to independence. Zanzibar also became a focus of Swahili cultural development. The Stone Town area of Zanzibar city is the largest and best example of Southern Arabian architectural styles and urban layout in East Africa. Stone Town and some palace and other ruins in the countryside are important historic attractions for tourists. Other attractions are the pleasant tropical climate, good beaches, marine areas for diving and sport fishing, scenic beauty, traditional Swahili villages and clove farms.

Prior to the mid-1980s, tourism development was very limited with only a modest level of facilities and services available to tourists. Attraction features required conservation and development and infrastructure needed improvements. Only a limited number of holiday tourists visited the islands. Since then, there has been some development of beach resorts and other tourism improvements carried out.

TOURISM DEVELOPMENT POLICY

The Zanzibar regional tourism development plan was prepared in 1983 (UNDP and WTO. 1983. *Zanzibar Tourism Development Plan*, Madrid: WTO). The planning project was designed to prepare a comprehensive regional tourism development policy and structure plan, including the institutional elements. Detailed plans were prepared for specific priority development sites.

The tourism development policy recommended in the plan was quite comprehensive. This policy and its introductory statement, as extracted from the plan report, is as follows:

> Formulation and adoption of appropriate tourism policy is the essential first step in developing tourism. Tourism policy indicates the type and direction which the area wishes to take on tourism development and provides the general basis for planning tourism and making decisions on its continuing development. Adoption of tourism policy indicates that the area has made an official commitment to develop tourism, and the policy provides the legal basis for guiding the general type and extent of tourism to be developed.
>
> The major elements of a suitable tourism policy statement for Zanzibar are recommended as follows:
>
> - International tourism should be developed as an important means of achieving greater understanding and appreciation of Zanzibar's history, culture and natural environment by foreigners, and of residents' developing some understanding of other people's customs and cultures.
> - International tourism also should be developed to provide additional employment, income and foreign exchange for Zanzibar, and to help diversify the islands' economy.
> - Domestic tourism should be developed as an important means of recreation, increasing understanding by Zanzibaris of their own historical, cultural and environmental heritage, and by mainland Tanzanians of Zanzibar's rich historical and cultural heritage.
> - Domestic tourism also should be developed as a means of redistributing income within Zanzibar, especially from urban to rural areas and from mainland Tanzania to Zanzibar.
> - Tourism development should be integrated into the overall development policy, planning and strategy of Zanzibar, and receive appropriate priority and its necessary share of development resources.
> - Tourism should be developed and operated so that it promotes conservation of archaeological sites and historic places, conservation and revitalization of the desirable aspects of traditional cultural patterns, arts and handicrafts, and maintenance of the essence of religious beliefs and practices, all of which represent the historic and

cultural heritage of Zanzibar. Tourism should be planned, developed and organized so that it does not result in serious social problems or cultural disruptions.

- Tourism should be developed in a carefully planned, controlled and organized manner so that it promotes conservation of the natural environment, especially places of scenic beauty, indigenous flora and fauna, important natural ecological systems, outdoor recreation potential, beaches and underwater environments. Tourism development should not result in any type of serious air, water, noise and visual pollution.
- Tourism development should proceed on a controlled, systematic basis, according to a staged programme of allocating development resources to specified places. The pace of tourism development should be kept in balance with the number and type of tourist arrivals, the development of infrastructure and with Zanzibar's economic and social capability of absorbing tourism growth.
- Tourism should be developed so that it will serve as a catalyst for increased development of related economic activities such as handicraft production, agriculture and fisheries and other related industries, and help in supporting improvements of transportation facilities and services and other infrastructure.
- Tourism should be planned and developed so that it makes maximum use of existing infrastructure, and that improved and new infrastructure should serve general purpose needs as well as tourism.
- Tourist accommodation and other facilities should be designed to reflect and represent Zanzibar's distinctive architectural styles, the islands' tropical environment and utilize local building materials to the extent possible. Maximum use should be made of renovated existing buildings which have architectural and historical significance for tourist facilities.
- All aspects of tourism development and operations should be organized so that tourism functions in an efficient and integrated manner to meet the needs of international and domestic tourists and achieve the objectives of tourism development. Especially important is the coordination of tourism development among the various government agencies and parastatals.
- Tourist facilities and services should be designed to meet the range of needs of various tourist market segments, including international and local standards, without being unduly expensive to develop, on the one hand, and always meeting minimum requirements of sanitation, safety and comfort on the other.
- Emphasis should be placed on employment of local persons in tourism. The persons working in all aspects of tourism should be properly

trained to function effectively in their employment, and be given maximum opportunity for career development and job satisfaction.
- The general public should be educated to understand tourism and its role in Zanzibar's development policy, and be given all possible opportunities to use and enjoy tourist facilities and attractions while still respecting and maintaining suitable standards of these facilities and services.

The plan report recommends that this policy be carefully reviewed by the government, modified if needed, and incorporated into the proposed policy statement then being considered by the government. Alternatively, it should be adopted as part of the tourism plan.

CRITERIA FOR SELECTING TOURISM DEVELOPMENT AREAS

In determining the tourism development areas in the structure plan, several selection criteria are specified. These criteria are as follows:

- One or more important attractions within or near the area.
- Suitable and environmentally attractive sites for development of tourist accommodation (or existing buildings suitable for renovation), without creating undue social or environmental problems, for example, availability of sites which do not require substantial relocation of people or major economic activities.
- Adequate transportation access now or in the future to the area from the tourist entry points (airport and seaports) in Zanzibar and Pemba islands.
- Adequate transportation linkages to other development areas and to important tourist attractions elsewhere in Zanzibar.
- Availability of other infrastructure now or in the future, especially of adequate potable water, electric power, sanitary sewage disposal and telephone service.
- Availability or potential to develop the necessary other tourist facilities within the area (often these can be provided in the hotel or resort environment).
- Existing or proposed development of accommodation in the area – the existing patterns of tourism development.
- Interest of local residents in having tourism development in or near their area.
- Need in the general area for employment and economic activities.

Based on these criteria, several tourism development areas, mostly urban places and resorts areas, were selected and designated on the tourism structure plan.

CONCLUSIONS

The plan report first indicates why policy is important to formulate and adopt. This educates the government about the need for policy. The actual policy statement is comprehensive and refers to all the basic relevant themes of developing tourism. One theme is why international and domestic tourism should be developed, and both economic and social reasons are indicated. The importance of integrating tourism into overall development policy and patterns is emphasized. Another major theme is that tourism should be used as a technique for environmental and cultural conservation, and not generate socio-cultural or environmental problems. The approach to be taken of controlled, staged and integrated development is specified in the policy. Economically, the policy stresses that tourism should be a catalyst to overall economic development, as well as generating its own immediate benefits. The points are made that tourist facilities should be architecturally integrated into their cultural and natural environment, and make use of multi-purpose infrastructure.

Institutional elements are included in the policy. Reference is made to the need for effective organization of tourism including coordination among the various government agencies and with the private sector. The importance of training and employing local residents is stressed. The need for public education about tourism is indicated. The point is made that residents should have access to tourist attractions and facilities. The concept of developing quality tourism that meets the expectations of tourists is set forth.

The criteria applied for selecting tourism development areas reflect a specific and systematic approach to preparing the structure plan. The selection criteria consider all the important physical factors – tourist attractions, environmental suitability, transportation access and linkages, availability of other infrastructure and existing development patterns. Socio-economic considerations, about the interest of local residents in developing tourism and local economic development needs, are also indicated. Not listed here, but also applied as a criterion in the plan, was that tourism should not pre-empt places or resources that are more important for other types of uses and development.

Chapter 15

Tourism planning in Bhutan

Policy and planning for tourism in Bhutan are based on the concept of maintaining high value, special interest and adventure tourism, which is developed in a very controlled and staged manner. There is much involvement of the government and religious leaders in the planning and management process.

BACKGROUND

Located in the eastern Himalaya Mountains of South Asia, the Kingdom of Bhutan is mostly high and mountainous. Bordering India on the south are foothills with subtropical wildlife and vegetation. The country contains a population of about 1.5 million, most of which is agricultural. Only about 5 per cent of the people live in urban places. Nomadism is still practised by certain groups in the higher elevations. Many Bhutanese live a relatively secure and comfortable subsistence life style that is not, to a great extent, integrated into the modern cash economy.

Attractions for tourists are the spectacular mountain scenery and strongly traditional Buddhist cultural patterns. The distinctive Bhutanese architectural styles of monasteries, palaces, shops and homes are a major feature. The castle-monasteries called *dzongs* are particularly striking features of the cultural landscape. Handicrafts are available. Cultural tours and mountain trekking are the most popular activities of tourists. Access to the country for tourists is primarily by air to the international airport at Paro in western Bhutan. The airport is at a relatively short distance from the capital city of Thimpu, and connects to the country's road network. There is also one road access from India in the southwest.

Tourism in Bhutan commenced after the Royal Coronation of the present king in 1974, when it was realized that the hotels developed for that event could be utilized for tourists. The objectives of tourism at the time of its introduction were to:

● Generate revenue, especially foreign exchange.

- Publicize the culture and traditions of the country to the outside world.
- Play an active role in the country's socio-economic development.

However, the government was concerned that the unrestricted flow of tourists could lead to socio-cultural and environmental problems, and it applied a strict policy of controlling tourism development. Until the mid-1980s, the maximum number of international holiday tourist arrivals, excluding the neighbouring Indians, was maintained at 2,000 annually. In 1986, 2,500 arrivals were targeted. Arrivals have remained at about the 2,500–3,000 level into the early 1990s.

THE TOURISM PLAN

A national tourism development plan was completed in 1984 and, after long debate by the government, adopted in 1986 (UNDP and WTO. 1986. *Tourism Development Master Plan for Bhutan*. Madrid: WTO). The plan indicates that Bhutan's resources present potential for three types of tourism, each in a different geographical zone, as follows:

- Himalayan zone for mountaineering and high altitude trekking.
- Central zone for cultural tours, including trekking.
- Southern foothills zone for wildlife tourism in conjunction with Indian winter tourism

The plan states that, 'The central cultural zone has unique attractions by world standards, and creates great potential as a focus for all aspects of Bhutanese tourism development.'

The plan recognizes the government's desire to continue the policy of controlled tourism development, gradually opening up new areas as infrastructure is developed. The overriding aim is to ensure that the type and rate of growth of tourism does not damage the natural environment nor degrade the cultural heritage. In fact, the tourism plan views controlled tourism as an important vehicle for conserving and enhancing the cultural assets of the country.

In the tourism plan, growth targets for international tourist arrivals were set at 3,000 for 1990 and 5,600 for 1995 under the preferred strategy. The National Seventh Five-Year Development Plan for 1992–96 closely follows and further refines these market targets.

The tourism development strategy set forth in the plan is to focus development around tourism service centres in the main potential areas, linked by tourist excursion routes. Eight such centres are recommended for the long-term period in the western, central, eastern and southern regions of the country. The strategy identifies three time phases, which are illustrated in Figure 15.1, and described as follows:

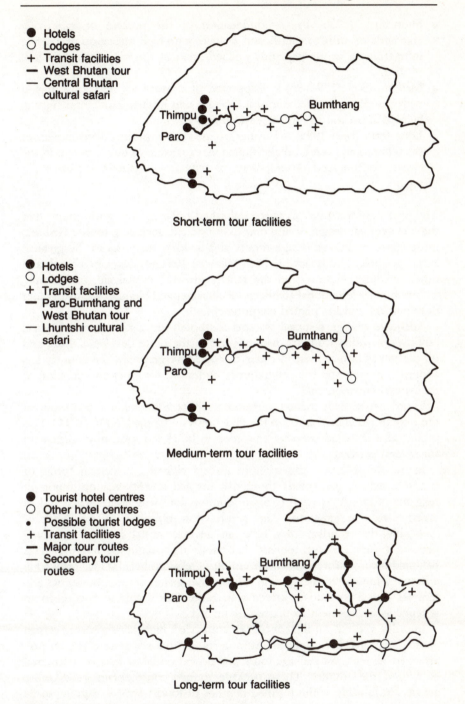

Short-term tour facilities

Medium-term tour facilities

Long-term tour facilities

Figure 15.1 Bhutan tourism development plan

- Short-term (1986–90) – Continuation of the process of improving standards of tourist facilities and services with high utilization of existing infrastructure in the presently opened areas in the western and central regions.
- Medium-term (1991–95) – Expansion of tourism in the central region with development of some new facilities and infrastructure, and starting cultural safari tourism in the eastern region.
- Long-term (post 1995) – Further expansion of tourism development in the western and central regions, gradual expansion of development in the eastern region, and development of wildlife tourism in the southern region.

The plan reinforces that already established policy of the government that the architectural design of any new development, including tourist facilities, must utilize traditional design motifs and building materials to the greatest extent possible. This policy has been followed. Recently developed hotels and other buildings, especially in the rapidly growing capital city of Thimpu, incorporate the traditional architectural character and blend in well with older development and the natural environment.

Adequate sewage disposal systems for hotels are also required. Electric power is provided from the national grid in the more developed areas and on-site generation is used in other places. More generally, the country has adopted a policy, and has programmes underway, for strict conservation of the natural environment.

In order to provide trained tourism personnel, a training unit was set up at the Bhutan Hotel in Thimpu in the mid-1980s under the UNDP/WTO. This project also included overseas education in hotel and tourism management for several persons.

In the mid-1980s, some religious leaders objected to certain forms of tourist activities, particularly those that involve tourists visiting important religious sites. A special tourism commission was established and it investigated the situation. The commission reported to the National Assembly that tourism may have an adverse moral impact on young people, if they observe tourists' behaviour that might be interpreted as belittling the mystical power of the country's religious beliefs. This resulted in a Royal Command to the tourism office to designate certain monasteries and temples closed to tourists, effective in 1988. This seems to have been an acceptable arrangement to the parties involved.

In order to carry out the concept of controlled, high value tourism, certain approaches have been applied. All non-Indian tourists must come on pre-arranged, all-inclusive package tours, and no individual tourists are permitted entry into the country. These package tourists must obtain visas before arrival. Presumably, if the planned number of tourist arrivals is going to be exceeded in a particular year, no more tour groups would be allowed in during that period. Also, marketing of tourism for the country is kept very limited and targeted to special interest groups, so as not to encourage casually interested tourists. Minimum daily expenditures per tourist have been established. These vary depending on the season and type of tour and are periodically increased. These required minimum expenditures are much higher than the average expenditures of tourists elsewhere in South Asia.

Contacts are maintained with overseas tour operators who specialize in Bhutan tours. These operators handle the visa arrangements and receive the tourists' tour payments before arrival in the country. Approximately 80 per cent of the tourists come for cultural tours and most of the remainder for trekking, including cultural treks to visit monasteries and historic places. A very limited number of mountain climbing expeditions are allowed.

CONCLUSIONS

The Bhutan plan demonstrates the application of establishing tourism zones, in this case based on different geographical areas which are related to different types of tourist attractions and activities. The plan also applies the concept of establishing tourism centres. An important aspect of the plan is logical staging of development during successive five-year periods. Although specified by time periods, in fact, this staging can be carried out within a flexible time frame depending on future circumstances, especially development of infrastructure.

The plan reflects the strong government policy to control tourism so that any undesirable impacts on the natural and cultural environment are minimized. Controlling impacts is achieved primarily through limiting the number of tourist arrivals. In Bhutan, the limitation on tourist arrivals is maintained by requiring that all tourists come on package tours and obtain visas before arrival. This approach is in contrast to some countries which remove visa requirements, or allow visas to be given on arrival, to many types of tourists, in order to encourage more tourism. The package tours also provide the opportunity to control the travel movements of all tourists. In order to receive substantial economic benefits from tourism, Bhutan somewhat compensates for the limited number of tourists by requiring a high level of tourist expenditures.

As another controlled tourism technique, the limited and targeted marketing – as well as the high spending levels required – will tend to attract only those tourists who have a serious interest in, and respect for, the country's culture and environment. Impacts are also controlled and tourism development environmentally integrated by requiring compatible architectural styles of tourist facilities and proper development of infrastructure. An important impact control measure is prohibition of entry of tourists to certain culturally sensitive religious monuments.

The tourism education and training programme and training unit were particularly important to develop in Bhutan because of the lack of tourism trained personnel in the country. This programme provides the skills and knowledge necessary to operate good quality tourist facilities and services, and to manage highly controlled development.

The approach in Bhutan includes the strong involvement of the government and religious leaders in the planning and management process. In this manner, the plan recommendations reflect government and religious policy, and the plan will receive good support. As should be done in any tourism area, continuous monitoring of tourism is maintained in Bhutan. When problems arise, as they did in 1987, the situation is investigated and remedial measures taken. Thus, tourism can be continuously responsive to local people's concerns while still generating benefits to the country.

Chapter 16

Tourism development plan of Bangladesh

The tourism development policy and strategy of Bangladesh represent a regionalization approach to developing tourism. They are based on a realistic appraisal of the opportunities and constraints of developing tourism.

BACKGROUND

Bangladesh is located in South Asia within the eastern part of India. The country contains somewhat more than 115 million people, most of whom live in densely settled rural and agricultural areas. The landscape of Bangladesh is dominated by the major river systems that flow through it – the Jamuna (Brahmaputra), Padma (Ganges) and Meghna Rivers. Most of the land is flat with some hills in the east and northeast. The two main cities are the capital of Dhaka in the central part of the country, and Chittagong, a major port in the eastern area. There are numerous towns scattered throughout the country.

The attractions for tourists relate to both natural and cultural features. There are major beaches at Cox's Bazar and the Teknaf Peninsula on the eastern coast, and elsewhere. A beach resort is already developed at Cox's Bazar. The Rangamati and Chittagong Hill Tracts, also in the east, offer scenic landscapes, indigenous tribal life and lake recreation. Some interesting forests, tea plantations and birdlife lie in the Sylhet district in the northeast. The Sunderbans in the south contain vast mangrove and tidal forest with ample wildlife including the Bengal tiger and crocodiles. More generally, the extensive river system offers opportunities for developing riverine tourism.

The country's historical heritage reflects various cultural influences. Dhaka contains a number of buildings from the Mohgul and British periods, and has a national museum. A major historic palace in Dhaka has recently been restored and will be available for tourist use. Near to Dhaka, a major historic town heritage site has been developed. Of much archaeological and historic interest are some impressive Buddhist monuments dating from the third century BC at various inland sites. There are major Islamic monuments, and other places of historic importance. The popular culture of Bengali music, song and dance, religious festivals, arts, crafts and cuisine are all of considerable touristic interest.

Bangladesh has limited tourism development. There were 115,000 tourist arrivals in 1990, of which the majority were travellers on business, official mission or visiting friends and relatives. A substantial proportion of the arrivals are from India and other countries in South Asia, with most of the remainder from Europe and the Americas. The level of tourist arrivals fluctuates considerably from year to year, particularly depending on the incidence of natural disasters (flooding) experienced by the country. Slightly over 3,000 accommodation rooms were reported to exist in the country in 1990. There are two major international hotels situated in Dhaka.

Infrastructure for tourism is still limited, and access to some attraction areas can be difficult. However, there are two international airports – the main one at Dhaka and the other at Chittagong – and several regional airports within the country. Various areas are served by roads and railways, as well as by boats on the extensive river system. Because of the many wide rivers, river crossings are often by ferry boat.

The Bangladesh Parjatan Corporation (BPC), the national tourism organization and a semi-autonomous body, is responsible for the marketing, regulation and several of the operational activities of tourism. The private sector is also involved in commercial tourism operations.

TOURISM DEVELOPMENT POLICY

The tourism development plan for Bangladesh was prepared in 1988 (UNDP and WTO. 1988. *Strategic Master Plan for Tourism in Bangladesh*. Madrid: WTO). This is a comprehensive plan that examines and makes recommendations on all aspects of tourism. It gives consideration to both international and domestic tourism. In the plan, tourist attractions, facilities, services and infrastructure are described and evaluated. A detailed market analysis is presented of both international and domestic tourists. This analysis establishes market targets for the year 2000. The total target is 300,000 arrivals, with the majority from other South Asian countries, and lesser numbers from Europe, Southeast and East Asia, North America and elsewhere. About two-thirds of the arrivals are expected to be business-related. Domestic tourism is foreseen to expand rapidly. The plan reviews the institutional elements of tourism in detail. It also examines environmental, economic and socio-cultural considerations.

With respect to the objectives of developing tourism, the plan identifies several ways in which tourism can bring benefits to the country, as follows:

- Increased foreign exchange earnings to improve the balance of payments.
- Provision of income to people working in tourism.
- Increased employment in this generally labour-intensive industry.

- More intensive use of existing investments in airports, the national airline, transport and accommodation.
- Reaffirmation and development of local culture and national identity.
- Stimulation of the conservation of historic monuments and preservation of the remaining natural reserves.

The tourism development policy and strategy were formulated to respond to the principal economic, social and cultural objectives for tourism in the country. The important policies are summarized in the plan as follows:

- Pursue the gradual and controlled development of domestic and international tourism.
- Concentrate marketing resources on selected source markets and market segments, and integrate international marketing initiatives with those of other agencies and countries in the region.
- Establish zones of tourism development within which tourism investments could be consolidated and attractions clustered.
- Promote conservation and preservation of land, wildlife and cultural heritage.
- Develop an attractive tourism environment, through the relaxation of controls restricting entry into and travel within Bangladesh.
- Promote and foster culture and sport, and encourage participation from international and domestic visitors (particularly youth).
- Strengthen domestic inter-sectoral economic linkages; reduce the import content of tourism; and increase foreign exchange earnings.
- Strengthen and improve the tourism infrastructure including transportation.

The plan states that implementation of these policies entails provision of an appropriate framework within which tourism can develop.

TOURISM DEVELOPMENT STRATEGY

The tourism development strategy is based on the regionalization approach of establishing tourism zones, each focused on a cluster of attractions. Each zone is based on different types of tourist attractions and related tourist activities, facilities and services. Figure 16.1 shows the six tourism zones which are designated in the plan. The Dhaka zone will also serve as the major international gateway and staging area for the country. As indicated in the figure, the major types of attractions, priority improvements required and time frame for development are specified for each zone. The plan states that development strategies should be centred on a unique tourism theme appropriate to each zone, such as the following:

- River tourism – This will capitalize on Bangladesh's many rivers and waterways, and can provide good access to various points of interest.

- Village tourism – This will complement the development of river tourism in many places. Several villages close to Dhaka could be developed for day excursions from the capital. Village tourism can assist the local people in developing their communities.
- Cultural heritage – This has an important education element and can be divided into several categories – archaeological sites; historic monuments and buildings; museums; and fine and performing arts. Conservation is of utmost importance in developing cultural heritage tourism.
- Forests and wildlife – The development of this type of tourism should proceed in tandem with, and help justify, a preservation strategy for the country's forests and wildlife. This strategy has several components – upgrading the Dhaka zoo; increasing interpretation at selected sites; opening animal breeding stations to visitors; encouraging camping vacations and picnicking excursions; and introducing river tours in the Sunderbans forest and wildlife sanctuary.

In order to support the development of these types of tourism in the designated zones, the plan states that the strategy should seek to improve the tourism product. Product improvements should be aimed at accommodation, handicrafts, speciality shopping, nightclubs, urban-type products and sports. An important part of the strategy is to strengthen the institutional framework, and attract the required levels of investment needed in both the public and private sectors. The plan indicates that the public sector should take responsibility for tourism planning, provision of essential physical infrastructure and conservation, and protection of tourism's natural and cultural assets. The private sector should bear the responsibility for operation and management of commercial tourist facilities and services.

The plan examines ways to strengthen the organizational structures for tourism. It recommends that, toward the end of the planning period, a tourism development corporation be established. This would absorb the investment division of the BPC, and provide a vehicle to channel equity and local capital from the public sector to individual private sector enterprises.

To implement proper development within the designated tourism zones, the plan recommends a coordinated planning approach, as follows:

- Control and prohibit illegal and unplanned development in tourism areas.
- Safeguard the landscape and natural environment.
- Conserve the historic fabric of the country.

The plan recommends that there be close coordination among all the agencies responsible for the respective aspects of implementation. Town planning ordinances and powers should be extended to control development in the tourism zones. All forms of development within the zones should require planning permission and conform to the overall development plan. Institutional support should be given to the private sector, including

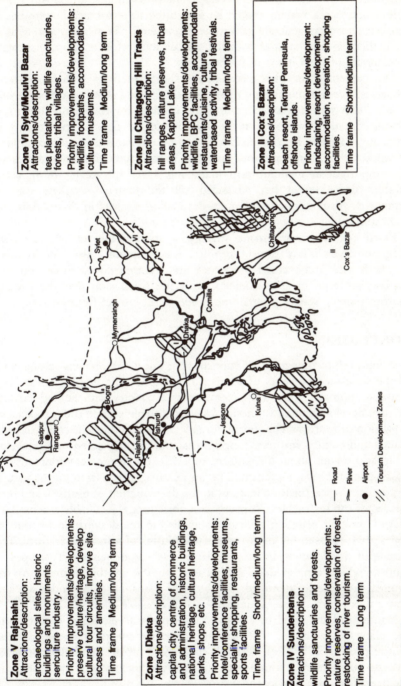

Zone VI Sylet/Moulvi Bazar
Attractions/description:
tea plantations, wildlife sanctuaries, forests, tribal villages.

Priority improvements/developments: wildlife, footpaths, accommodation, culture, museums.

Time frame   Medium/long term

Zone III Chittagong Hill Tracts
Attractions/description:
hill ranges, nature reserves, tribal areas, Kaptan Lake.

Priority improvements/developments: wildlife, BPC facilities, accommodation restaurants/cuisine, culture, waterbased activity, tribal festivals.

Time frame   Medium/long term

Zone II Cox's Bazar
Attractions/description:
beach resort, Teknaf Peninsula, offshore islands.

Priority improvements/development: landscaping, resort development, accommodation, recreation, shopping facilities.

Time frame   Short/medium term

Zone V Rajshahi
Attractions/description:
archaeological sites, historic buildings and monuments, sericulture industry.

Priority improvements/developments: preserve culture/heritage, develop cultural tour circuits, improve site access and amenities.

Time frame   Medium/long term

Zone I Dhaka
Attractions/description:
capital city, centre of commerce and administration, historic buildings, national heritage, cultural heritage, parks, shops, etc.

Priority improvements/developments: hotel/conference facilities, museums, speciality shopping, restaurants, sports facilities.

Time frame   Short/medium/long term

Zone IV Sunderbans
Attractions/description:
wildlife sanctuaries and forests.

Priority improvements/developments: nature reserves, conservation of forest, restocking of river tourism.

Time frame   Long term

— Road
~ River
● Airport
/// Tourism Development Zones

Figure 16.1 Bangladesh tourism development zones

provision of suitably serviced development sites within the tourism zones. The country's tax system should be structured to encourage investment in tourism, as well as generate government revenues. The strategy also aims at strengthening tourism links with the agricultural sector in order to increase local inputs of food items to tourism.

On marketing, the plan recommends short-, medium- and longer-term strategies. For the short term, marketing should be limited to domestic and South Asian source markets until some product improvements are made. During the medium term, marketing should be directed particularly at attracting travellers from countries served by the expanded national airlines network. Other airlines and tour operators in the source market countries are also important in medium-term marketing. Over the longer term, when product development has advanced, all the targeted markets can be promoted. Also, stopovers of multi-destination tourists in South Asia can be encouraged.

Based on the development strategy, a specific ten-year development programme, including project profiles, was prepared. Also development standards and architectural guidelines are recommended. Education and training for tourism are examined, with the conclusion that the present tourism training school programme is adequate to meet future needs.

CONCLUSIONS

The approach to preparing the tourism plan was a comprehensive one, with all the necessary elements of tourism considered. The emphasis was on a strategic approach. This is appropriate for a country with limited existing tourism development and various obstacles to overcome in order to achieve expansion of tourism. The tourist attractions identified take account of both natural and cultural features. Emphasis is appropriately given to capitalizing on what is unique about the country, especially the riverine environment and possibilities for village tourism. The importance of conservation of natural and archaeological/historic features in the development of tourism, and how this sector can help achieve conservation objectives, is justifiably emphasized.

An important planning principle is applied in the designation of tourism zones, each focused on its own particular cluster of attraction features. The staging of development in these zones is also recommended. The types of tourism which can be developed, based on the specific features of the country, are logically identified. The types of tourism recommended are also practical ones which can be developed at reasonable costs.

Institutional and regulatory ways to implement development according to the plan are indicated. The tourism development programme includes project profiles. It is often desirable to prepare project profiles in order to give the government a sound basis for justifying inclusion of the projects in the overall country development programme.

The marketing strategy is realistic in that it recognizes the value of selective marketing, and that product improvements will need to be carried out before substantial promotion can be undertaken. It is also an appropriate strategy in realizing that Bangladesh can be marketed as a stopover visit for some tourists who are making a multi-country tour of Asia. Recommending cooperation on marketing efforts with other South Asian countries is a sound approach. The marketing strategy could also include the need to portray a favourable but realistic image of the country. Image building is especially important in Bangladesh because of the international publicity that has taken place about the natural disasters which periodically occur in the country.

Chapter 17

Tourism development strategy of Cyprus

The tourism development strategy for the Republic of Cyprus reflects the approach of aiming for sustainable development of an already substantially developed tourist destination, while still expanding tourism as a major economic sector of the country.

BACKGROUND

Cyprus is situated in the eastern Mediterranean Sea south of Turkey. The population of the Republic is close to 600,000. It has an extensive coastline with numerous beaches and coastal plains. Much of the southern interior is occupied by the scenic, forested Troodos Mountains. These are flanked by the central plain, where the capital city of Nicosia is located, and the coastal lowlands.

The country has a long history of prehistoric development, followed by successive periods of Classical and Hellenistic Greek, Roman, Byzantine, Frankish, Turkish and British occupation, and now independence. This history has left a rich heritage of archaeological and historic sites, picturesque villages and cultural traditions. The mild climate of Cyprus is one of the major general attractions for tourists.

Tourism in Cyprus in the twentieth century has undergone several changes. Before independence in 1960, tourism was small scale, based on the cool mountain environment. During the early post-independence years, there was greater emphasis on coastal tourism, appealing to a wider international market. Since partition of the island in 1974, coastal tourism has experienced dramatic growth, making the country a mass tourist destination by the early 1980s. By then, concern was being expressed about the future direction of tourism, and the emphasis was shifted somewhat away from quantitative to more qualitative development.

Expansion of tourism has been considerable since the early 1980s, with tourist arrivals reaching almost 1 million in 1987 and 1.7 million in 1990. The great majority of tourists are from Western Europe, with much smaller numbers from the Middle East and North America. Domestic tourism, mostly day trips, is also substantial in the country.

By the mid-1980s, there was still concern about the direction that tourism was taking. Environmental degradation was commencing in the more developed tourism areas, and coastal tourism, focused on the beaches, was by far the dominant form.

Most tourism development had taken place in five main coastal regions. The typical form of development was that the higher class multi-storyed hotels occupied prime sites adjacent to the best beaches. Lower category accommodation of smaller hotels and hotel apartments were situated on the less desirable sites, often with poor access and views to the beaches. There was very limited tourism in the mountains despite their scenic beauty, interesting historic villages and cool temperatures. The central plain area attracted few holiday tourists, although conference tourism is being developed in Nicosia. Often visited by tourists, the archaeological and historic sites were not primary attractions, and were not always well interpreted to tourists.

TOURISM PLANNING APPROACH

The continued concern about tourism led to preparation of a comprehensive tourism development plan for the country in the late 1980s (UNDP and WTtO. 1988. *Comprehensive Tourism Development Plan for Cyprus*. Madrid: WTO). The planning approach takes into account economic, social and environmental considerations. First, the macro-economic aims of the government up to the year 2001 are analysed, and the economic growth implications are translated into development requirements. Market analyses for international and domestic tourism are made and the product changes needed are assessed.

An important element of the planning approach is an environmental and planning analysis. This includes carrying capacity studies. An appraisal of existing development was carried out of each of the tourism areas, including assessment of the infrastructure. Based on these background analyses, the major development opportunities and constraints are identified. The tourism development strategy is formulated, first as alternative options, and then finalized. Implementation techniques are specified. Environmental improvement plans are presented for certain priority tourism areas in order to demonstrate the local planning approach that could be applied.

The three major objectives of tourism are specified based on present government policies, as follows:

- Growth of tourism's contribution to the Gross Domestic Product (GDP).
- Protection of the environmental and cultural qualities of Cyprus.
- Attraction of higher expenditure tourists.

The potential conflict between the first two objectives is recognized in the plan – that growth might take place at the expense of the environment and culture. This is envisaged to be somewhat reconciled by the third objective of higher spending tourists. Also, the plan's recommendations on improving and controlling development will result in environmental and cultural quality improvements and protection.

The market growth targets are prepared for five-year periods up to 2001. These targets are quantified and expressed in five different ways – contribution of tourism to the GDP; gross expenditures of tourists; number of tourist arrivals; number of total bed-nights; and number of additional tourist beds required. The emphasis of market mix is on attracting higher spending tourists. This implies improving and diversifying the tourism product.

The environmental and planning analysis is approached primarily from the tourist viewpoint – what tourists expect in terms of an interesting, attractive, non-polluted and non-congested environment, and how the environmental quality of Cyprus compares to that of competing destinations. In analysing the environment, the tourism areas were divided into two distinct categories – the coastal areas and the mountain hinterlands. The mountain area is examined generally and the coastal urban tourism areas are analysed in detail, noting the development opportunities and problems. Overall social impact is also evaluated with existing and potential problems identified.

In the environmental analysis, the plan indicates that the beaches form an essential element of the tourism product. Therefore, the quality and capacity of beaches are analysed in detail. The quality analysis is related to whether the beach is sand or shingle, its accessibility and the safety of the adjacent water for bathing. In assessing capacity, the area of beach suitable for tourist use was surveyed, and the beach length and width recorded. Different standards were adopted for different beach qualities, and high and low capacity estimates made. The high and low capacity estimates provide guidelines which show the differences between intensive and non-intensive use of the beach. For example, for sand beaches, the plan uses the standard of 8 square metres per person using the beach as the high estimate, and 12 square metres per person as the low estimate. The beach carrying capacities are calculated for each beach area and for the entire country.

The plan summarizes the major development problems and opportunities. The most significant problem is identified as the threat of environmental degradation in most existing coastal tourism areas. The major opportunities are seen as being the resource capacity to further expand coastal tourism and to expand the tourism product and development areas. More tourism development can be undertaken in the mountain region, including the traditional villages there, and presentation of archaeological and historic sites can be improved.

TOURISM DEVELOPMENT STRATEGY

Various alternative development strategies are considered in the plan, of which two basic options are presented:

- Continuation of present trends, which represent a *laissez-faire* approach toward development and limited government intervention.
- Controlled growth, which would involve a greater degree of government control on location, quantity and the types of development.

The controlled growth strategy is adopted as the best approach. This strategy implies that much stronger links be forged between the public and private sectors. It aims at providing a sound basis for participants in tourism development to work jointly in achieving balanced and coordinated growth. The plan indicates that the controlled growth strategy defines the amount of development that should take place to meet targets, and makes proposals on its type and location within the context of market and physical planning criteria.

Within the framework of the controlled growth strategy, the plan states that there are two distinct ways in which regional development strategies can be formulated – from the physical planning and environmental viewpoints. One is to open up new tourism areas where new types of development take place to meet the requirements of an up-market improved product. The second way is to consolidate development within the existing tourism areas, where new types of development can be used to intensify the built environment, to give it more form, structure and identity than at present. The development strategy of consolidation is recommended for the following reasons:

- Existing underutilized infrastructure would be more efficiently used.
- Opportunities would be created to give definition, form and identity to specific areas instead of an anonymous 'could be anywhere' image.
- The tourism areas would provide a better range of accommodation and facilities and be more attractive to tourists than at present.
- Revenues to the district and improvement boards would be increased from the intensified development.
- Improvements could be undertaken because more funds would be available for the more developed areas.

The plan emphasizes that the strategy of consolidation would make an important contribution to the much needed environmental improvements necessary to upgrade the product. A strategy of dispersal would appeal to land speculators and developers, and leave most of the existing tourism areas in their present environmentally poor condition. Based on this controlled strategy of consolidation, the projected number of tourist beds needed to meet the market targets are distributed among the existing tourism areas.

This allocation is made according to the results of the environmental and planning analysis. The plan states that a much greater diversity in the range of facilities and activities offered to tourists will be required to attract higher spending, as well as more tourists during the lower seasons. Some possible new facilities and activities are suggested. Also to reduce seasonality, new types of market segments are identified. These include retired persons, winter sun market, conference tourists, incentive markets, and special interest groups.

In the development programme, recommendations are made on several factors – the quantity, location and type of development; investment incentives; tourism institutional structures; development controls; need for preparation of detailed tourism development plans and beach improvement schemes; environmental issues; product improvements needed; improving the presentation of archaeological and historic sites; and village upgrading schemes. Recommendations are made on tourism employment and training needs. A marketing strategy and promotion programme are recommended. The plan emphasizes that successful implementation of the controlled development strategy will depend on controlling the quantity, type and location of development, effective institutional structures, and the incentives offered for development of new tourism products.

CONCLUSIONS

The Cyprus plan is an interesting example of formulating future development strategies for sustainable tourism in an already substantially developed and successful tourist destination, but one that is overly dependent on a single type of tourism and commencing to suffer from environmental problems in the tourism areas. These strategies are established within the framework of the government's objectives to continue expanding tourism for its economic benefits and, at the same time, improve environmental and cultural quality.

The planning approach is a comprehensive one which examines all the major aspects of tourism. An important element of the approach is the environmental and planning analysis, including carrying capacity analysis, of the existing and potential tourism areas. It is important to understand present environmental problems as a basis for recommending how to improve the areas. It additionally provides the environmental parameters for recommending the type and extent of suitable future development.

As is the case in many beach resort areas, the capacity of the beaches in Cyprus is the critical factor in establishing carrying capacities. Infrastructure is also examined with respect to carrying capacities of tourism areas. Although the environmental analysis is focused on maintaining tourist satisfaction levels, consideration is also given to the social impact of tourism on residents.

Based on evaluating alternative options, the plan rationally recommends the controlled growth development strategy as the best one to achieve the development objectives. Within that framework, the plan recommends controlled growth at the regional levels through consolidation of the present tourism areas as being the best way to improve the environmental quality of these areas. Controlled growth is a general concept and not necessarily easy to accomplish. The plan provides specific guidelines by specifying the number of tourist beds that should be allowed within each of the tourism areas.

The plan emphasizes that implementation of the strategy will require more government intervention. It rightfully points out that application of development controls will be particularly important to implement controlled growth. Investment incentives will be needed to encourage development of new products. In addition to proposing future strategies, the plan recognizes that improvements need to be made in existing tourism areas. It makes recommendations on the types of improvements that are required.

The plan justifiably takes account of the opportunity to diversify the tourism product based on the tourism resources of the country. This diversification can expand the tourist markets and reduce the seasonality factor. Through both product improvements and marketing strategies, the objectives of attracting higher spending tourists can be achieved.

Chapter 18

Tourism development strategy of Mongolia

The tourism development strategy for Mongolia is related closely to the particular natural and cultural attractions of the country. It aims at giving tourists direct exposure to traditional Mongolian life styles and the distinctive environment of the country.

BACKGROUND

Mongolia is located in central Asia, bordered on the south, east and west by China and on the north by the Federal Republic of Russia. The country is large, extending almost 2,400 kilometres east and west. The western half of the country is very mountainous, with much of this region having elevations above 2,000 metres and some mountains rising above 3,000 metres. Dense forests and grasslands cover large areas of this region. A great variety of wildlife, including elk, various species of deer and gazelles, bear, sable, wolf, boar, fox and the rare Argali sheep and snow leopard live in the mountains.

Across the eastern part of the country stretches the vast grasslands of the Asian steppe. The steppe grades into the Gobi Desert, which extends through southern Mongolia and into northern China. The Gobi is mostly gravelly, but also contains large areas of sand dunes in the drier portion of the desert near the southern border. The country experiences long, cold winters, but most days throughout the year are clear and sunny.

Although large in size, Mongolia has a small population of about 2.2 million. About a quarter of the people live in the capital city of Ulan Bator. Other cities and towns including provincial capitals are widely dispersed throughout the country. Nomadic herdsmen live on the steppes. Traditionally, Mongolians are Buddhist. Agriculture, mostly animal husbandry, is the basic sector of the economy. Industry is expanding rapidly and is based on processing of agricultural products and mining of coal and minerals. The economic system of Mongolia is currently undergoing change from socialist to free market.

The attractions for tourists in Mongolia are the wide variety of landscapes and wildlife, historic features including monasteries, temples and palaces, and the living traditions of the nomadic way of life. Although now in ruins, an important archaeological site is Karakorum, capital of the Genghis Khan empire. More generally, the mystique associated with Mongolia's large-scale landscapes, interesting history and nomadic way of life is appealing to tourists.

In the late 1980s, some 10,000 holiday tourists were visiting Mongolia annually. Somewhat over a half of these were from the Western countries and Japan. A relatively small but economically important type of tourists are hunters who pay very high prices for hunting arrangements and permits. The remainder of tourists were mostly from the former USSR and Eastern European countries. Most tourists came on group tours. In addition to the holiday tourists, there is official travel by delegations from other countries.

Access to the country is by air to the international airport at Ulan Bator and by rail connections to Moscow and Beijing. Although roads are being improved, most long-distance travel within the country is by domestic air flights. In 1988, there were about 1,200 tourist beds available – in two hotels in Ulan Bator and three tourist camps, including a camp in the Gobi Desert.

TOURISM PLANNING APPROACH

The national tourism plan for Mongolia was prepared in 1989 (UNDP and WTO. 1989. *National Tourism Plan for Mongolia.* Madrid: WTO). The plan examines all aspects of tourism. It recommends a development strategy for 2005, implementation policies, development programme for 1990 to 1995, and plans for demonstration projects. The objectives of the planning study are stated in the plan, as follows:

- Identify a concept for tourism which reflects the particular characteristics of Mongolia in relation to international market opportunities.
- Increase the scale of international tourism with a view to earning more foreign currency.
- Develop tourist centres in parts of the country with different characteristics to widen visitors' choice and to assist in the dispersal of economic activity.
- Devise forms of tourism development which are most cost effective in terms of the level of investment required in relation to the length of the season, and to minimize foreign exchange leakage.
- Improve existing services and facilities for tourists, and establish future standards appropriate to the identified markets.
- Provide opportunities for the diversification and restructuring of the economy and for the creation of cooperatives and small business enterprises.
- Minimize in the process any adverse social, cultural or environmental impacts.

Basic studies are presented first in the plan – geographic analysis; review of the overall economy; examination of all types of transportation; description of the present status of tourism; survey and evaluation of tourist attractions; evaluation of the institutional framework; and planning parameters and guidelines. Tourist attractions are categorized into scenic and natural, historic, architectural and archaeological. The planning parameters identify constraints, opportunities and special problems.

The development strategy is divided into the development concept, development of market targets, communication (transportation) and socio-economic implications. Several types of implementation policies are recommended – institutional structures; marketing and promotion strategy; improvement in services; collection and analysis of tourism statistics; and import substitution and new supply industry opportunities. The development programme is divided into the promotion programme and programme of projects and policy implementation. The demonstration projects include two tourist camps and visitor facilities at a major historic monument.

The market analysis considers general world tourist market trends and analyses several specific national markets. The views of the international travel trade are taken into account. Problems seen by the travel trade are the lack of information about tourism in Mongolia and a weak image of the country as a destination. The plan concludes that future tourism growth must be supply led. The overall tourism product needs improving, expanding and diversifying before much further growth can take place. Also there is a problem of extreme seasonality, with half of the holiday tourist arrivals occurring during July and August.

The plan identifies Western Europe, North America and Japan as the major source markets for Mongolia. Market targets, based on achieving an optimum supply/demand balance, were established by year from 1990 to 1995 and for 2000 and 2005. The 2005 target figure is about four times the present number of arrivals. This represents an annual growth rate of 8 per cent. Accommodation bed needs are projected based on the market targets.

TOURISM DEVELOPMENT STRATEGY

The tourism development strategy is illustrated in Figure 18.1. The plan explains the key elements of the development strategy. It states that the central feature which makes Mongolia special to tourists is the quality of the rural environment, coupled with the traditional life style of its inhabitants. The image that should be promoted is multi-faceted – the range of different landscapes; the richness of flora and fauna; places of exceptional scenic interest; the absence of development except in traditional nomadic camps; and the overall sense of isolation and tranquillity. To experience this ambience of Mongolia, tourists should be able to visit different parts of the country and pursue their general and special interests. Therefore, product

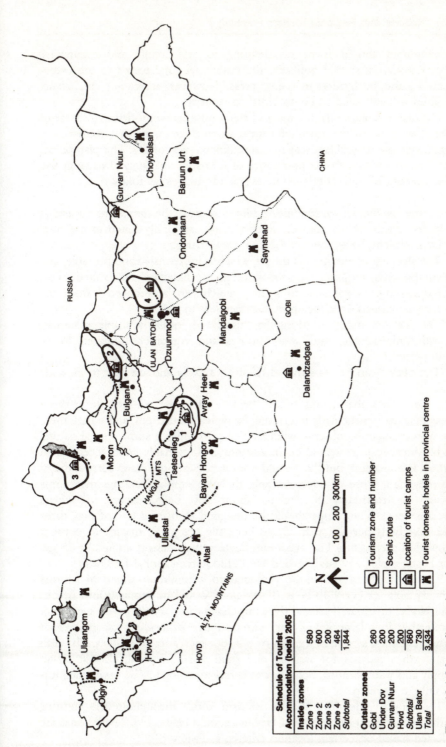

Schedule of Tourist
Accommodation (beds) 2005

Inside zones	
Zone 1	580
Zone 2	600
Zone 3	200
Zone 4	464
Subtotal	*1,844*
Outside zones	
Gobi	260
Under Dov	200
Gurvan Nuur	200
Hovd	200
Subtotal	*860*
Ulan Bator	730
Total	*3,434*

Key:
- ⬭ Tourism zone and number
- ⋯⋯ Scenic route
- 🏠 Location of tourist camps
- 🏛 Tourist domestic hotels in provincial centre

0 100 200 300km

Figure 18.1 Mongolia tourism development strategy map

development should focus on devising tourist circuits and excursions. Accommodation should duplicate the traditional rural forms to the extent possible, and be located in scenic areas. However, recreation and leisure facilities will still need to be provided for tourists.

The plan recommends that most of the tourist accommodation (outside of Ulan Bator) be in the form of camps in rural areas, so that tourists can experience the natural landscapes and traditional way of life. The plan points out that, in addition to the preference of tourists, expansion of existing and development of new camps offer several advantages, as follows:

- Formed as they of *gers* (traditional tented homes), the camps are somewhat characteristic of the nomadic life style and are ideally suited to the rural environment, being low profile and unobtrusive.
- The sleeping component is the *ger*, which is inexpensive and portable, and components requiring use of permanent materials are limited. This reduces the capital cost to a level which can be recovered from the revenue earned over the short summer season.
- The *gers* are made in Mongolia, mainly of locally available materials, with only sanitary and utility fittings and equipment required to be imported.
- The camps can be constructed relatively rapidly and are easy to expand.

The plan states that camps should be located in the countryside in those areas that have particularly interesting or typical landscapes, and where there are opportunities to observe wildlife. The proximity to some special natural or historical features would be an advantage. Reasonably good access to an airfield is important, but this should not intrude into the camp surroundings. To prevent a sense of overcrowding, the plan emphasizes that the camps should be restricted in size to about 200 beds, except in special circumstances. The camps should be designed to offer a mix of two, three and four beds per *ger*, with 75 *gers* generally being the maximum number allowed in each camp. The maximum development density should be 25 *gers* per hectare, plus any land needed for outdoor recreational facilities.

Sanitary facilities should be provided to a minimum standard of one sanitary unit for every 10 beds. These units would be grouped into two to four blocks distributed around the camp. Each camp would have a restaurant (preferably in a large *ger*), a bar, administrative offices, stores and indoor leisure facilities, as well as a range of outdoor recreational facilities. The plan sets forth standards for sanitary and solid waste disposal, electric power supply and water heating. Solar power is recommended to be used when it is feasible to develop.

The strategy identifies various tourism zones throughout the country, within which most of the tourist facilities should be located. These zones are selected based on certain location criteria, as follows:

- Combination of high environmental quality and a relative concentration of historical/architectural features.
- Exceptional environmental quality.
- Distinctive landscape forms and a variety of wildlife habitats.
- Availability of several locations suitable for the development of tourist camps.
- Capacity to absorb a number of facilities.

Consideration is also given to the location of existing facilities or firm proposals for new ones.

Four inner tourism zones are designated relatively near to Ulan Bator in the north central part of the country, and four outer zones are recommended in more remote places including the Gobi Desert and western mountains. The projected accommodation beds are distributed among these zones. Some new beds are allocated for expansion of existing camps. A total of some 13 camps (six existing and seven proposed) are envisaged. Some accommodation is also allocated to Ulan Bator. The plan states that small hotels for use by holiday tourists and local business travellers could be developed in the provincial capitals.

An important part of the development strategy is to make Mongolia more attractive to tourists in those aspects where it has special advantages. To achieve this, various types of activities are recommended to be developed – horse riding, pony trekking, wildlife observation and fishing. Facilities and services would be developed in the camps for tourists to engage in these activities. Special interest tours and hunting are also identified as having potential. The plan examines excursion itineraries that can be made from the camps. Because of the limited extent of improved road network and substantial travel distances, it is difficult and not always interesting for tourists to undertake long excursions. However, excursions can be organized to visit local features near to the camps – horse and camel farms; nomadic encampments; some outstanding monasteries; archaeological sites; and areas of scenic and environmental interest.

The plan makes recommendations for transportation, noting that air access to and within the country is already good, as is the rail access. However, the present condition of the road network and the distances involved do not make long-distance land travel by tourists feasible. Therefore, the strategy is designed so as not to rely on extensive road travel. The domestic air service will remain the primary means for tourists to visit various parts of the country and reach the camps.

The marketing strategy emphasizes that marketing efforts should be directed to enhancing the appeal of Mongolia across a broader spectrum of tourist types, both general and special interest tourists. Priority should be given to image-creation of the country as a destination. During the short term, it is envisaged that group tours will continue to be the appropriate market to target. Over the longer term, more independent tourists can be attracted, as tourist facilities and infrastructure are improved. During the short term, the existing major markets of North America, Western Europe and Japan should receive the main thrust of promotional efforts. Over the longer term, more attention can be given to emerging markets in Asia.

CONCLUSIONS

The tourism development strategy for Mongolia logically focuses on the unique features of the country and how these can best be experienced by tourists. Other important considerations are to minimize the investment capital required for development, and to provide opportunities for cooperatives and small business enterprises. The approach of developing traditional tented camps is an imaginative one that will allow tourists to experience life in rural Mongolia. Such camps are relatively inexpensive to develop and Mongolians already have some experience in their operation. Using the camps as a base, activities can be organized for tourists. These will give them some exposure to nomadic life styles, horse riding for which Mongolia is well known, scenic places, wildlife and important archaeological and historic sites.

The plan applies the basic planning principle of designating tourism zones, with Ulan Bator being maintained as the gateway and staging area for the country. Ulan Bator has hotels, museums, theatre performances and other attraction features which can induce tourists to stay there for one or two days on their entry to and departure from the country. The zones are located based on application of realistic criteria, including accessibility utilizing the existing airport network. The more specific location criteria set forth for the tourist camps will provide a valuable guide for the government to use in selecting new camp sites in the future. The standards recommended for planning the camps are ones which will help maintain the tourist sense of isolation and contact with the environment. At the same time, the plan recommends appropriate utility standards so that the camps do not generate any serious environmental problems.

It should be noted that Mongolia has a progressive nature conservation programme. This will reinforce the nature-oriented concept of the tourism development strategy. Several important environmental areas have already been established as national parks and nature reserves, and more parks and reserves have been proposed. Although hunting is allowed and is an important source of tourist income, it is very carefully controlled. The number of permits sold each year for the taking of individual animals is based on maintaining a sustainable population level of those animals. A census of animals is carried out annually as a basis for deciding how many permits to issue in that year. Conservation is also being applied to historic monuments, in some cases with international assistance.

The marketing strategy is realistic. It emphasizes the importance of initially developing a definite image of Mongolia as a tourist destination, and the need to broaden the types of tourist markets. It recognizes, however, that because of presently limited product development, promotional efforts should first be directed to group tours. When the product is improved in the future, including better tourist services and road infrastructure, promotion can be directed more to individual tourists.

Implementation of this strategy will provide a firm foundation for developing sustainable tourism, at minimal cost, in Mongolia. When this planning period is completed, then further development of tourism can take place based on circumstances prevailing at that time.

Chapter 19

Tourism development strategy of Uganda

The tourism development strategy of Uganda applies sound planning principles in establishing a foundation for revitalizing the tourism sector in a country that has limited existing facilities, but much long-term potential.

BACKGROUND

Uganda is located in east-central Africa, inland from Kenya, east of Zaire and north of Tanzania and Rwanda. The population of the country is somewhat over 17 million, and includes several cultural groups. The capital city of Kampala has about half a million inhabitants. The country contains the northern part of Lake Victoria, the source of the Nile, Murchison Falls, the high snow-capped Ruwenzori Mountains (the Mountains of the Moon) and mountain gorilla reserves.

The primary attractions for tourists are outstanding scenic areas, including lakes, rivers, mountains, rainforests and savanna, and a variety of wildlife. Uganda generally has wetter, more upland and more forested landscapes than do other eastern and southern African countries. This environment offers numerous opportunities for boating, trekking and wildlife viewing. The upland climate is very pleasant for tourists. Ten national parks have been designated although most of these still have limited tourist facilities. Some historic places and traditional cultural patterns comprise interesting secondary attractions.

Tourism was relatively well developed in Uganda in the late 1960s and early 1970s, when it made a significant contribution to the country's economy. Then, because of changes in government policy and political turmoil during the 1970s and early to mid-1980s, tourism became virtually non-existent. Much of the tourist facility development was seriously damaged or deteriorated from lack of maintenance, as was the country's infrastructure. Much of the wildlife was killed. Commencing in the late 1980s and continuing to the present, rehabilitation of the economy and infrastructure, including revitalization of tourism, is taking place. Programmes for conservation of wildlife are being vigorously pursued. The animal populations are now expanding, although some species are not yet up to their previous levels.

By the early 1990s, some hotels of international standard were available in Kampala, Entebbe and Queen Elizabeth National Park, but not yet elsewhere in the country. However, there are limited facilities for business travellers and the more adventurous tourists in the towns and in or near most of the national parks. Plans are underway for continued rehabilitation of accommodation and development of new hotels and lodges. Roads are being improved and the parks are becoming more accessible to tourists. The international airport at Entebbe is also being upgraded. Several tour and travel agencies and some other tourist facilities are now in operation.

In 1991, Uganda received 68,000 international tourist arrivals. Only about 10,000 of these were holiday tourists, and the remainder were travellers on business and official missions. Many of the holiday tourists are of the budget type, including 'backpackers' and 'truckers' – tourists travelling overland by truck or van through several countries in Africa. The large international aid community in the country provides many of the present visitors to the national parks.

Recognizing the potential importance of tourism as a source of economic development, the government has adopted a policy for developing tourism. Along with tourism, the government has some major national park programmes underway, including developing visitor facilities in the parks.

TOURISM PLANNING APPROACH

A comprehensive tourism planning project for Uganda was carried out in the early 1990s. This included preparation of a national tourism plan (UNDP and WTO. 1993. *Integrated Tourism Master Plan – Republic of Uganda, Vols 1, 2 and 3.* Madrid: WTO) and training of government staff in tourism management. A separate project is also underway on establishing a tourism training school for training Ugandans in hotel, catering and tour and travel operations.

The tourism plan is composed of several elements. Various background studies were conducted – an overview of the economy and economic policies; review of tourism-related projects and studies, of which there were many; survey and evaluation of tourist attractions, accommodation and other tourist facilities and services; market prospects; analysis of financial and manpower resources; and the institutional system. Planning parameters and guidelines are established, including identifying the development opportunities and constraints.

The general objective of developing tourism is stated in the plan as follows:

To develop the tourism sector of the economy to the maximum extent possible, consistent with the protection of environmental and cultural

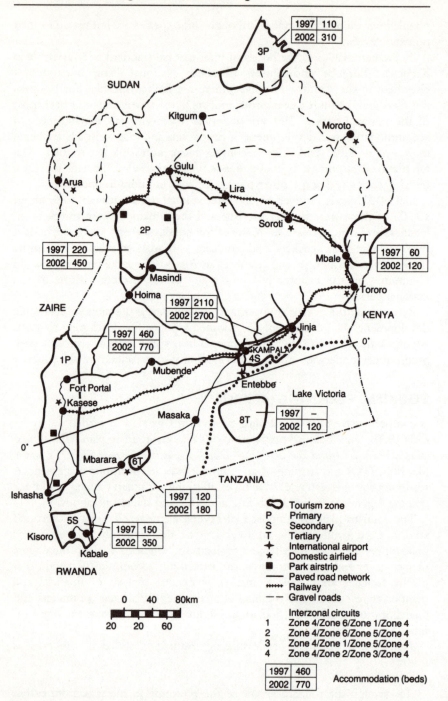

Figure 19.1 Uganda tourism development concept

values, as a means for generating wealth, foreign exchange earnings, employment, a public awareness of the international community, and that community's understanding of the attributes of Uganda.

This general objective was further elaborated and specified in the plan.

Based on the background studies and objectives, the national tourism structure plan was prepared. The horizon year of the plan is 2002, with an intermediate period for 1997. Part One of the structure plan deals with the spatial and development strategy – general policy and planning principles; development concept; market development; tourist accommodation and facilities; transport; economic impact analysis; and environmental and social impacts. Part Two of the structure plan comprises planning and development policies – management of tourism planning and development; development of a tourism data base; manpower analysis and training; managing the environment; and implementing the plan.

Plan implementation is given emphasis. The implementation section includes several elements – selection of priority areas; detailed planning for Queen Elizabeth National Park; a development programme for 1993–97; a policy action programme; an implementation manual; and pre-feasibility analyses for several priority projects.

TOURISM DEVELOPMENT STRATEGY

The development concept is based on phased development of attractions and related activities as a tourism product of high quality and diversity. The plan states that, during the short and medium term, game viewing, whilst being the prime attraction, will be an inferior experience to that available elsewhere because the game populations are still being rejuvenated. Game viewing should, however, be combined with other attractions – the general scenic beauty of the country and specific natural features such as Murchison Falls and the river trips on the Nile to reach the falls. Also very important is the adventure tourism potential of the Ruwenzori Mountains, which are excellent for trekking and of much botanical interest. Similarly, the rainforests offer opportunities for different forms of ecotourism, including controlled viewing of primates – mountain gorillas and chimpanzees.

Therefore, the strategy is to create a multi-faceted tourism product while game populations are recovering. This diverse product will provide a special image for Uganda's tourism, which can be further strengthened when the game have reached their former levels.

The plan establishes tourism zones. These are depicted in Figure 19.1 and described as follows:

• Three primary zones – The Rift Valley Zone, which includes Queen Elizabeth and Ruwenzori Mountains National Parks and other national parks and game reserves; the Murchison Falls Zone, which includes

Murchison Falls National Park and forest and game reserves; and the Kidepo Valley Zone, which includes Kidepo Valley National Park, a forest reserve and controlled hunting areas.

- Two secondary zones – The Capital Area Zone which includes Entebbe as the entry point of tourists, Kampala as the country's staging area and focus of business travel, and other points of interest such as the source of the Nile; and the Southwest Mountains Zone which includes two gorilla-based national parks and some outstanding scenic areas of mountains, lakes and forests.

- Three tertiary zones – Lake Mburo Zone, which is focused on Lake Mburo National Park; Mount Elgon Zone, which contains Mount Elgon National Park, a major waterfall and scenic beauty; and the Ssese Islands Zone, which includes a group of islands in Lake Victoria known for their scenic beauty and birdlife.

The plan sets forth several tourist circuits which link the zones and will assist in prolonging the stay of tourists. Seven inter-zonal circuits, ranging from four days to three weeks, are recommended. Possibilities for intra-zonal circuits are also identified.

Based on the market analysis (described below), the plan projects the type and number of accommodation required – a total of 5,000 beds by 2002. The projected accommodation beds are allocated to each of the development zones for 1997 and 2002. Figure 19.1 shows the allocation of accommodation for each of the tourism zones for 1997 and 2002. Because of its importance as the business and government centre and the staging area for tourists, the Capital Area Zone receives more than half the beds.

There is a further breakdown of accommodation allocation by year from 1993 to 1997. Because of the time required to build accommodation, no new beds are shown for 1993. A crash programme is recommended to provide additional beds by 1994. These would be in the form of safari camps of high standard. The additional accommodation required after 1994 would be composed of renovated and new hotels and safari lodges and camps. The accommodation would all be developed to medium- and high-quality standards, depending on their locations. The plan describes the types of safari lodges and camps that should be developed.

The plan recommends provision of other tourist facilities. These would be in the form of tourist service centres located at the national parks and other major destination points. Three levels of tourist centres are proposed, as follows:

- Principal tourist centres – providing a comprehensive range of facilities including a reception and information lobby, a nature interpretation centre, a general service outlet for the issuance of park permits and arranging guides, excursions, transport and tours, a medical clinic and emergency evacuation services, public lavatories and retail services such as a cafe, bar and craft shop.

- Subsidiary tourist centres – providing a more limited range of functions and smaller in size.
- Minor tourist centres – providing only basic facilities of reception and information, small interpretation displays and public lavatories.

The tourist centres that serve the special needs of adventure tourists would be slightly different. These centres would also include porterage services, a grocery shop and equipment and clothing for sale and rental. Emergency evacuation services will be particularly important for these centres.

The plan sets forth a ten-year programme for development of the tourist centres. Six of these are scheduled for 1993–97 and 11 for 1998–2002.

Recommendations are made for transport. The plan notes that the international airport facility at Entebbe will have adequate capacity when the present programme for renovation is completed. International air links, however, will need to be expanded. The domestic airports are not greatly important for tourism. More important is pursuing the programme for upgrading and continuing maintenance of airstrips in various national parks, in order to provide better access for tourists.

The plan indicates that substantial progress is being made on rehabilitation of the road network, and several tourist destinations can now be comfortably reached by road. The plan lists other roads which still require improvements for tourist use.

On market development, the plan states that, during the short-term period, the marketing and attraction of tourists should be carefully approached. The current restricted capacity of facilities in the tourism zones and the limited possibilities for game viewing will not meet many typical tourists' expectations. When these conditions are improved, marketing can be more aggressively pursued. The projection of tourist arrivals is based on the proposed programme of new accommodation being developed in the tourism zones. Simultaneously, the game populations will have increased, based on present conservation programme objectives. Holiday tourist arrivals are projected to reach 33,000 by 1997, and 66,500 by 2002. Also, there will be substantial numbers of business and other types of arrivals.

By region of origin, the main source markets are identified as Western Europe and the USA. The major market countries to be targeted will be the UK, Germany and the USA, with France and Italy as subsidiary targets. The plan specifies the major market segments – single-destination general interest tourists; multi-destination general interest tourists; regional tourists (residents of neighbouring countries); trekkers; truckers; and special interest tourists. The marketing objectives are stated as follows:

- Cooperate closely with all neighbouring countries.
- Develop as wide a spread of market segments as possible.

- Encourage a wide seasonal spread of tourist arrivals by attracting shoulder and off-peak traffic.
- Attract, where possible, market segments which offer a longer length of stay to obtain an optimum return on marketing costs.
- Direct, where possible, marketing resources to segments that tend to have higher spending patterns.

A subsequent case study examines the promotion strategy and programme for Uganda, based on these market projections and marketing objectives.

The plan reviews environmental impact with respect to several considerations – types of impacts; biological carrying capacity; tourist carrying capacity; and visual and physical impacts. No serious environmental problems are foreseen if the recommendations of this plan and other programmes are followed. However, some types of tourist use must be highly controlled. For example, the viewing of gorillas and chimpanzees must observe strict carrying capacities. For gorilla viewing, visitors should be limited to a party of no more than six over the age of 15, for a period of no more than one hour a day, for any habituated group of gorillas. This control is necessary to avoid unduly disturbing the habits of family groups and to protect the animals from the transmission of potentially fatal human diseases.

Social impact is briefly examined in the plan. No serious social problems are anticipated. However, it is recommended that there be information given to tourists, and that the local population be educated about tourism. This public education will be especially important to make local communities aware of the need to conserve important natural areas from being misused. The plan states that part of this exercise should consist of involving these communities in the introduction of control measures, in the planning of development proposals and in encouraging their participation in the benefits of tourism development.

CONCLUSIONS

The Uganda plan examines all aspects of tourism as an integrated system. On the growth of tourism, the plan is justifiably cautious. It recognizes that market projections must take into consideration the need to improve and expand the tourism product of facilities, services, attractions and infrastructure. If tourist expectations are raised to an artificially high level and not then met in reality, this can do long-term damage to the image of the country. Therefore, marketing development is kept in harmony with the capabilities of achieving the necessary product improvements.

In formulating the development strategy, the plan applies the fundamental principle of establishing tourism zones based on the attractions available in the zones. This zoning further specifies the different importance levels of the zones. These zones then logically provide the basis for identifying various types and lengths of tourist circuits. The concept of developing tourist service centres – as places where tourism services are consolidated – seems to be an appropriate one that has been successfully used elsewhere. In the project analysis section of the plan, pre-feasibility analyses are conducted for three of the service centres. These analyses will give the government some guidance for development of the centres.

The plan observes that if local communities located near to national parks and conservation areas are involved in tourism, and receive benefits from it, they will more likely be cooperative in supporting the necessary conservation measures. This is an important concept that could be elaborated in the future, and some pilot community projects undertaken.

Implementation of a tourism plan is challenging in a newly developing tourism country. The Uganda plan includes a manual as a specific guide for implementation. This manual is summarized in a subsequent case study.

Chapter 20

Tourism development plan of the Philippines

The national tourism development plan for the Philippines is a comprehensive one. It provides short-, medium- and long-term objectives, policies and strategies that aim at correcting current deficiencies while, at the same time, providing the basis for the continued expansion of tourism.

BACKGROUND

The Republic of the Philippines is situated in Southeast Asia and is a member of the Association of Southeast Asian Nations (ASEAN). It is a relatively large multi-island country with a population of more than 65 million, comprising various ethnic groups and religions. The Philippines encompasses a diversity of tourist attractions located throughout the country. These attractions are related to both the natural environment – particularly scenic mountain areas and an extensive coastline offering beaches and marine recreation – and its history and culture.

Tourism is already considerably developed in the country. There were more than 1 million international tourist arrivals in 1990 and some 2 million domestic tourists. About half the foreign tourists come from other countries in East and Southeast Asia, and most of the remainder are from North America and West Europe. The average length of stay of tourists is about 12 days. In 1990, tourism generated approximately US$ 2.5 billion in gross revenues and more than US$ 1 billion in net foreign exchange earnings. Tourism accounted for close to 5 per cent of the Gross Domestic Product and employed an estimated 660,000 persons.

In the 1980s, various problems with respect to tourism development were identified. For the size of the country and its extent of attractions, tourism was still rather small scale. Most of the limited tourism that did exist was concentrated in the National Capital Region of Manila. The growth of tourism had been quite erratic, with rapid reversals in tourist flows, depending on unpredictable events.

TOURISM PLANNING APPROACH

In order to provide the basis for rectifying existing problems and a logical framework for the expansion of tourism, a tourism development plan was prepared in 1991. (UNDP and WTO. 1991. *Tourism Master Plan for the Republic of the Philippines*. Madrid: WTO).The planning study was organized based on formulating a long-range plan, medium-term development programme, and destination area plans. The long-term horizon year was set for 2010. Planning is based on division of this time frame into a short-term period of 1991–93, medium-term of 1994–96 and long-term of 1997–2010.

The plan uses the integrated approach of examining all the physical, socio-economic and institutional aspects of tourism, with the main report backed up by separate technical reports. Background surveys and analyses were conducted, the major opportunities and constraints for improving and expanding tourism were identified, and objectives, targets, policies and strategies were formulated. The analysis includes a comparative evaluation of ASEAN destinations, and consultations were made in key market areas such as East Asia and Europe. Also important was analysis of transportation access to and within the country. In the review of the current situation of tourism, economic, socio-cultural and environmental impacts were analysed. Alternative strategies were evaluated to arrive at the optimum ones.

A series of workshops were held with the tourism industry and other groups, including the Tourism Committee of the House of Representatives. These workshops focused on identifying the strengths, weaknesses, opportunities and constraints facing tourism, and the strategies that should be applied to develop this sector.

The main conclusions of the background studies on the potential of tourism to expand at a macro level are as follows:

- The tourist markets, and attractions to match these markets, are available and the tourism product can be delivered at a quality standard and price that are competitive in ASEAN.
- The capacity of the economic, social and ecological environment to handle growth is still considerable despite the fact there are certain problems.

However, the physical capacity of the tourism sector is limited by:

- Its ability to move large volumes of tourists to other parts of the Philippines outside the Capital Region.
- The lack of trained human resources at the required standard and quantity.
- Institutional overlap and human resource shortages in the tourism planning, development, financing and management areas.
- Strong competition for public and private sector finance.
- Inappropriate land use planning and development policies that make it difficult to readily develop large resorts.

- Unpredictable events such as earthquakes, volcanic eruptions, regional conflicts, internal political disputes and insurgency.

The plan indicates that these factors limit the total volume of foreign and domestic tourists that the country can expect to host, unless a programme of action is undertaken to remove these constraints to expansion.

TOURISM DEVELOPMENT OBJECTIVES, STRATEGIES AND POLICIES

The long-range objectives of tourism development are designed to balance economic interests with socio-cultural and environmental issues. These objectives are stated as follows:

- Optimize the contribution of tourism to economic growth at the national and regional levels (including spreading the benefits of tourism throughout the country).
- Enhance and contribute to social cohesion and cultural preservation at the local level (including encouraging development that is sensitive to the needs of local people and conservation of cultural heritage).
- Develop tourism on an environmentally sustainable basis (including limiting development to the carrying capacity of the environment and encouraging environmental conservation).
- Develop a diversity of destinations, attractions and markets to minimize exposure to major internal and external threats to tourism activity.

The plan observes that the expansion of tourism will depend greatly on the level of investment that can be made, especially of scarce public sector resources.

After evaluation of alternative development strategies to achieve these objectives, the study recommends a three-point strategy as follows:

- Adopt a cluster development approach based on the establishment of three main international gateways and associated satellite destinations.
- Adopt a niche and mass market approach based on a diverse mix of special interest, vacation, resort, convention, exhibition, touring and incentive travel products.
- Work toward a balance of development between foreign and domestic tourism.

Based on the development objectives and strategies, domestic and foreign tourist market targets are established for the short-, medium- and long-term periods. These are expressed in terms of both tourist arrivals and tourist nights, with domestic tourist targets calculated only for those using commercial accommodation. The targets indicate considerable growth of tourism for 2010 – about five times the 1990 figure for foreign tourists and

10 times the 1990 figure for domestic tourists. The main source of foreign markets are targeted from East Asia, with the majority of foreign tourists being resort oriented.

The plan recommends implementation of development strategies for the short-, medium- and long-term periods. Short-term development should be focused on several actions – completing key infrastructure projects; making use of existing tourist attractions, facilities and markets; planning future infrastructure and resort projects; removing policy constraints; and streamlining the institutional structure. During the medium term, emphasis should be placed on expanding key infrastructure and developing new resorts according to the development strategy, and establishing tourism training facilities. In the longer term, the development strategy should be consolidated with continued development of emerging and potential destination areas in each of the clusters.

The cluster development strategy is based on the concept that each cluster is served by one or more international gateways, linked to a variety of satellite destinations. Each satellite would have its own unique theme. Figure 20.1 illustrates this development approach. One cluster is the Luzon- or Manila-based cluster, with Manila as the gateway, and includes several destinations in the northern and eastern parts of the country. Another cluster is the Visayas- or Cebu-based cluster, with Cebu as the gateway, and includes the central Philippines. The third is the Mindanao- or Davao-based cluster, with Davao as the gateway, and includes destinations in the southern part of the country. Short-, medium- and long-term targets of tourist arrivals are established for each of these tourism regions.

The plan recommends implementation policies for various major elements of tourism. Accommodation policies are focused on developing accom-modation outside the capital region, especially in the Visayas and Mindanao clusters. Incentives should be offered to upgrade existing and develop new accommodation in these regions. New resorts would be developed in these regions, as well as the northern part of the Luzon region, and infrastructure constructed to serve the resorts. Marketing should be directed to promoting places outside the Manila area.

Transportation policies relate mostly to air transport. The plan recommends that a more flexible approach be adopted to approve charter and scheduled air services, and that additional domestic and international air carriers be allowed to serve secondary airports in the country. Domestic and international terminal facilities at the main gateways should be expanded. Also, domestic air operation should be deregulated and more competition encouraged among domestic carriers. Recommendations are made on road, sea and rail transportation within the country.

The plan recommends that marketing policies be implemented in three phases. During the short-term period, the focus should be on several efforts – raising the present low accommodation occupancies; improving the

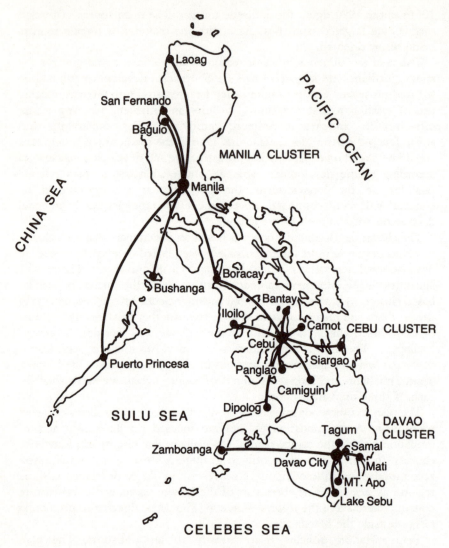

Figure 20.1 Tourism cluster development areas and satellite destinations, Philippines

international tourist image with regard to stability and security; improving the image for tourism investors; and improving service and access to entertainment, restaurants, shopping and tours. Over the medium term, the marketing policy should be to start to project the Philippines as a major and revived tourist destination aiming at a wide spectrum of markets, but particularly at the emerging domestic and East Asian markets. For the long term, the policy should seek to build upon the initiatives established previously, but diversify the Philippines into a major world destination.

The main thrust of the product development policy should be to upgrade and diversify the existing range of products in various ways. One recommended approach is to focus on properly developing one or two attractions in each of the gateways, including creating at least one major attraction in or near each of these. Another policy is to improve access to and information about existing products, and upgrade the standard of existing tour products and programmes. Other policies are also recommended – encouraging the development of additional day visitor activities at destination areas; improving the reliability of domestic transportation services; and creating new resort, special interest and tour products based on the particular features of the country.

The plan points out that the existing training system will not be able to produce the trained manpower needed in the future. The main thrust of the training policies is to establish a Tourism Industry Training Board, regional training centres in the three tourism regions, an internationally acceptable standard facility and certification programme, and faculty development.

The policies recommended on development standards and guidelines are reviewed in detail in a separate case study in this publication.

CONCLUSIONS

The approach to the Philippines plan is a comprehensive and integrated one that is adapted for a country which already has a somewhat established tourism sector, but one that requires stabilization and appropriate policies to guide its future development. The plan is particularly focused on identifying the present opportunities and constraints of tourism as a basis for recommending objectives, strategies and policies. The planning analysis reveals a problem (and opportunity) that is common to many tourism countries – the need for diversification of the tourism product, especially of tourist attractions and activities, in order to attract a broader base of tourist markets and effectively compete with destinations elsewhere. The plan also makes the important point that tourism should be developed for sustainable use of resources.

The plan identifies another common problem – the concentration of tourism in a single area and the neglect of other tourism areas that have potential for development. As the plan emphasizes, this leads to limited distribution of the benefits of tourism, as well as a limited tourism product. The plan also recognizes the disruption that natural disasters and political disturbances can have on maintaining consistent tourist arrival patterns.

To overcome these problems and take advantage of opportunities, the plan uses the principle of establishing tourism regions, called clusters in this plan, each of which is focused on a regional gateway. Within the regions are designated development areas or satellite destinations. At the regional level, emphasis is placed on development of integrated resorts, another important planning principle for large-scale tourism. This development strategy provides a rational basis for dispersing development, whilst still containing it in specific places for ease of providing access and infrastructure and other reasons.

The national level market targets are allocated to the various regions. This provides not only a guide for the specific level of development in each region, but also allows for flexibility of development within the regions. The multiple regional gateways allow for flexibility of arrival and departure access points to a relatively large country, also a basic planning principle.

In the implementation of the strategy, the plan applies a very useful approach of recommending policies for each of the key elements of tourism, including institutional factors. This provides the government and private sector with guidelines for actions that need to be taken. For example, the need to improve the international tourism image of the country is an important marketing strategy that is recommended to be undertaken, as well as specific promotional techniques. The plan further sets forth a detailed medium-term development programme and destination area plans as specific guides for decision-making.

In the staging of development implementation, the plan recommends a realistic short-term approach that focuses on making better use of existing facilities. At the same time, it lays the foundation for change through infrastructure planning and development and institutional improvements. Then, over the medium and long term, there is gradual implementation of the regional cluster concept and controlled dispersal of tourism.

This plan provides the overall basis for rational development of tourism. It will need to be followed by other studies such as for development of special interest and ecotourism, as part of the product enrichment programme.

Chapter 21

Resort development strategy of Mexico

The strategy for development of integrated resorts in Mexico represents a national level policy approach adopted for developing beach resorts as a major form of tourism in the country. An important aspect of this strategy is the financial and organizational mechanisms established to implement it.

BACKGROUND

Situated in North America, Mexico is a relatively large country of some 90 million people. It has extensive coastlines facing onto the Pacific Ocean, Gulf of Mexico and Caribbean Sea. With many beaches and marine areas, scenic landscapes, pleasant climate, major archaeological and historic sites and highly interesting cultural patterns, Mexico offers a full range of attractions for tourists. Its location next to the USA and not far from Canada provides the country with large nearby tourist markets.

Mexico has a long tradition of domestic tourism with beach resorts having been particularly popular with Mexicans. International tourism, based mostly on the American market, commenced substantial development after World War II. The west coast beach resort of Acapulco became especially popular with both domestic and foreign tourists. Also, tourists were, and still are, attracted to the major cities and archaeological sites. There was, and still is, considerable 'border' tourism developed near the boundary with the USA. However, by the 1960s, it became clear to the government that tourism in the country was lagging behind Hawaii, the Caribbean and other destinations.

In examining the country's potential for development, the government identified tourism as a sector that could generate substantial employment, income and foreign exchange earnings. A detailed analysis of tourism was carried out by the Bank of Mexico during 1966–68. This revealed that tourism was developing rapidly internationally, with much potential for continued growth, but that Mexico was not adequately participating in tourism. The study identified several problems – the country had no long-term tourism policy; no tourism programme existed that established concrete objectives; there were no functioning financial instruments for development and promotion; and no criteria had been adopted for planning and development. Tourist facilities were excessively concentrated in Acapulco. Some newer resort areas had occurred spontaneously and possessed obvious weaknesses. This situation led to adoption of a resort development policy and strategy.

Since the late 1960s, tourism has grown considerably in Mexico. By 1990, there were more than 6 million foreign tourist arrivals, plus a much larger number of excursionists who visited the border zone for short stays. Most foreign tourists are Americans and Canadians, with a limited number from Europe. The average length of stay of foreign tourists is slightly more than 10 days. International tourism receipts contribute more than US$ 5 billion to the national economy. Domestic tourism also has remained an important tourist market.

RESORT DEVELOPMENT STRATEGY

Following on from the study of the late 1960s, diversification of tourism was considered to be the priority approach. (This description of the development strategy is taken from the publication *Tourist Resorts – a Mexican Strategy for Development*, published by FONATUR in 1988 in Mexico City.) Within that framework, the policy was decided to be that of upgrading existing resorts and developing new ones. The new resorts would be developed based on the concept of building complete and integrated resort cities from 'the ground up' on undeveloped sites. Over a period of several months, the Bank of Mexico conducted a detailed investigation of Mexico's coastline, evaluating several dozen potential sites.

These site studies involved many considerations – land ownership; climatological conditions; environmental impact; types of soil; transportation access; telecommunications; nearby population centres; socio-economic levels of the local population and their past experience in tourism; and other factors. The climatological and related surveys included average hours of sunshine, levels of ocean tides, distribution and strength of prevailing winds, frequency of natural disasters and other characteristics.

Based on the site studies, the Bank of Mexico in early 1969 recommended the creation of five integrated tourist resort cities, each for specific reasons. These resorts are as follows:

- Cancun (on the Caribbean coast in the state of Quintana Roo) – selected because of its strategic location in the Caribbean as a region that was already attracting many tourists, its potential for reinforcing the limited existing tourism development on the offshore islands of Cozumel and Isla Mujeres, and to strengthen the regional development of Quintana Roo.
- Ixtapa (on the Pacific coast in the state of Guerrero) – selected in order to relieve the tourism concentration in Acapulco which is located about 200

kilometres to the southeast, because of its location near to Zihuatanejo which already had some tourism that would help support marketing of the resort, and to provide impetus for regional development of the state.

- Los Cabos and Loreto (two sites on the Pacific coast in the southern part of the peninsula of Baja California) – selected in order to reinforce the limited existing tourism development in that area, publicize this area more to the American market, and stimulate regional economic development along with attracting more people to this underpopulated region.
- Bahias de Huatulco (on the Pacific coast in the state of Oaxaca) – selected because of its great tourism potential and to revitalize the weak economy of Oaxaca.

All these places met the immediate site selection criteria, including good beaches, scenic surroundings, climatic desirability and availability of land for development.

The president then issued a policy statement on the need for encouraging tourism development for its economic benefits. This was immediately followed by the creation in 1969 of the National Fund for Tourism Infrastructure (known by its Spanish acronym of INFRATUR). This agency was organized to implement the following objectives:

- Conceive and implement tourism infrastructure projects that complement investments of the federal government.
- Develop tourism infrastructure projects that generate private investment.
- Acquire, develop, sub-divide, sell and lease property associated with tourism projects.
- Collaborate with other government agencies in the promotion of tourism.

INFRATUR was assigned the primary mission of initiating the construction of the first two resorts – Cancun and Ixtapa. The first activity undertaken was to specify the guidelines for the resort development and prepare the resort master plans. These plans are integrated and comprehensive. They included land use zones – for hotels, residential, commercial, public facilities and conservation areas – the transportation network, and the utilities system of water supply, electric power, sewage collection and disposal and telecommunications. In the case of Cancun, an international airport was sited. The Cancun plan includes a large new town for the resort support population, in keeping with the concept of developing resort cities.

The resort plans contain detailed projections and recommendations – characteristics of tourist arrivals; numbers of hotels and hotel rooms; hotel occupancy levels; number of daily air flights expected; and investment procedures. The master plans also establish the quality of construction, building heights, density limits and architectural styles.

The first step in the development process was acquisition of sufficient land for short-, medium- and long-term needs. Field work commenced at Cancun in early 1970. One year later the initiation of work at Ixtapa was authorized. The underground infrastructure – water supply and sewer pipes, electric and telephone lines, and drainage – was installed first. Then the above ground infrastructure of roads, the airport (at Cancun), sewage and water treatment plants, streets, etc., was constructed. The infrastructure was designed and developed according to international standards.

At Cancun, INFRATUR did the planning, acquisition of land and construction of basic infrastructure for the new town (Cancun City), located next to and integrated with the beach resort area. Housing at Cancun City was developed largely through the existing programmes of various housing and financing agencies of the national government. INFRATUR carried out an excellent programme for training local inhabitants in construction skills. This included language training in Spanish because many of the Mayans living in the Cancun area speak only their own language. The agency also implemented a training programme in hotel operations. This eventually became successful in producing several hundred graduates annually.

Concurrent with the development of infrastructure, INFRATUR conducted a promotion campaign to attract investment from the private sector for development of hotels and recreational facilities. The first hotel was opened in Cancun in 1973 and, in 1974, the first hotel opened in Ixtapa.

With the impetus of the successful commencement of these two resorts, in 1974 the government upgraded the Department of Tourism to the cabinet level status of State Secretariat. At the same time INFRATUR was merged with the Tourism Guarantee Fund. The new agency was named FONATUR. In addition to acquiring sites and developing the resorts' infrastructure and implementing the plans, FONATUR was given the responsibility of granting loans for hotels and making direct investments in commercial facilities throughout the country. In the mid-1970s, the resorts of Los Cabos and Loreto in Baja California were launched. The government continued giving strong support to development of tourism and, in 1984, the Bahias de Huatulco resort in Oaxaca was started.

Funding for FONATUR is primarily from the institution's own resources. In addition, substantial loans were made by the Inter-American Development Bank and the World Bank, with the first loan granted in 1971 (to INFRATUR). An important concept of this public type investment is that it attracts much private investment. Each peso (the Mexican currency) invested by FONATUR is estimated to attract 10 pesos of private investment. In addition, a programme of co-investment with Mexican and foreign capital has been promoted, chiefly for the construction of the first hotels at each resort. In the 1970s and 1980s, FONATUR financed the great majority of hotels in Mexico (within and outside the five resorts). The agency also maintains direct investment in many tourism enterprises – hotels, restaurants, golf courses and tennis complexes. FONATUR is operating on a financially positive basis, and has continued to meet its obligations in repayment of loans.

The government considers that the resorts have generated substantial economic benefits in their regions. It estimates that each hotel room generates 2.5 jobs directly, and the same number indirectly in the tourism supply sector. The direct resort employees earn, on average, 1.5 times the country's minimum wage. In addition, the resorts' construction, which is still on-going, employs large numbers of people. The infrastructure developed for the resort cities has also stimulated overall regional development.

By the late 1980s, FONATUR estimated that the total hotel room capacity in the five resorts accommodated about a quarter of all tourists visiting Mexico. Development of the resorts continues at present. In the case of Cancun, largest and the most internationally recognized of the five resorts, 112 hotels providing approximately 18,000 hotel rooms were in place by the early 1990s. Cancun has a small convention centre, a championship golf course, retail centres, and a variety of water sports facilities. The type of accommodation varies widely, with 72 beach-front hotels on Cancun Island and another 32 mid-level and budget accommodation enterprises in Cancun City. The city has grown to about 300,000 persons with an ultimate population anticipated to be some 400,000 to 500,000.

The range of accommodation in Cancun allows it to attract a diversity of tourists, including a large proportion of domestic tourists. Although tourists come mostly for beach and marine activities, many also visit the Mayan ruins that are located in the region, as well as important nature conservation areas. The resort has stimulated other tourism development along the Quintana Roo coast and some additional development on the offshore islands.

CONCLUSIONS

The resort development strategy for Mexico did not evolve from a comprehensive tourism plan. It was, however, based on identifying problems, establishing objectives, formulating policy and then a strategy for developing a particular form of tourism. The country also has policies for development of other forms of tourism, such as urban and rural tourism.

The concept of developing well planned and integrated resorts was particularly progressive for its time of the late 1960s, when integrated resort development was rather a new idea. The government appreciated that well planned resorts would generate less negative environmental and socio-cultural impacts and offer a much better product for tourists. The government expanded this concept to that of resort cities, which integrate well designed communities for the support population. The fact that Cancun City also has developed some accommodation and other tourist facilities, in addition to the large beach-oriented hotels, reflects the extent of integration. This approach broadens tourist markets because of the greater range of facilities available. It is also advantageous for city residents who can live near their jobs, and participate in ownership and management of smaller-scale facilities and services.

Selecting the resort sites was carried out in a methodical manner, according to specific criteria. The sites selected reflect careful consideration of the immediate environmental and social characteristics, as well as the importance that resorts can play in stimulating regional development. All the regions in which the resorts are situated need the economic impetus which tourism can offer. The resorts were developed on a phased basis. This approach provided the opportunity for the more recent resorts to learn from the experience gained in developing the older resorts. Phasing is also important to maintain a balance between market demand and product development.

In determining the development approach, the government realized the importance of establishing a strong agency – first INFRATUR and then FONATUR – with adequate funding for planning, financing and carrying out development according to the plans and development programme schedules. The responsibilities of this agency were enlarged and streamlined over time to meet the development process needs. It was realized that considerable public expenditure would be required for the construction of infrastructure, as a basis for implementing integrated development and to attract the private investment required. However, this investment is well justified with respect to achieving substantial economic development of the country. Much of this investment can also be recovered over the long-term period.

It is interesting to note that these resorts, in addition to providing a variety of their own recreation and entertainment facilities, also serve as bases for tourists to visit attractions in their regions. This expands the tourism products and markets, and spreads the economic benefits of tourism more widely. These regional relationships reflect the important principle that resorts should be planned and developed within the context of their regions.

From the market standpoint, the Cancun resort has probably attracted some foreign tourists who otherwise would have gone to Caribbean Island destinations. However, this may provide the competitive stimulus for those islands to improve their product. In the case of Cancun, it appears that hotel room rates had to be somewhat lowered in order to attract the large volume of tourists needed to support the hotels.

Inevitably, some problems were encountered in implementing development. These problems were recognized and resolved over a period of time. As concluded by FONATUR, the resort development strategy in Mexico has been economically and environmentally successful. The strategy has greatly assisted the country in commencing to realize its tourism potential.

Chapter 22

Village tourism in Senegal

The village tourism programme in Senegal is an example of a national tourism policy applied to effect a particular type of regional tourism development. It is also a good case study of community involvement in tourism that provides exposure of tourists to local life styles and generates benefits directly to local villages.

BACKGROUND

Senegal is located in West Africa and is the westernmost of all the continental African countries. Geographically, the country is composed mostly of low-lying plains and marshes laced by several rivers. There are some highlands in the far southeast. The separate country of The Gambia occupies the Gambia River area extending through the west-central part of Senegal. The population of more than 7 million is French speaking and mostly Islamic. Dakar, the capital and a major seaport, contains more than 1.2 million inhabitants.

The country offers a variety of attractions for tourists – the cosmopolitan ambience of Dakar with its good hotels and restaurants; several excellent beaches and beach resorts along the coast; the historic slave centre heritage complex on Goree Island; a large national park with wildlife viewing in the southeast; an important bird sanctuary in the northwest; and the cultural traditions of the people. Also a major attraction is the Casamance region, in the southern part of the country, where village tourism offers the opportunity for exposure to the traditional African way of life in an interesting riverine environment. In the early 1990s, Senegal had about 250,000 tourist arrivals annually, the largest amount of all the West African countries. Most tourists are from Western Europe.

VILLAGE TOURISM PROGRAMME

The village tourism programme was conceived in the early 1970s. (This case study is taken from 'Tourism for discovery: A project in Lower Casamance,

Senegal' by Christian Saglio in the book *Tourism – Passport to Development?* [published for the World Bank and UNESCO by Oxford University Press, 1979], and updated from more recent sources.) Its inception was in response to various concerns being expressed by the government and others during the late 1960s and early 1970s. At that time tourism was based primarily on beach resorts and urban hotels with organized excursions sometimes taken into the countryside. This type of tourism did not offer tourists the opportunity to experience the African way of life and meet Africans on a spontaneous basis. It was also seen by some residents as being socially degrading. Local people often felt that they must meet the expectations of the tourists. They were worried about the demonstration effect of tourists on their young people and the loss of traditional values.

Also there was concern about the need to provide a variety of jobs and income to young people in the villages. Many young villagers were migrating to the cities in order to improve their lives economically. Additionally, the villages needed money to finance community development facilities and services. The village tourism programme was not viewed as the only desirable type of tourism for the country. Rather it was intended to supplement more conventional forms of tourism with an alternative type.

First a model of the village tourism programme was formulated. This called for simple accommodation to be built, managed and operated by the local village people. The lodgings would be designed in the traditional style and built of local materials. They would offer only minimal comforts to small groups of tourists. According to the model, management of the lodgings (called camps) was to be left entirely to the villagers. Cooperatives would be organized to be responsible for the operation of the camps, as well as the allocation of profits. Meals would be planned around the use of local food products and traditional cuisine. The cooperatives would organize tourist activities. Tourist promotion would be based on straightforward descriptions of what the villages had to offer.

The next step was to select a suitable place to commence the project. After many reconnaissance trips were made to examine possible sites in Senegal, the final selection was the Lower Casamance. This region lies between The Gambia and the southern border of the country. It includes the Casamance River and its tributaries. In this region, distances are short, the environment is interesting and the climate is agreeable. The area is well populated. The regional capital already offers comfortable hotel facilities, and a major beach resort was in operation on the coast of the region. These existing tourist facilities would provide a base for tourists to visit and explore the region, staying overnight in the proposed camps.

The project was, and still is, strongly supported by the national and regional governments and tourism offices. Technical advice was provided by an international specialist who had had field experience. The regional coordinator for tourism supervised operations, taking part in all meetings, and encouraging the villagers by making many visits. He also helped run an in-service training programme for the village management teams. An international agency (Canadian University Service Overseas) provided some financial assistance for salaries, an all-terrain vehicle, and travel expenses. Only villages receptive to the project were invited to join it.

The model, as described above, was closely followed in implementation. Four village projects were initially developed. However, some problems were inevitably encountered. During the first year, a serious drought resulted in many people leaving the villages, with a consequent shortage of labour. The remaining workers were distracted by their immediate drought problems, and it was difficult to interest them in the project and train teams for operation and construction.

A second problem related to the major effort required to inform people about the new project and gain their cooperation. Also some local administrative authorities, accustomed to large-scale tourism development, were often suspicious of the project. They criticized the small amount of investment being made, feared problems in the villages, and wondered if tourists would stay in clay houses. There was a reluctance to show visitors some of the traditional life styles, which many of the educated officials tend to believe is backward. Many of both the officials and villagers thought the lodging should be constructed of modern materials and have hotel amenities.

Selecting sites for the lodging was difficult because of rivalries among the village leaders, especially between village heads representing government and the still influential traditional chiefs. These disagreements were resolved only after many meetings and discussions. The sites chosen were deliberately isolated and away from major tourist routes. Access was often only by boat or footpath which presented travel problems. Once a site was selected, a well had to be drilled to provide a water supply. These wells helped win support from the villagers because they provided them with additional water sources. Much effort was put into faithfully reproducing the traditional house styles and arranging for purchase of local building materials. These problems were overcome and, by 1974, the first camp had opened. The initial four camps were completed by 1976.

Management and operation of the camps are carefully organized. Under the authority of the village chief, the work of serving visitors is assigned to young people of the village. A management committee supervises three operating units of two persons each – these units are respectively in charge of meals, accommodation and excursions. Tourist prices are set by agreement, as are the wages of each worker and the share allocated to the cooperative. The employees are paid after each visit according to the number of tourists and the services rendered.

The profits that accrue to the cooperatives are distributed by boards composed of members appointed by the village. These members are typically community leaders. This money is used for community facilities – health and maternity clinics, youth centres and schools. It is also used to initiate new business activities, such as vegetable farming, livestock raising, fishing and crafts. These activities provide more jobs for local young people.

The village tourism programme was an immediate success with tourists. Some of the guests staying at the beach resorts take tours of the Casamance and make overnight stays at the camps. Other tourists come for longer stays. In order to diversify the tourist markets, the national tourism office has encouraged several travel agencies to sell tours that include the Casamance camps. Agencies specializing in youth groups arrange for stays of up to three weeks in the camps.

In order to avoid saturation of the camps and villages, which could lead to social problems in the villages and weaken the sense of tourists' contact with villagers, certain size controls have been established. Camps are located in villages with at least 1,000 inhabitants. Accommodation is limited to 20-30 beds in each camp. As more facilities are needed, the existing camps are not expanded, but new ones are built elsewhere in the region.

By the early 1990s, a considerable number of camps have been developed in the Casamance region. These are located in various places north and south of the river with two on the coast. Reservations can be made to stay in the camps through the *Campements Rurals Integres* system. The camps are quite popular and reservations are typically required during the high seasons of July–August and December–January. The success of these camps has stimulated private investment. Attracted by the modest outlay of capital required, ease of construction, and quick return of revenue, several small-scale regional business persons have developed private camps. They are competitive in pricing and are also popular with tourists. However, they may not provide as much revenue to the villages for community development.

CONCLUSIONS

The Casamance village tourism project represents a successful approach to developing community-based tourism that directly benefits the villagers, and brings more cultural understanding and interesting experiences to tourists. The success of the programme depended on several factors that can be applied in many other local tourism development projects. The initial careful modelling was essential, even though this was somewhat adapted in application. The strong support of both the national and regional governments was very important. The technical and financial assistance, as well as some dedicated involvement of outside officials, was invaluable. Education of the villagers and local officials was a necessary aspect of implementing the programme. Patience and persistence in pursuing the programme objectives were necessary. The local organization of labour and finances seemed to work well in this social environment. Use of the profits for community projects and expanding economic activities results in the entire villages receiving the benefits of tourism.

The policy of not allowing the camps to become too large in any one village has been a wise choice. The original concept of the programme has been maintained and, by developing new camps, more villages can benefit from the programme. The programme has also served a purpose in stimulating private investment in camps. This has helped reinforce tourism development in the region. Additionally, the Casamance village tourism programme has introduced a new type of tourism product to the country. This has resulted in greater overall tourist flows.

Although successful, continuous monitoring of this type of programme must be pursued. Monitoring will give greater assurance that any problems which arise will be quickly resolved. It also provides a basis for refining techniques which can then be applied to new village tourism projects.

The Casamance programme has evoked much interest from other places in the world, and has served as a model for similar type projects elsewhere. As is always the case, of course, the model must be adapted to the governmental, socio-cultural, economic and environmental situations where it is being applied. This type of programme can result in developing an imaginative new and successful type of tourism that is responsive to certain market demands and brings benefits to local residents.

Chapter 23

Enhancement of economic benefits in the Tibet tourism plan

Particular emphasis was given to ways of enhancing economic benefits in the tourism plan for Tibet. This is a good example of the many techniques that can be applied to increase the economic opportunities from tourism.

BACKGROUND

Tibet is an Autonomous Region of the People's Republic of China, located in south-central Asia north of India, Nepal and Bhutan. The region's southern boundary lies in the Himalaya, where mountains rise to more than 8,000 metres. Much of Tibet occupies a high plateau averaging some 4,000 metres in altitude. The landscape is largely treeless with grasslands in the upper valleys and cultivated fields in the lower valleys. Isolated forests occur on the approaches to the Himalaya. In the southeast, which receives the summer monsoon rains, the grasslands merge into rainforests which contain a diversity of flora and fauna. Despite the high altitude, the climate of southern Tibet is equable, with long hours of sunshine in both the summer and winter.

Most of the population of about 2.2 million inhabit the sheltered valleys, lying between 3,500 and 4,000 metres, which thread the mountainous plateau. Most people live in villages and engage in agriculture and animal husbandry. The capital of Lhasa and the few other towns are situated in this more settled area. Buddhism has been the focus of Tibetan culture for well over 1,000 years. The region has a rich heritage of cultural traditions and historic and religious monuments. Although many of these places were damaged in recent years, much remains and an active restoration programme is underway. People are gradually returning to formerly abandoned monasteries and temples.

Tibet offers both cultural and natural attractions. The villages provide exposure to traditional architecture and life styles. Of the towns, Lhasa and its Potala Palace is by far the most interesting. Many of the historic monuments of monasteries, temples and palaces scattered through the countryside are significant attractions. Traditional dress, customs and festivals comprise important features. Most of southern Tibet is scenically and environmentally interesting, and provides opportunities for trekking and sightseeing. There is much potential for developing mountaineering along the northern flanks of the Himalaya, with 22 peaks legally open (in 1990) to foreign expeditions. More generally, the mystique of Tibet holds a fascination for many tourists.

Tibet was first opened to foreign tourists in 1980, and a peak of 43,500 tourist arrivals was reached in 1987. Because of civil strife in the late 1980s, the number of arrivals greatly decreased, but again picked up to an estimated 8,500 in 1990. Most tourists come from Western Europe with lesser numbers from the USA, Japan and Australia. The majority of tourists are independent travellers and the remainder come on group tours. The authorized tourist hotels are considered to provide satisfactory accommodation. Access to the region is by air to Lhasa from where transportation is by road to other parts of the country. The road network is being improved but access to many attraction places is still difficult. Other infrastructure is limited. The marked decrease of tourist arrivals in the late 1980s resulted in considerable excess capacity of accommodation and a surplus of tourism employees.

TOURISM PLANNING APPROACH

The regional tourism plan for Tibet was prepared in 1990 (UNDP and WTO. 1990. *Tourism Plan for Tibet Autonomous Region, People's Republic of China*, Madrid: WTO). This is a comprehensive plan that examines all the elements of tourism. It recommends a development concept, improvements required to accommodation and other tourist facilities, services and infrastructure, and a marketing strategy. Economic, social and environmental impacts are evaluated. Implementation policies are recommended on procedural and technical issues – the institutional framework for tourism; development of key tourism services; development of economic opportunities; and manpower development and training. A detailed development programme for 1991–95 is recommended. Physical plans are presented for various demonstration projects including an improvement plan for Lhasa. Design guidelines for development of tourist facilities are recommended in the plan.

The plan proposes market targets by five-year periods up to 2010. For that year a total of 170,000 arrivals are targeted. These targets are composed of about three-quarters general interest tourists, and the remainder are trekkers and a small number of mountaineers. Source markets would continue being primarily Western Europe, the USA and Japan.

The development concept of the plan is focused on the coordinated realization of the tourism potential of the cultural, historic and environmental resources which are special to Tibet. It emphasizes the consolidation and further development of those cultural features and tourist activities which currently attract tourists. At the same time, new attractions of a different type should be opened up to widen the appeal of Tibet to general and special interest groups. The concept defines several tourism zones, each with distinctive characteristics suitable for different touristic pursuits. The major zones are linked by a system of touring circuits to facilitate visits to a wide range of destinations offering a variety of experiences.

The plan designates three cultural zones – one primary zone (focused on Lhasa), one secondary zone, and the third zone being of minor importance to general interest tourists. Four trekking areas are defined, with trekking routes shown on the plan. Two environmental zones are designated. These are areas of outstanding environmental quality, based on their scenic beauty and wealth of flora and fauna, with particular appeal to general interest tourists for relaxation and recreation. The projected accommodation rooms needed are allocated to the various zones.

Touring circuits are defined in the plan as circular road routes which link a number of destinations and take tourists several days to accomplish. Stopovers are made at different places along the route. Three touring circuits are recommended, with possible combinations of these for the longer-stay tourists. The plan examines the potential for developing mountaineering, pony trekking, white-water rafting and mountain biking. Ways to give tourists greater exposure to the Tibetan culture are suggested – organized presentations of song and dance; exhibitions in museums; and visits to villages, nomadic camps and traditional festivals.

In the marketing strategy, the plan indicates that the initial step is to establish an image of Tibet as a viable tourist destination. The strategy emphasizes that a programme must be instituted for removal of constraints on marketing, improving the tourism product and informing the world of these changed circumstances. Image-building would then focus on establishing Tibet as a mystery land of scenic beauty, great mountains and old monasteries, peopled by agriculturalists and nomadic herdsmen. Promotion should be primarily through selected tour operators and travel agents.

DEVELOPMENT OF ECONOMIC OPPORTUNITIES

An important element of the Tibet tourism planning project was to propose ways in which the present and future economic benefits of tourism could be increased to the local population. The plan includes a section on development of economic opportunities, in addition to conducting the standard economic impact analysis of tourism. This element is given emphasis because of Tibet's present economic underdevelopment and low income of the population. The plan points out that, although Tibet has considerable natural resources, their development is difficult because of the huge size of the region, its mountainous geography and small population. The relatively few number of people provides only a limited local market for manufactured goods.

The plan points out that the general opportunities for economic development in Tibet are mainly in the fields of agriculture, animal husbandry, forestry and minerals, plus tourism. Development of tourism can provide substantial foreign exchange for the region and help diversify the economy. It can create new markets for local products and services. Tourism will also act as a catalyst and help pay for the improvement of infrastructure which will benefit the total economy.

The plan sets forth an economic strategy for tourism, as follows:

- Given the large investment and excess capacity in tourist accommodation, aim in the short term to increase tourist numbers and length of stay as fast as possible, but without jeopardizing the reputation for quality and future sustainable growth.
- Given the limited capital available for investment and the limited infrastructure, minimize the capital costs of developing tourist facilities.
- Maintain prices and value in relation to revenue above the levels of competitors to reflect Tibet's premium status and to maximize revenues, subject to the need to improve the reputation for quality of services.
- Increase the length of stay of tourists.
- Increase retail and incidental spending per tourist which, with increasing the length of stay, offers the greatest potential for increasing revenues.

Improving regional economic linkages, resulting in greater use of local products and services, is also identified as an important means of enhancing local economic benefits.

For increasing the number of tourist arrivals during the near-term period, the plan makes several recommendations – more promotion of tourism, some reduction in prices, improvements in quality of services, and relaxation of restrictions on independent travellers. The plan states that it will be difficult to reach the market targets solely from group tours, and independent travel should also be encouraged. The plan emphasizes that a substantial increase in the average length of stay can be achieved only by developing new activities and locations. This will require new investment. Trekking, however, offers the potential to develop new activities at a relatively low cost and should be expanded rapidly.

In order to minimize the capital investment costs of tourism development, the plan recommends:

- Coordinating the development of tourist facilities with infrastructure improvements.
- Making the best use of existing facilities, for example upgrading the Tibetan (locally owned) hotels rather than building new hotels.
- Not providing costly facilities for seasonal peak demands, and choosing low cost solutions for seasonal use, such as tented camps, where appropriate.

- Once capacity of facilities is reached in the peak months, focus efforts on increasing occupancy at other times through pricing and promotion before investing in additional capacity.

When capital resources are needed, the plan indicates that they can be drawn from the central government, profits of existing tourism enterprises, local bank loans and international sources.

On pricing of facilities and services, the plan recommends that present premium prices be maintained (except for a slight reduction to attract more tourists), as a means of increasing tourism income. As Tibet becomes better known, it will have to offer more competitive prices.

The plan indicates that raising the spending per tourist can be encouraged in various ways. The range of goods available for tourists should be expanded, including imported goods where necessary. The items related to Tibetan culture, such as handicrafts and books, can be increased for sale to tourists. Tourists can be allowed more opportunities in their itineraries for retail shopping and incidental spending.

On improving regional economic linkages, the plan makes several recommendations:

- Use local materials, to the extent possible, in the construction of hotels and other tourist facilities.
- Increase the production of local food items used in tourism. Opportunities exist especially for local production of poultry, eggs, milk products, bakery goods and fresh vegetables.
- Expand the production and sales of locally produced handicrafts through extending the range of items produced, adapting designs to tourists' tastes, and establishing training programmes in craft skills and quality controls. Some assistance will be needed to expand local production of crafts.
- Provide more supplies and services for trekking, including fresh and processed food items and some equipment such as Tibetan style tents.

CONCLUSIONS

The planning approach of the Tibet tourism plan is comprehensive, with particular attention given to priority issues. The development concept applies the principle of establishing tourism zones for different types of tourism areas. Additionally, the plan recommends touring circuits for sightseeing tourists. These circuits are related to the tourism zones.

The emphasis given to development of local economic opportunities reflects the concern that tourism should generate maximum benefits to Tibetans. The plan's proposals for expanding these opportunities include ones which are applicable in many places – attracting more tourists in the near future in order to make use of existing excess capacity of tourist facilities; increasing the length of stay of tourists; making effective use of limited capital resources; maintaining high pricing levels; increasing spending per tourist; and improving regional economic linkages. However, they have been adapted to the Tibetan situation so that they are more likely to be effective.

An interesting approach recommended is that of not providing costly facilities only for peak season use, because this does not make effective use of capital resources. Rather, the plan recommends that seasonality be reduced through promotion and pricing techniques, and that low cost facilities such as tented camps be used to absorb the extra needs during the peak season.

Some of the recommendations made, such as locally producing more food items and handicrafts, will require detailed programming, developing some pilot projects and technical and financial assistance. Attention will also need to be given to effective marketing of these products. However, experience with application of these approaches elsewhere indicates that such investments can be very worthwhile in increasing local production.

Chapter 24

Environmental management of tourism in the Maldives

Tourism development has been carefully managed in the Maldives so that it does not generate any serious environmental or social problems, while still making a major contribution to the economy. This has been achieved through careful planning and application of strict controls.

BACKGROUND

The Republic of Maldives is situated southwest of India and west of Sri Lanka in the Indian Ocean. The country is composed of 26 atolls containing about 1,200 low-lying islands spread over a north–south distance of approximately 800 kilometers. About 200 islands are inhabited. The total population is somewhat more than 200,000, with about 50,000 living in the capital city of Male. The society is Islamic, and religious values and customs are strictly maintained. There is a single local language. Natural resources are limited and the economy is based mostly on fishing and tourism.

The primary attractions for tourists in the Maldives are the warm, sunny tropical climate, scenic island beauty and activities related to the extensive beach and marine environment. Snorkelling and scuba diving are especially popular. Tourism commenced in 1972, when two resorts were opened and about 1,000 tourists visited the islands. In 1990, there were nearly 200,000 tourist arrivals. The major tourist markets are Western European countries. The Japanese market is also becoming important. The average length of stay of tourists is about nine days. International tourism receipts constitute the single most important source of foreign exchange for the country, and tourism contributes about 20 per cent to the Gross National Product. There is a high import content of goods used in tourism.

The physical configuration of tourism development in the Maldives is an unusual one. Virtually all development is composed of resorts, about 75 of them, which vary in size from six to more than 150 rooms. Each resort occupies a separate island and is totally self-contained. The resort islands are accessible only by boat from the international airport, also on its own island. The capital of Male extends over another entire island. The majority of resorts are developed in Kaafu Atoll where Male and the airport are located. There are some resorts on other atolls, mostly on Alif Atoll situated west of Kaafu.

A tourism plan prepared for the Maldives in the early 1980s provided some ideas for development. However, most of the tourism planning and environmental management for the country has resulted from government initiatives, based on its evaluation of the best forms and standards of development. (The material in this case study is taken from information provided by the Maldives government, other publications and field observations.) Many of the government's present approaches and standards have evolved through monitoring of the earlier phases of development to determine what is most suitable. Approaches and standards are refined – and some may be discarded – based on the experience gained from previous types of development.

PLANNING OF TOURISM DEVELOPMENT

The Ministry of Tourism (then a department) was organized in 1978. The Ministry has been very active in guiding the growth of tourism and applying strict development and operating standards on new and existing resorts. The Ministry, for example, has the power to close substandard resorts if, after imposing fines, operating standards have not been improved. One of its important functions is to formulate and implement environmental protection policies and regulations. The coral island and reef ecosystem is extremely fragile, and the government recognizes that both fishing and tourism are dependent upon preservation of this ecosystem. The Ministry also coordinates closely with the private sector. It regularly holds meetings with the resort owners and managers, tour operators and others involved in tourism.

By government policy, the resorts are located on uninhabited islands, in order to reduce any possible socio-cultural impacts. Also most islands are too small to contain both resorts and traditional villages. These islands are owned by the government and it can allocate them for resort use as needed. The resort developer receives a long-term lease and pays an annual rent that is calculated individually for each island. The resorts must provide their own infrastructure of electric power, water supply, sewage and solid waste disposal, boat dock and recreation facilities. They must also provide housing and related facilities for the resort employees. The families of employees remain on their home islands, often some distance away.

The government policy has been to expand tourism for its economic benefits, but in a systematic manner of staged development. In the late 1980s, Kaafu Atoll was considered saturated with resort development. This decision was made within the framework of maintaining high environmental standards for the existing resorts, and retaining sufficient land for village and urban expansion and recreation parks. In fact, one of the older resorts located near Male city is being phased out to allow for development of a satellite community of Male, to absorb urban expansion of the capital.

All new resort development is programmed to take place in Alif Atoll, which is accessible by boat from the international airport. In 1988, 16 islands in Alif were designated for resort development. These were allocated to developers based on approval of their development plans, financial arrangements and other considerations. By the early 1990s, most of these new resorts had been developed. During this period of expansion in Alif, no new resorts are allowed elsewhere in the country.

Additionally, the government policy is to encourage upgrading of existing older resorts to higher standards, including meeting present environmental quality standards. This upgrading is considered necessary to maintain the viability and competitiveness of these resorts. Also the aim is to maintain all tourism development at a reasonably high quality level, catering to quality tourist markets. Much of this upgrading has been accomplished.

Because of limited availability of local financial resources, the government encourages foreign investment as needed. As the country develops, especially the tourism sector, there will be a greater amount of local capital available for investment.

ENVIRONMENTAL STANDARDS AND CONTROLS

As an important basis for deciding the number of rooms and extent of resort facility development allowed on each resort island, the government has established carrying capacity standards. These are based on several factors:

- Control of tree cutting so that the natural appearance and facade of the island are maintained with no buildings allowed to appear above the tree tops.
- The maximum island area to be occupied by buildings is 20 per cent, with two-storey buildings allowed to conserve land area if there is sufficient vegetation to conceal these buildings from the ocean view. Equal space will be left open on the island for every building developed on the lagoon. (Based on the experience of actual development, buildings on the lagoon are not now being encouraged.)
- In order to preserve the tourists' perception and image of beach orientation, all guest rooms should be facing the beach, with a minimum of 5 metres of linear beach available in front of each room. Sixty-eight per cent of the total length of beach on the island is allocated for guest room frontage, 20 per cent for general resort facilities, and the remaining 12 per cent left as open space.

The exact capacity of each resort island is decided after reviewing the proposed resort layout, and determining how well the plan meets the above guidelines and fits into the overall environment.

For environmental protection, the government applies various measures. These include the following:

- Architectural control of resort buildings – so that they are well integrated into the island environment, take advantage of the tropical climate and use local building materials, such as thatch roofs, to the extent possible. Previously many buildings of all types were constructed from coral stone mined from the reefs. However, the mining of coral is now restricted to a few isolated reefs in order to prevent any further environmental damage to the remaining reefs. The use of imported building materials is now being encouraged, although these are expensive by local standards.
- Controls on the heights of buildings – no more than two storeys.
- Setbacks of buildings from the shoreline – a minimum of 5 metres, with suitable landscaping to complement the natural vegetation.
- Design of boat piers – in such a manner that they do not result in beach erosion or deposition. Previously, solid-based piers were developed which led to some environmental problems. Now piers must be built on pilings with free flow of water under the piers.
- Provision of adequate potable water supply – usually a combination of restricted use of the limited groundwater, roof catchment and storage, and desalination using the reverse osmosis technique.
- Provision of proper sewage disposal systems – the actual system used will depend largely on the size of the resort.
- Provision of proper solid waste disposal systems – utilizing controlled incineration, compaction and disposal in deep water sea areas. Empty cans must be compressed and plastic materials cannot be disposed in the sea. Recycling of some waste material is being experimented with, but this requires shipping the material outside the country.
- Encouragement given to undergrounding utility lines – installation of overhead lines is discouraged.
- Controls on the marine ecology – prohibition of collection of coral, seashells and even rocks from the sea, reefs and beaches and use of harpoons and guns to kill fish (spear-fishing) by tourists; and prohibition of purchase by the resorts of turtles and tortoises under a certain size and young lobsters and female lobsters ready to lay eggs. Sport fishing by tourists with lines and hooks is permitted.
- Controls on turtle products – prohibition of the display and sale of stuffed turtles and tortoises in shops and the export of turtle and tortoise shells and black coral in whole form. Ornaments made out of these materials are allowed to be produced, sold to tourists and exported.

There are plans to establish marine conservation areas or reserves where more stringent environmental controls would be applied. For the safety of tourists, the government applies strict regulations on wind surfing and diving operations. Resorts are required to employ internationally qualified diving instructors and dive masters. These may be Maldivians who have passed international examinations.

SOCIO-CULTURAL AND ECONOMIC CONSIDERATIONS

Several policies and controls have been established which relate to socio-cultural and economic considerations. Islamic codes and customs are carefully maintained. Nude bathing is prohibited and fines are imposed on both the bather and resort management if this regulation is violated. Tourists visiting inhabited islands for picnics or excursions are not allowed to go swimming on those islands. Locally acceptable dress codes must be observed by tourists when they visit Male or the island villages.

Cruises for tourists can be conducted only in atolls where tourist facilities are available and tourists are not allowed to visit other atolls. The atolls approved for visits are listed by the government. Tour groups can be taken to certain traditional villages on a prearranged basis for sightseeing and to purchase local handicrafts made in those villages. These regulations have been respected by tourists and resort management, with very few exceptions.

With permission, alcoholic beverages can be imported and served in the resorts. However, Maldivian employees are not allowed to handle and serve these beverages. Most bartenders are from Sri Lanka. Maldivian employees (except waiters and other employees required to do specific work) and Maldivian visitors to the resorts are prohibited from entering the bars and shops where liquor is sold. Maldivians, foreign employees and tourists are not allowed to carry liquor with them when leaving the resort islands. No pork is produced in the islands, and pork may be imported, by permit, only for consumption in the resorts. Pork dishes must be labelled when served in buffets. It is prohibited for pork to be sold, given or served to Maldivians.

To ensure that Maldivians, and especially the urban residents of Male, have sufficient recreation facilities, an island in Kaafu Atoll near Male has been designated and developed as a recreation park for Maldivians. This park is quite popular with the Maldivians on weekends and holidays. A similar island recreation park is being developed in Alif Atoll for use by the residents there. The land areas of these island parks are limited, and therefore they can be visited by tourists only on days when there is little demand for use by Maldivians.

Preference must be given to Maldivians for employment in resorts. Work permits for expatriate employees are granted only for bartenders and others who have special skills not yet available locally. Through education, training and experience, Maldivians are commencing to assume higher level technical and managerial positions in the resorts.

Because most fruits and vegetables must be imported for resort use, one large resort has taken the initiative to develop a hydroponic farm. This has been successful in supplementing the resort's needs for certain imported vegetables. A chicken farm has been established to provide some locally produced poultry, although its production costs have been higher than imported poultry. Locally caught fish and other sea food items are used extensively in the resort menus, as are some locally grown fruits. Beef and pork must be imported.

The resorts must provide suitable housing, community and religious facilities and services for the employees who live on the resort islands. These are typically located in the interior of the islands. The fact that those employees who work in resorts located some distance from their home islands may see little of their families does not seem to cause any serious problems.

The Ministry of Tourism has implemented a public education programme to inform Maldivians about tourism. The programme emphasizes the economic importance of tourism, and attempts to raise the environmental awareness of Maldivians. This education programme is conducted in the public school system and on the radio, the islands' primary communications medium. The local television station also includes news items about tourism.

Traditionally not attuned to structured regular employment, more Maldivians are being attracted to work in tourism. By policy, the government encourages Maldivian employment in tourism in order to reduce the previously high rates of unemployment and underemployment, increase income levels, and decrease the number of foreign employees. At the same time, some concern is being expressed that, over the long term, tourism should not deplete the labour supply necessary to maintain the fisheries industry, the other major sector of the economy.

Training persons to work in tourism is being promoted. A hotel and catering school, assisted by the WTO, UNDP and European Community, was opened in Male in 1987 and is operating successfully. Also, several of the government tourism staff have been involved in internationally sponsored local and overseas tourism management education. Some of the hotel staff are sent overseas for training by the larger resorts.

CONCLUSIONS

The Maldives have developed a very suitable form of tourism – it is appropriate for their small-island environment; does not generate any serious environmental or socio-cultural impacts; creates substantial economic benefits; and meets tourist expectation and satisfaction levels. It is interesting to note that this has been accomplished through government commitment, initiatives and application of strict regulations over a period of time. Success has been based on government policy, but not a particular tourism plan. The techniques applied by the Maldives government in developing sustainable tourism, however, are those which tourism planners typically use in their plans for island destinations.

Many of the present environmentally suitable standards in the Maldives have resulted from experimentation with various approaches – discarding those which were seen to be unsuitable, and adopting and refining those which were deemed to be appropriate. A wise move, in recent years, has been upgrading of the older resorts and ensuring that new resorts meet good quality standards. The Maldives have thus become a 'quality' destination. With respect to demands on the reef system from both general development and tourism, several appropriate measures have been taken, but continued monitoring of any further reef deterioration will need to be maintained.

Much of the effectiveness of the approach in the Maldives has derived from having a competent government tourism office, with a good working relationship and coordination established between the public and private sectors. This public–private sector cooperation is one which is always encouraged in contemporary tourism management. Success has also been assisted by other factors – a strong central government; a homogeneous population with a single set of religiously-based social values; and government control of land.

With respect to socio-cultural considerations, a minor issue is the separation of many of the men working in the resorts (most resort employees are men) from their families and communities. However, employees are allowed to visit their home villages during the Moslem fasting month of Ramadan (foreign workers are employed during that period). The government is investigating the possibilities of developing complete new communities on uninhabited islands located near to resorts, where employees can live with their families and commute to work by boat. Also, a consideration to be made in the future is whether, within the framework of Maldivian Islamic values, to encourage more women to work in the resorts.

An economic issue is the extent to which goods must be imported for use in tourism. Efforts are being made to produce more items locally, but the Maldives have very limited resources and few manufacturing industries. It will not likely be possible to achieve complete import substitution. Even with a high import content, however, tourism still brings substantial benefits to the society.

The government recognizes that it will need to decide whether and how much to expand tourism in the future. It wishes to maintain a diversified economy based on both tourism and fisheries. It also does not want to encourage any more migration of foreign workers. If tourism is developed to the extent that tourism depletes the local labour supply, to the detriment of maintaining fishing activities, the economy will become too dependent on a single economic sector.

Chapter 25

Environmental impact management in the Tibet tourism plan

The Tibet tourism plan includes an assessment of environmental and social impacts. Various suitable policies and control measures are recommended to manage impacts, including a Tourist Code of Conduct.

BACKGROUND

The background of tourism planning in Tibet was described in a previous case study, and so is only summarized here. Tibet is an Autonomous Region of the People's Republic of China located in south-central Asia. The southern boundary of the country lies in the Himalaya Mountains. Much of Tibet is composed of a high plateau of grasslands averaging some 4,000 metres in altitude. Most of the population of 2.2 million live in villages situated in the sheltered valleys on this plateau. The capital of Lhasa and the few other towns are also located in these valleys. Some forests lie on the approaches to the Himalaya and in the southeastern part of the country. Despite the high altitude, the climate of southern Tibet is equable with long hours of sunshine in both the summer and winter. The region's economy is based primarily on cultivated agriculture and animal husbandry.

The cultural attractions for tourists in Tibet are the traditional patterns of the villages and towns, and many religious and historic monuments of monasteries, temples and palaces. Buddhism has been the focus of Tibetan culture for well over 1,000 years. The natural attractions relate to scenic beauty and environmentally interesting areas that offer opportunities for trekking, mountain climbing and sightseeing. Tibet was first opened to tourists in 1980 with a peak of 43,500 arrivals reached in 1987. Because of civil strife, tourism sharply dropped in the late 1980s and then picked up somewhat to an estimated 8,500 arrivals in 1990. Access to the region is by air to Lhasa, and from there by road to other parts of the country. Most authorized tourist accommodation is considered to be satisfactory. Infrastructure is limited and some attraction areas are not easily accessible.

The regional tourism plan for Tibet was prepared in 1990 (UNDP and WTO. 1990. *Tourism Plan for Tibet Autonomous Region, People's Republic of China.*

Madrid: WTO). This is a comprehensive plan that examines all aspects of tourism. The market targets established indicate a substantial growth of tourism over a 20-year period. About three-quarters of these tourists will be of the general interest type and the remainder will be trekkers and mountaineers. The development concept in the plan is focused on coordinated realization of the tourism potential of those cultural, historic and environmental resources which are special to Tibet. Present attractions will be improved and new ones developed. The plan designates three cultural tourism zones, two zones of environmental interest, and four trekking areas. Three touring circuits are recommended. The near-term marketing strategy focuses on image-building and selective promotion.

ENVIRONMENTAL IMPACT ASSESSMENT

The plan considers the impact of tourism on both the man-made and natural environment. Based on the market targets and expected distribution of tourists, the average number of daily visitors to historic monuments is calculated. The plan concludes that these numbers of visitors will not likely exceed the monuments' visitor carrying capacities. The example is given of Potala Palace in Lhasa, which will receive the largest number of tourists – about 600 daily during peak periods. This level of use will not congest the palace, although a better means of access will need to be devised.

The plan explains that the development of tourism could possibly cause damage to the natural environment in four principal ways:

- Ecologically sensitive areas may be subjected to greater pressure by being opened up for tourist visits and activities.
- In less sensitive areas, the introduction of relatively large numbers of people on defined routes or at specific places (engaging in activities such as trekking and mountaineering) may cause a general degradation of the immediate environment, and generate large quantities of refuse and sanitation problems.
- The penetration of roads into previously inaccessible forest areas may encourage settlement to take place on slash and burn principles – removal of vegetation for cultivated agriculture – or the commercial extraction of timber.
- Erosion could arise as a consequence of building operations and the construction of roads in mountainous areas of heavy rainfall.

The plan states that the last point is mainly a matter of ensuring good design that takes into account the characteristics of the environment. The other points are reviewed with respect to the tourism zones designated in the plan – the two zones of environmental interest and the four trekking areas.

Calculation of the peak daily use in the environmental zones indicates that the numbers of tourists using these zones at any one time will be relatively small – 600 and 850 respectively in each of the zones. Therefore, there will not be any immediate problems associated with overuse. However, in the smaller zone, capacity may be reached by 2005, and environmental impact there should be carefully monitored. The improvement of access roads and tracks in these zones is not considered to generate any negative impacts, if they are properly designed. However, the plan recommends that cutting of timber, except for domestic use such as fuel and housing, should be prohibited in these zones. To accomplish this, the zones should be declared as natural protection areas under environmental conservation legislation.

The two potential environmental problems of trekking and mountaineering – ecological damage from overuse and poor disposal of refuse – are examined. Because of the plan's development strategy of spreading trekking over various large areas, the use of each track will be limited and general environmental damage is not considered likely to be a problem. However, there could be damage from removal of rare plants, the cutting of vegetation for fuel and the grazing of pack animals on the thinly grassed upland areas. The latter two could lead to erosion and resentment among the nomadic people and local residents.

The plan recommends that collection of all plants by tourists be prohibited, in order to ensure that rare plants are not removed. The cutting of firewood by trekking groups should also be prohibited, with use of portable fuel such as kerosene made obligatory. This rule could be relaxed in densely forested areas. Tourist groups should be required to carry sufficient fodder for their pack animals in any area where there is a danger of depleting local supplies or creating erosion conditions.

The plan indicates that refuse disposal is a particularly difficult problem in remote areas. A couple of places are already becoming seriously polluted by refuse that has been discarded by trekkers and mountaineers. The plan suggests that either of two approaches could be used. One is that refuse bins be placed along the trails and at camp sites. The refuse would be periodically removed for disposal in an acceptable manner. The other approach would be to require trekkers to carry out their refuse or to bury it in pits of sufficient depth. The present practice of covering refuse with rocks should not be allowed. Also, as an important measure, both the trekkers and their Tibetan staffs should be educated not to litter trails and camp sites. The plan states that littering of mountaineering camps and trails must also be controlled.

For sanitation, the plan recommends that use of toilet tents and pit latrines should be required for all trekking groups. At more intensively used places, permanent sanitary facilities should be developed. Detailed designs for these facilities are illustrated in the plan.

It is recommended that design standards for tourist facilities reflect Tibetan styles and make use of local building materials. This will help integrate the facilities better into the cultural and natural environment, thus lessening their environmental impact.

TOURIST CODE OF CONDUCT

The plan states that tourists' activities should be regulated by a Code of Conduct to be observed by trekkers, mountaineers and any visitors who journey into the open country for such purposes as picnicking. The recommended code is summarized as follows:

- Not to kill any animal, except under licence, nor cut or remove any growing plant for fuel, except in exempt areas, or for any other purpose.
- Not to damage growing crops nor to harass domestic animals.
- Not to pollute any river, stream, spring or other source of water.
- Not to dispose of any litter, refuse or other items except in authorized refuse containers or in pits dug in accordance with the regulations.
- Not to dispose of human wastes except in accordance with established sanitary procedures.
- Not to permit the grazing of pack animals, except in exempt areas.

This code should be distributed to every tourist, and especially those going trekking or mountaineering. The responsibility for policing the code should be placed with the Tibetans who accompany the tourists as guides, organizers or liaison officers. As part of their training, they should be instructed on how to enforce the code in an effective but tactful manner. The local government authorities would be responsible for maintaining refuse containers.

The plan recommends that all trekkers be required to obtain a trekking permit. The permit fees should be established at a level that will pay for the cost of maintaining trails, collecting and disposing of refuse, and servicing the sanitary facilities. The money collected from permit fees should be specifically allocated for these purposes.

SOCIAL IMPACT CONSIDERATIONS

The plan reviews possible social impacts from tourism. It concludes that there will not be any substantial negative impacts because of the relatively modest level of tourism proposed and the strong Buddhist-based cultural values of Tibetans. The plan points out that there are now many outside influences on the Tibetan culture, in addition to tourism. However, it indicates that there will undoubtedly be some influence by tourists on the Tibetans' attitudes, values and ways of life. Also in the tourism areas, some moderate problems will likely arise – non-traditional begging by children from tourists; petty theft; prostitution; and overly aggressive selling of items by vendors to tourists.

The plan recommends that there be a public education programme about tourism – its nature, benefits and problems – using television and other media, and organizing annual tourism weeks. Tourism education programmes should also be included in the public school system at the primary, lower middle and second middle levels. These school programmes would include giving students information about job opportunities in tourism. Teachers will need to have some special training in tourism studies in order to implement this programme. The plan also recommends that tourists be informed about the local culture and possible social problems, and asked to refrain from encouraging begging or to place temptation in the way of petty thieves. Tourists should also be sensitized about adopting proper behavioural patterns at religious places.

CONCLUSIONS

The Tibet plan systematically identifies the types of environmental impacts that may result from tourism. This provides a logical basis for recommending preventative measures. A basic policy approach is to spread tourism throughout various places in the region, within the framework of the designated tourism zones. Thus, no one area or specific place becomes overcrowded with tourists, which could lead to serious environmental or social problems. The plan uses a quantitative approach in calculating peak period daily use by tourists, and relates that to carrying capacities. This provides a sound basis for evaluating whether overuse will likely take place. In one area where there might be an excess of tourists in the future, the plan justifiably recommends that environmental impacts be monitored and future development be controlled.

In order to reduce environmental problems along trekking trails and at camp sites, the plan recommends specific environmental control techniques – proper refuse disposal and sanitation; prohibition of tree cutting; and control of use of the local grasslands by pack animals. These are regulations which have been successfully applied elsewhere, for example in Nepal and other mountain tourism areas. Proposing a Tourist Code of Conduct incorporating these regulations is a very useful technique. This gives responsibility to the tourists and their Tibetan entourage for applying and enforcing the regulations. The requirement for trekkers to obtain permits with the fees used for maintenance of the trekking areas is a reasonable approach which has worked well in other places.

The plan also notes that some environmental problems are being caused by misuse of the landscape by local residents. It recommends the sound approach of designating environmentally important areas for environmental protection, but with controlled private use allowed to continue in these places.

The plan identifies the likely social impacts of tourism, indicating that these should not become serious. It makes the important point that there are various outside influences on the Tibetan society, of which tourism is only one type. The development concept of spreading tourism throughout different areas in the region is very valid for social, as well as environmental, reasons. This reduces the number of tourists and possible adverse social impacts in any one place. The dispersal approach also spreads more widely the economic and social benefits of tourism.

The plan recommends carrying out public education programmes about tourism – including incorporating tourism studies in the public school system – and informing tourists about the local culture and how to behave in their interaction with Tibetans. These are basic approaches which are always important to apply in tourism areas. The next steps would be to organize and implement specific public awareness programmes utilizing local communications media, write and distribute teaching guides on tourism to be used in the school system, and prepare and have available for distribution a tourist information brochure.

Chapter 26

Socio-cultural programme in the tourism plan of Nusa Tenggara

The socio-cultural analysis, policies and programme component of the regional tourism plan for Nusa Tenggara reflect an effective approach to achieve selective cultural conservation, reduce negative impacts and integrate tourism into the local societies.

BACKGROUND

Nusa Tenggara is located in southeastern Indonesia, east of Java and Bali. It is composed of the two provinces of Nusa Tenggara Barat and Nusa Tenggara Timur. The region includes numerous islands, the largest of which are Lombok, Sumbawa, Flores, Sumba and the western part of Timor. The islands are topographically rugged, with steep-sided mountains, valleys and some coastal and inland plains. Along the coasts are numerous beaches and offshore coral reefs. The climate is tropical with a monsoonal rainy season that varies appreciably from one place to another.

The vegetation is tropical but not jungle, with savanna landscapes of grasslands and scattered trees prevailing in the eastern islands. Nusa Tenggara lies immediately east of the Wallace Line which divides the Asian and Australian types of flora and fauna, although there is considerable overlap of these two types. The most famous animal of the region is the Komodo Dragon, a giant monitor lizard whose main habitat on Komodo Island has been designated and developed as a national park.

The population of Nusa Tenggara is somewhat over 6 million. Several cultural groups live in the region. Each one has its own language, customs and building styles. The cultural patterns of these ethnic groups are based on principles of mythological thinking, in which the sense of belonging to a collective group and family kinship is very strong. In most islands, traditional beliefs have been overlain by the Islamic and Christian religions, but there are some isolated Animist villages. These cultural groups vary in their degree of openness to outside cultural contacts and attitudes. This openness also varies greatly between the urban and rural areas.

In the early 1980s, when the plan was prepared, modern development was in its early stages in the region. Tourism was not developed to any great extent, except for limited facilities on Lombok Island where some tourists would visit from nearby Bali. A relatively small number of special interest groups and individual tourists toured the other islands. Basic accommodation existed in the towns for use mostly by business and government travellers.

Nusa Tenggara contains both natural and cultural tourist attractions. The most important specific natural feature is Komodo National Park. Also of much interest are the three coloured crater lakes in central Flores. Other natural attractions include good beach and marine environments – which offer possibilities for development of beach resorts – scenic beauty and opportunities for mountain hiking and camping. Cultural attractions relate to some highly traditional villages and their distinctive layouts and architectural styles, and the traditional dress, music, dance and ceremonies of the various cultural groups. The best developed handicraft is textile weaving, including tie-dye textiles, produced in the traditional manner. Each cultural area has its unique type of textiles, many of which are internationally known among textile connoisseurs.

SOCIO-CULTURAL ANALYSIS, POLICIES AND PROGRAMME

A comprehensive regional tourism development plan was prepared for Nusa Tenggara in 1981 (UNDP and WTO. 1981. *Tourism Development Plan for Nusa Tenggara, Indonesia.* Madrid: WTO). This planning study includes a major socio-cultural component prepared by an Indonesian development sociologist on the planning team. The objectives for developing tourism in the region incorporate a statement on socio-cultural considerations, as follows:

> Promote the conservation of traditional cultural patterns and their artistic expressions and places of specific historic and cultural importance which represent the heritage of Nusa Tenggara; and minimize any adverse impact of tourism on the traditional cultures and the general society through carefully controlled development.

The socio-cultural patterns of the region were carefully analysed relative to tourism development. Field trips were made to many places and the existing literature on the various cultural groups was reviewed. As stated in the plan report, socio-cultural considerations in tourism include:

- Traditional aspects of the Nusa Tenggara cultures – their unique characteristics which provide attractions for tourists and a sense of cultural identity to the people.
- The historically isolated nature of the cultures – although politically and religiously influenced by early contacts of Portuguese, Dutch and Islamic cultures, Nusa Tenggara did not undergo rapid change until national

independence. Change and modern influences are taking place in a non-selective manner, especially among young people, with a loss of some traditional patterns and sense of cultural heritage.

- Constraints imposed by Christian and Islamic religions – many traditional ceremonies and other cultural elements associated with Animist beliefs are being lost. There is a need to separate traditional elements from religious beliefs so that some aspects of traditional culture can be maintained.

The plan states that tourism will result in both positive and negative socio-cultural impacts. Types of possible positive impacts include:

- Conservation of some traditional cultural patterns because they are attractions for tourists, thus maintaining a sense of cultural heritage and enriching national cultural diversity.
- Improvement of the socio-economic standards of communities through the economic benefits of tourism.
- Encouragement of cross-cultural exchange, both nationally and internationally, through contacts between tourists and residents.

Possible negative socio-cultural impacts include:

- Commercialization of traditional cultural elements.
- Demonstration effect on the cultures, brought about by tourists, resulting in non-selective imitation by residents of outside cultural traits.
- Disruption of cultural continuity.
- Weakening of cultural identities resulting from the above-described sectors.

The plan makes the point that negative socio-cultural impacts result from many outside influences, not only from tourism.

The plan explains that a socio-cultural programme should be organized and implemented. This programme would focus on conservation of certain selected elements of traditional cultures, and on the controlling of the negative effects of tourism. The sequence of the conservation strategy should be: 1) inventory of traditional cultural elements; 2) selection of the appropriate elements for conservation; and 3) applying conservation measures. The plan indicates that the traditional elements which should, and feasibly can be, conserved and their conservation techniques are:

- Dance and music – training at all levels and organization of performances and contests, including tourist performances.
- Textile weaving and other handicrafts – maintenance of quality control, development of a greater variety of crafts, and improvement of production and marketing through village cooperatives and handicraft centres, with sales to tourists.
- Special cultural events – organization of traditional special events and ceremonies on a regular basis, and maintenance of their authenticity.

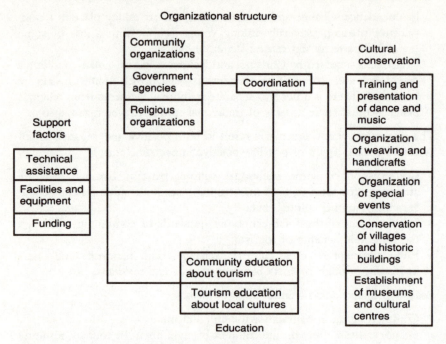

Figure 26.1 Socio-cultural programme for Nusa Tenggara

- Traditional villages, historic buildings and archaeological sites – application of conservation measures, including to culturally representative villages.
- Traditional and historic artefacts – establishment of museums and organization of special cultural and historic exhibits.

The plan indicates that establishment of cultural centres can be an important technique for cultural conservation, because they provide suitable physical facilities and can organize cultural programmes.

Based on this approach, the plan sets forth a socio-cultural programme. This is reproduced in Figure 26.1. The various organizations and agencies which should be involved in implementing this programme are specified in the plan.

The plan also recommends that there be community education about all aspects of tourism. This should be carried out in two ways – through formal government channels such as the tourism offices providing information to the media of newspapers, radio and television and to towns and villages in the tourism areas; and through non-government channels of local cultural, youth, religious and community organizations, and traditional leaders. Holding meetings on tourism in towns and villages is recommended as an important communications technique.

The plan emphasizes that it is necessary to inform tourists properly about the socio-cultural characteristics of the Nusa Tenggara people before they visit the region and during their tour. In this manner, tourists will have a more meaningful experience and more respect for the local cultures.

Other recommendations of the tourism plan also relate to socio-cultural considerations. The overall policy is for gradual, controlled growth of tourism according to staged and programmed development. Also, no intensive type of tourism development was recommended, except for some low-density beach resorts. Many recommendations are made for conservation of specific archaeological, historic and cultural sites, including certain traditional villages. The importance of incorporating traditional design motifs and local building materials in the development of tourist facilities is stressed.

The plan recommends that there be a follow-through project on village tourism. The concept is that local villages develop, own and manage small-scale tourist facilities for visitors who wish to gain a better understanding of the village culture by living there for a while. The facilities, such as simple accommodation and a restaurant, would be built in the local architectural style, and visitors would eat local cuisine and participate in village activities. Some of the villages in the Nusa Tenggara village tourism programme would be organized to serve as base camps for tourists hiking and camping in the nearby mountains. In these villages, in addition to development of accommodation and restaurants, the villagers would rent camping equipment and provide guide services.

CONCLUSIONS

The socio-cultural element of the Nusa Tenggara tourism plan represents a systematic approach. The local socio-cultural characteristics are surveyed and analysed relative to developing tourism. The possible positive and negative impacts of tourism are identified. Cultural conservation policies and a strategy are set forth, and the traditional elements to be conserved are specified. A recommended socio-cultural programme is presented in diagrammatic form and explained in detail in the plan. Such a specific programmed approach is more likely to be understood and implemented than if merely a list of policy recommendations had been presented.

Important recommendations are to educate residents about tourism and inform tourists about local traditions. It is noteworthy that in both the socio-cultural and education programmes, the plan emphasizes that community, religious and traditional organizations and leaders, as well as the government, should be involved. In the case of this region, and many others in the world, these non-government organizations and leaders exercise much influence in their societies. Although not mentioned in the plan, education about tourism could also be included in the curriculum of public and private schools.

More generally, the plan recommends ways to minimize negative impacts and integrate tourism into the society. The gradual, staged approach to developing tourism will give residents time to adapt to it, and learn how to participate in its development and benefits. Conservation of important physical sites, which are attractions for tourists, will also preserve significant symbols of the various societies' cultural heritage. Use of traditional styles in tourist facilities reinforces the local architectural heritage, integrates the buildings into the cultural environment and makes these facilities more acceptable to local residents.

Conserving culturally representative villages and buildings is an important recommendation. In this region, as well as many other places, traditional village buildings are being lost. This is happening, in part, because traditional buildings are now often more expensive to construct and maintain than modern buildings. Also, they typically do not offer the amenities that their occupants want. Therefore, there is a tendency to completely discard traditional styles for modern ones. By deliberately conserving representative examples of traditional villages – including their layouts as well as buildings – residents can appreciate this major aspect of their cultural heritage. They become major attractions for tourists, and tourism helps pay for their conservation. Also an important approach, now being used in some places, is to adapt traditional building styles to modern living, thus evolving a new vernacular architecture in these areas.

The village tourism programme provides the opportunity for tourists to have contact with local residents and participate on a equal basis in their life style. This helps expand cross-cultural understanding. At the same time, it generates direct employment and income to residents and the opportunity for them to develop entrepreneurial skills. However, such programmes must be carefully organized and managed to be successful – with training, advice and often financial assistance made available to the villagers.

Chapter 27

Investment incentives in the Cyprus tourism plan

The investment incentives proposed for Cyprus represent an effective and imaginative approach to encourage the types of tourism projects that reinforce the tourism development strategy of the country. The incentives are specifically tailored to the investment needs of the strategy.

BACKGROUND

The background of tourism in the Republic of Cyprus and the tourism planning approach and development strategy were presented in a previous case study, and so are only summarized here. Cyprus is an already substantially developed tourist destination based primarily on coastal and beach tourism. Development of tourism has been quite rapid since the mid-1970s, reaching 1.7 million arrivals in 1990. However, concern had been expressed since the early 1980s that there was too much dependency on coastal tourism and that some of the coastal tourism areas were beginning to experience environmental problems. If these problems were not remedied and the present trends shifted, they would continue to become worse in the future. However, tourism was also viewed as an important economic sector that would need to expand. The three main objectives of the government on tourism development are to accomplish:

- Growth of tourism's contribution to the Gross Domestic Product.
- Protection of the environmental and cultural qualities of Cyprus.
- Attraction of higher expenditure tourists.

The attraction of higher expenditure tourists would result in increased income from tourism without a corresponding increase in the number of tourist arrivals, thus assisting with environmental and cultural protection.

In order to achieve these objectives, a national tourism development plan was prepared in 1988 (UNDP and WTO. 1988. *Comprehensive Tourism Development Plan for Cyprus*. Madrid: WTO). The planning approach is a comprehensive one that examines all elements of tourism. It includes a detailed environmental analysis and carrying capacity study of the beaches.

Market growth targets are established based on the government's economic development objectives, as well as the proposed development strategy. Institutional elements are given careful consideration, and implementation techniques are specified.

The proposed tourism development strategy is that of controlled growth. Within that framework, consolidation of the existing tourism areas, with new development being located in these areas, is recommended. Consolidation, as opposed to dispersed development, is seen as the best way to provide the resources necessary to carry out environmental quality improvements in these areas. In addition, the plan strongly recommends that a programme of tourism product diversification and improvement be undertaken. This is important in order to attract the desired higher spending international tourists, broaden the tourist markets generally, and better serve domestic tourism needs. Product diversification can also reduce the problem of the seasonality of tourist arrivals that currently prevails.

As part of the institutional considerations for implementation of the overall development strategy, the plan carefully examines the investment incentives needed. In order to understand the investment incentives that are recommended, it is first necessary to review the product improvement strategy.

PRODUCT IMPROVEMENT STRATEGY

Since the early 1980s, the government has recognized the need for tourism product enrichment. The 1988 tourism plan reinforces this need. It states that, although Cyprus currently has a successful tourism sector, the tourism product is limited compared to that of competing destinations. The accommodation facilities and services are generally good, but only a narrow range of recreational and entertainment facilities are available. Competing destinations are developing accommodation tailored to specific market segments and offering diversified products. They achieve economies of scale through development of larger-scale projects. The plan also notes that the domestic market in Cyprus is changing from its traditional pattern of non-active tourism in the hinterland villages to more active holidays requiring recreational facilities.

The plan emphasizes that Cyprus possesses a wide range of both natural and man-made resources that have potential for greater development. There is much opportunity to enrich the tourism product in order to achieve qualitative growth of tourism, for the benefit of both international and domestic tourism. The plan indicates that the strategy for product improvement lies in the following areas:

- Diversification of accommodation and associated facilities aimed toward both existing and new market segments – these can include holiday villages and club-type developments offering a wide range of recreational and leisure facilities.

- Further improvements of archaeological sites, historic buildings and other cultural attractions, utilizing imaginative interpretation techniques.
- Greater promotional efforts directed to encouraging use of the mountainous hinterland for overnight stays, sightseeing and other activities, and development of village tourism including village conservation programmes.
- Development of yachting and sailing facilities and related marine tourism environments and golf courses, pending determination of their market and financial feasibility.
- Encouragement of the organization and promotion of festivals and special events.
- Promotion of opportunities to enjoy a wide range of peripheral activities.
- Encouragement of developments that generate higher tourist expenditure in entertainment, shopping, etc.

The plan elaborates on this product improvement strategy.

PRODUCT DEVELOPMENT INCENTIVES

The plan examines investment incentives with respect to how these can be used to encourage development of the product improvements needed. The existing incentives are reviewed. The plan determines that they have not been particularly successful in attracting investment in the desired types of product diversification. The main reasons for their lack of success are stated as follows:

- Uncertainty about the likely returns on investment due to its non-accommodation nature.
- Large land area requirements in appropriate locations.
- Lack of local knowledge and experience regarding the type of projects, their planning, organization and operations.
- Scepticism of banks to support projects with an apparent high degree of risk.

The first point is considered of particular importance. If ancillary facilities, such as golf courses or marinas, are not included as part of an accommodation project, they are likely to be less attractive as investments. Consequently, future product improvement schemes should include accommodation along with the desired ancillary facilities.

Leading from this analysis, the plan recommends that all government incentives for tourism development not relating to the product improvements needed should be removed. Furthermore, allowances for those projects consistent with the product improvement strategy should be approached as follows:

- Increasing investment allowances for buildings in new products and product improvement schemes.
- Providing accelerated depreciation allowances for capital expenditures incurred for the acquisition of fixed capital assets comprising new plant and construction of buildings in relation to product improvement projects.
- Providing ten-year tax holidays for tourism enterprises undertaking large-scale product improvement projects. The plan states that this overlaps the investment and depreciation allowances but has an important psychological effect and can be especially attractive to foreign investors.

The plan observes that many types of product improvement projects, such as integrated resort hotels, require relatively large land areas. In order to overcome the problems of land assembly and high land costs, the plan recommends that government should consider entering into joint venture arrangements by providing land and infrastructure for key projects. Also, public land could be made available on a selective basis to encourage the desired type of development. This would reduce the private sector investment required, with the government (or local authority) receiving an equity share, based on the value of the land and infrastructure contributed. Eventually, the private company could buy out the government's equity share.

The plan indicates that limited local capital is available for large-scale projects. Also there is lack of local experience in developing and managing these projects. Therefore, it recommends that more foreign participation be allowed in the investment and management of those projects which provide product enrichment.

The plan also recommends that the existing Fund for Financing Priority Projects, which has been used for financing some accommodation projects, be more specifically oriented to encouraging tourism product improvements. This should include allowing accommodation financing only when it involves a major ancillary facility such as a golf course, marina or water sports facility. The Fund already allows financing for tourism development in hill resorts, supplementary tourist facilities that provide entertainment, and camping sites. Concurrently, disincentives should be adopted to discourage development of accommodation that is not compatible with the qualitative growth image. These disincentives include high licence fees for developments which do not contribute to product improvements, and other techniques.

Many local investors in Cyprus have only sufficient capital to make investments in small-scale accommodation projects, but these projects typically do not improve the tourism product. The plan recommends ways in which these investors can participate in larger-scale product enrichment projects. Also, the plan indicates that small investors can make a contribution to product improvement by developing high quality and specialized accommodation – such as retreat type marine and mountain resorts and village tourism. The plan suggests that the government set up some pilot projects suitable for small investors.

CONCLUSIONS

The plan, as well as the government, recognizes that Cyprus must diversify and improve its tourism product. If it does not accomplish this, the country will not be able to continue competing effectively with other tourist destinations, or achieve its objective of attracting higher spending tourists. This represents a progressive approach in that it anticipates possible future problems, even though tourism is currently successful in attracting tourists. The product improvement strategy is very much in keeping with present tourism trends – more tourists now want to be involved in recreation, sports, cultural and other activity and learning experiences; there is increasing market segmentation of tourists including many special interest tourist markets; the older and retired persons tourist markets are rapidly growing with many of these tourists seeking activity-oriented holidays; more tourists are taking shorter but more frequent vacations throughout the year.

The investment incentives recommended for Cyprus reflect the principle that incentives should be specifically designed to achieve the desired type of development – in this case to diversify and improve the tourism product. In the Cyprus plan, incentives are formulated as an integral element of the implementation programme for the proposed development and related product improvement strategy. Consequently, they are more likely to be effective than if they had been prepared in isolation from the strategy.

The approach to formulating the incentives is logical in that it first reviews the present incentives, and determines why they have not been very effective in attracting investment in the desired future types of projects. The approach is comprehensive in that it considers all possible types of incentives. It also considers the need to provide disincentives which will discourage the types of projects that are not compatible with the development strategy.

The plan recognizes that part of achieving product diversification is to encourage large-scale projects, such as integrated resorts, that include profit-making accommodation along with the less profitable ancillary recreation, sports and entertainment facilities. This presents a dilemma in Cyprus as well as many other island destinations in the world. These places often have similar problems – high land costs and difficulty in assembling large parcels of land; limited capital of local investors who are able to invest only in small-scale profit-making accommodation; and limited local experience in developing and managing large-scale tourism projects. The incentives programme in the plan addresses these issues. It indicates that government and foreign involvement in such projects will be necessary for the long-term benefit of tourism. In order not to discourage local small investments in tourism, which is highly desirable in most places, the plan suggests ways in which small investors can still participate in tourism development.

Although not related to provision of incentives, the government will need to make some direct investments in improving the tourism product. For example, archaeological and historic sites require improved interpretation, and additional cultural and public-type recreation facilities need to be developed. Admission fees can cover some of the cost of this type of investment. In any case, the increased overall benefits from tourism, including government revenues from this sector, usually justify the public investment required.

Chapter 28

Manpower planning and training in the Oman tourism plan

The manpower planning and training component of the Oman tourism plan represents the recognized approach to providing the trained personnel required for proper management and operation of the tourism sector. At the same time, it takes into account the particular constraints that exist in Oman.

BACKGROUND

The background of Oman and the tourism planning approach used there were presented in a previous case study, and so are only summarized here. Located in the southeastern corner of the Arabian Peninsula, the Sultanate of Oman offers a diversity of tourist attractions. Natural features include scenic beauty, beaches and other interesting environmental features. Cultural attractions relate to the long history of the country – the traditions of historic towns and villages; and numerous archaeological and historic monuments. During recent years, the production and export of oil has provided the country with the means for achieving rapid economic development.

Although business travel is well developed in the country, holiday tourism is new. International holiday tourists have been allowed into the country only since 1987, and still comprise a small proportion of total tourist arrivals. Now the country wishes to diversify the economy and develop tourism in a very carefully controlled manner. Tourism is to be developed based only on the inherent natural and cultural/historic features of the country, and not be aimed at attracting the 'mass' tourist markets. Protection of the environment and culture is of utmost concern in developing tourism.

The national tourism plan for Oman was prepared in 1991 (UNDP and WTO. 1991. *National Plan for Tourism – Sultanate of Oman*. Madrid: WTO). The planning approach is a comprehensive one, with emphasis on controlled development. Both international and domestic tourism are considered. The tourism development concept is based on providing opportunities for informed tourists to experience the special cultural and environmental features of Oman. Six tourism zones are designated – three primary zones of attractions and three secondary zones. The major types of attractions are indicated for each zone. The plan also identifies several special interest themes based on flora, fauna and the country's history. The plan recommends various tourist itineraries, circuits and excursions. A marketing strategy is proposed which emphasizes image-building and selective promotion.

Implementation of the plan considers several elements relating to organizational structures, procedural controls, promotional measures, planning actions required, and detailed planning of certain priority projects and areas. An important element of the implementation programme is manpower planning and training.

A particular characteristic of manpower planning for tourism in Oman is the relatively poor cultural, religious and social image of the hotel and catering industry as an employer. There is not a tradition in the country of working in many of the activities associated with tourism, and especially in food and beverage service. Additionally, it is difficult to attract Omanis to work in the private sector generally for various reasons, including the greater appeal of working for government agencies. However, the present government policy is for Omanization of the work force including in tourism, and decreasing the country's dependence on foreign workers. Other manpower planning considerations are that Omani women traditionally do not work outside their homes, although this is changing rapidly. Finally, with its small population and rapid economic development, there tends not to be a great oversupply of local labour available in Oman, especially in the urban areas.

MANPOWER SUPPLY AND DEMAND

The planning team reviewed an existing national study of labour supply and demand for the entire economy of Oman, prepared by the World Bank in 1985. That study revealed that there is a much higher proportion of males than females in the education system as a whole, but there is a more balanced distribution of students taking business and commercial courses. The World Bank study projected the number of persons completing various education levels and entering the work force from 1985 to 1995. This provided the tourism study team with a general basis for determining the availability of persons to work in tourism at various skill, supervisory and management levels.

As the first step of the manpower planning analysis of the tourism plan, a survey was conducted of existing employment in hotels. Based on this survey and the projected accommodation needs in the plan, manpower needs are projected to 1995, 2000 and 2005. The projection figures are based on employee/bed ratios and include accommodation for business as well as holiday tourists. This projection is distributed by occupation and education/ skills level categories as follows:

- General management – graduate, diploma/certificate and advanced skills levels.
- Specialist management – graduate, diploma/certificate and advanced skills levels.
- Food preparation and kitchen – advanced skills, skilled, and low skills levels.
- Food and beverage service – advanced skills, skilled and low skills levels.
- Reception/telephone/administration/clerical – advanced skills, skilled and low skills levels.
- Housekeeping – advanced skills, skilled and low skills levels.
- Other – advanced skills, skilled and low skills levels

For each of these categories, separate projections are made for Omani and expatriate workers. Total employment needs are projected to more than double from the present level, reaching almost 6,000 persons in 2005. A much greater proportion of Omanis are projected to work in hotels in the future, based on the recommended training and other programmes being carried out. The manpower needs for tour and travel operations, including tour guides, and tourism management in the government are also examined.

MANPOWER TRAINING

The plan reviews the present status of training of tourism employees. It identifies that there is no existing tourism training programme or institute, although such a programme had been proposed in the past. However, some training of hotel employees is carried out by the larger hotels within their own enterprises. The hotels also, of course, employ expatriates who may have had training elsewhere. There has been some overseas training of local tour guides and tourism management officials. Most of the tour and travel operations and management personnel are foreigners who have received their training elsewhere.

Various types of training needs are identified in the plan. The major need is for full-time vocational programmes designed to facilitate entry of Omanis to employment in hotels and other tourism enterprises. Another need is for part-time programmes to improve the skills of persons already working in tourism. This includes upgrading type training of supervisory and management level staff and advanced craft level training of technical staff. The plan indicates that education and training should be regarded as a continuous process throughout a person's life. The training needs of the government tourism office staff in tourism management are also reviewed. The plan recommends that these needs be met through sending the tourism officials outside the country for overseas university programmes and on-the-job attachments. The plan identifies the need for short-term training of tourism-related employees such as drivers of tourism vehicles.

The plan emphasizes the importance of English language training in all the programmes. It states that Omanis must be provided with the means to communicate effectively in an industry where English is the language medium. Otherwise, employers will continue to discriminate in favour of expatriates with fluency in English.

The plan proposes that an autonomous tourism training institute be established. This institute should be under the Directorate of Tourism, and funded by the government in partnership with the leading industry enterprises. The institute would initially require some international assistance, including international instructors who would work with and educate Omani counterpart teachers.

The plan states that the institute should have primary responsibility for training of Omanis in full-time programmes, and secondary responsibility for offering part-time and upgrading courses for existing industry employees. The full-time programme should include several specializations – food and beverage service; food production; housekeeping and reception at the operations and management levels; hotel management; tour guiding; and transportation ticketing. These subjects would be phased in over a period of time. The continuing training programme would include short courses in various specializations. Omanization of the tourism work force would be emphasized in the training programmes. A target is set of 500 Omanis trained by 1995. After that time, many more Omanis would be trained, to reach the target of 55 per cent Omanization of all tourism employees by 2005.

The plan calculates the cost of establishing the institute. It proposes that the existing industry employment levy be allocated to pay for allowances of students, salaries of Omani counterpart teachers and for the cost of the part-time training of industry employees.

The plan examines the factors relative to achieving greater Omanization of the tourism work force. It points out that, in addition to some reluctance of Omanis to work in tourism for cultural and other reasons, the private hotels prefer employing expatriates because they can be attracted for lower wages than Omanis will accept. However, the government-owned hotels by policy successfully employ Omanis. The plan notes that establishment of the training institute will give a greater sense of status to tourism as a desirable career to follow. Several approaches are proposed in the plan to induce Omanis to select tourism as a career and, at the same time, encourage the private hotels to offer more jobs to Omanis. These include various government initiatives, as follows:

- Undertaking a public awareness programme to educate the general population about the benefits of tourism as an economic activity and as a career.

- Providing proper training of Omanis in tourism skills and English language, with structured periods of industry exposure as part of the training.
- Developing standards of compensation and work conditions that compare favourably with government posts.
- Requiring that hoteliers employ and train Omani staff, but giving them the right to select candidates and to discharge them on reasonable grounds.
- Giving preference to hotels which encourage Omanization in allocating the sizable amount of government use of accommodation.

The plan emphasizes that Omanization efforts should also include attracting women to tourism employment. It points out that Omani female employees have a high reputation for productivity and punctuality. In effecting Omanization, the plan notes that the present expatriate employees should be assured that this policy will not threaten their jobs. There will still be need for expatriate employment for many years.

CONCLUSIONS

The type of analysis applied in the manpower planning and training component of the Oman tourism plan represents the logical approach to this subject. First the existing employment in tourism is surveyed and any particular problems and needs are noted. Then future manpower needs are projected based on the level of tourism targeted in the tourism plan. Employee/bed ratios are applied in making this projection. Next, the overall human resources available in the country are evaluated, including consideration of expected future education levels of the labour supply – this study had already been completed in Oman. Finally, the training needs are identified and the education and training programmes and recommendations are formulated based on these needs.

The approach used in the plan is comprehensive in that all the types of tourism employment and tourism education and training needs are considered – hotel and catering operations and management; tourism management; tour and travel operations; and employment in related tourist activities.

The major recommendation of the plan is to establish a tourism training institute. Such a specialized training institution is usually required to be established in countries or large regions developing tourism. In places with more limited tourism, a tourism training programme can sometimes be incorporated into an existing vocational school. The Oman plan provides some specification of the proposed institute's programme and a general cost estimate. This can form the basis for preparing the more detailed study of the institute that will be required before it can be developed. The plan justifiably indicates that the institute will require international technical assistance.

A specific consideration underlying this manpower and training study is government's policy for Omanization of the industrial labour force. For socio-cultural and economic reasons, this policy presents particular challenges in the tourism sector. Similar constraints have faced some other countries where there is traditional reluctance of the local population to work in tourism, and to consider it as a desirable career. The plan systematically examines this situation in Oman in order to understand thoroughly the obstacles to Omanization. Then it recommends suitable approaches which can be applied to overcome the obstacles and achieve gradual Omanization.

Chapter 29

Promotion strategy and programme in the Uganda tourism plan

The promotion strategy and programme for Uganda reflect a realistic approach to commencing the promotion of a country which currently has limited facilities and a weak image but excellent tourist attractions.

BACKGROUND

The background of Uganda and the tourism planning approach used there were described in a previous case study, and so are only summarized here. Uganda is located in east-central Africa, inland from Kenya. The population of the country is somewhat over 17 million and includes several cultural groups. The capital city of Kampala has about half a million inhabitants. The primary attractions for tourists are outstanding scenic areas, including lakes, rivers, mountains, rainforests and savanna, and a variety of wildlife. Important specific features include Murchison Falls, the Ruwenzori Mountains and mountain gorilla reserves. Ten national parks have been designated although most of these still have limited tourist facilities.

Tourism was relatively well developed in Uganda in the late 1960s and early 1970s. Then, because of political turmoil and changes in government policy, tourism became virtually non-existent. Much of the tourist facility and infrastructure development was damaged or deteriorated through lack of maintenance, and wildlife was decimated. Since the mid-1980s, rehabilitation of the economy has been taking place including of tourism development. Major conservation programmes are being implemented to rejuvenate the wildlife. Substantial progress has been made on rehabilitation, and game populations are recovering, but these programmes are still underway.

The government policy is now for revitalization of the tourism sector as an important source of economic development. Tourism is also seen as a means to achieve conservation objectives. In 1991, Uganda received 68,000 international tourist arrivals. Only about 10,000 of these arrivals were holiday tourists, with the remainder coming for business, official mission and other purposes. Most of the holiday arrivals were budget types of tourists.

The large international aid community in Uganda provides many of the present visitors to the national parks.

In the early 1990s, a tourism plan was prepared for Uganda (UNDP and WTO. 1993. *Integrated Tourism Master Plan – Republic of Uganda. Vols. I, II and III.* Madrid: WTO). The planning approach is comprehensive, and examines all aspects of tourism. The development strategy emphasizes that tourist market development must take place slowly because tourist facilities and the wildlife will remain rather limited for the next few years. The spatial development concept is based on establishment of tourism zones – three primary, two secondary and three tertiary zones. Several possible tourist circuits are identified which link the tourism zones. The plan recommends that tourist service centres be developed to provide tourist information, nature interpretation exhibits, tourism services, medical clinics and commercial facilities.

PROMOTION STRATEGY

The Uganda plan includes a major element in the implementation section on the promotion policy and programme. The national structure plan sets forth the overall marketing and product strategy. It identifies the market target segments, and the product development priorities. The overall target for international holiday tourists is set at a modest level of about 33,000 by 1997. In addition, there will be a sizable number of business type tourists. The holiday tourist market countries are identified as follows:

- Priority A – UK, Germany and USA.
- Priority B – France and Italy.
- Priority C – Australia, rest of Europe, other countries in Africa and Asia.

The promotion strategy notes the progress that is being made in expanding international airline services, hotel development, revival of wildlife resources and improving inbound tour operating services. It indicates that Uganda can be perceived as a newly emerging destination. The plan states that promotion has to tackle three critical problems:

- Image problem that most tourists and even the travel trade believe that Uganda is out of the tourism picture.
- Chronic shortage of any up-to-date informational or promotional material.
- Lack of confidence of the international travel trade that the country has a definite programme for, and commitment to, tourism development.

To overcome these problems, the promotion strategy to 1997 is composed of three elements:

- Project a new image for Uganda, mainly by means of public relations activities with the media and travel trade.
- Make information available to existing and potential tourists, so that

present tourists have a more enjoyable visit and offer better word-of-mouth recommendations about the country, and so that potential tourists are informed about what Uganda has to offer and are induced to visit.

- Mount systematic public relations and sales promotion activities, that present what Uganda is doing about developing tourism and generate sales leads for the private sector operators.

The strategy is established for three distinct time phases:

- 1993–94 – initial period during which the present Tourism Department (or its promotion functions) of the Ministry is transformed into a separate autonomous board.
- 1995–97 – full operation of the board with provision of an adequate budget, and implementation of promotional activities.
- Post-1997 – designing and implementing a more aggressive promotion strategy and programme based on an improved and expanded tourism product, including improved infrastructure.

The plan examines market positioning and product differentiation. It states that Uganda needs to position itself as a new destination, now rebuilding itself, which offers outstanding scenic attractions and exceptional wildlife and rainforests. Other advantages are that the country is English-speaking and a gateway to Zaire and Rwanda. The plan indicates that Uganda will be a 'niche' market for several years and needs to stress its product differentiation from competing or complementary destinations. The country should differentiate its product from that of the Eastern and Southern African plains – which are a different type of environment than that of most of Uganda – and stress the country's rainforests and mountains. The plan identifies several possibilities for combination tours with other countries in the Eastern and Southern African regions, with Uganda offering a somewhat contrasting, but complementary, tourism product.

In terms of tourism image, the plan explains that Uganda should project itself as a country of spectacular scenic beauty that includes interesting wildlife. It should also stress that it is rebuilding itself. The imagery to be projected should be inspirational and emphasize that Uganda is an uncrowded destination which possesses an element of remoteness and adventure. The focus should be on exotic places – Murchison Falls Park with its launch trip up the Nile to the falls; rainforests with mountain gorillas and ecotourism; and the Ruwenzori Mountains for trekking and mountaineering. This imagery should be projected through use of imaginative photography showing tourist activities related to these attractions, and emphasize that good accommodation and medical centres are available.

The plan recommends a promotional mix, but shifting from the present market of backpackers, truckers and adventurous independent travellers toward a mix of more affluent tourists. These include independent holiday travellers, inclusive tours for adventurers, inclusive 'mainstream' sightseeing tours, trekkers, conservation-oriented and special interest tourists, and regional (African and expatriate) travellers. The recommended promotion techniques are tailored for each type of market.

The plan also recommends an organizational structure to be responsible for promotion. It points out the deficiencies of the present system and lists six conditions necessary to carry out effective promotion:

- Establish a separate promotional entity, such as the already proposed Uganda Tourist Board, able to receive and disburse funds independently of the Treasury.
- House this board separately from the Ministry.
- Provide the board with its own properly maintained equipment.
- Pay adequate wages to the staff, so that they do not need to take second jobs.
- Provide technical assistance to the board.
- Provide a budget (from the government) to the board.

Recommendations are made on the office space and equipment which the board should have. The board could be organized, under a set of directors, into the departments of public relations, sales promotion and administration. Tourist information would be under the public relations department.

Various types of informational and promotional printed materials are recommended. They include guide leaflets, fact sheets, maps, promotional leaflets and a shell folder. Distribution of printed material should be at tourist information points, through direct mail and at exhibitions.

The plan specifies the several functions of the public relations department. It points out that public relations can be much more cost-effective and have longer-term impact than advertising. The opportunities for press coverage are identified. These include coverage of new hotel openings and wildlife conservation activities.

The plan emphasizes that use of mailing lists and direct mail promotion are particularly suitable for Uganda because it is initially aiming for niche markets. Direct mail would reach groups which are especially responsive to the appeals of the country. However, other techniques should also be applied. The plan recommends that Uganda features go into brochures of tour operators in the various market countries. Additionally, Uganda should participate in the major tourism trade fairs such as the WTM in London, ITB in Berlin and Travel Trade Fair in Brussels. A modest level of media advertising is suggested including in regional expatriate magazines, for example in Kenya, and specialist travel trade and special interest magazines.

The plan examines the various approaches to budgeting promotional activities. It indicates that a fixed rate ratio based on a percentage of the projected tourist spending provides a guideline for budgeting. A specific promotion and budget programme is set forth, by year from 1993 to 1997. In this programme, most of the first two years are devoted to organizing the separate promotion board. The recommended annual budget for promotion would represent about US$ 7 per holiday tourist in 1997. The plan states that this is not an unreasonable figure. In addition to attracting more tourists, it will also help open up new spending opportunities to tourists (by providing them with more information) and shift Uganda toward higher spending tourist markets. The plan notes that the private sector also provides valuable promotion, but that it is directed to promoting individual enterprises.

CONCLUSIONS

The promotion strategy and programme for Uganda are logically formulated. The formulation starts with the market targets and product development priorities, examines the current situation, identifies the problems to be tackled, determines a strategy in terms of approaches and time phasing, and sets forth a realistic promotion programme. The market targets are set at a modest level, within the framework of the realities of developing the tourism product, but they still represent a considerable increase over the present level of arrivals. The strategy recognizes the importance of creating a tourism image of the country as an essential basis for developing tourism in Uganda, as it is for any newly developing destination. It also recognizes that considerable public relations efforts are required to project a desirable image.

The image to be projected – that of exotic scenic beauty and wildlife with a sense of adventure travel – is an imaginative one. It reflects what is unusual about the country, and attempts to differentiate it from the better known Eastern and Southern African countries. It also will prepare the tourists not to expect highly developed facilities and tourism infrastructure. The approach that part of the image focus on the rebuilding of the country should help raise the interest and confidence of tourists to visit Uganda. The initial emphasis on niche markets, but higher spending ones than those who now visit the country, reflects a realistic approach. These markets will make use of the existing limited facilities and get tourism started in the right direction. Many of the niche markets, such as eco- and special interest tourism, will likely remain as important markets in the future even after more general interest tourism has been developed.

The strategy rightfully recognizes the essential need to establish an autonomous and properly organized, staffed, equipped and funded promotion board. This is a basic organizational ingredient in carrying out successful marketing in almost any country. Because of their importance, the public relations functions of this board are specified in detail.

The promotional mix of techniques to be utilized are those which meet the specific requirements of image-building and attracting the desired types of tourists. Many of the niche markets, for example, can best be tapped through direct mailing of information. The types of informational and promotional materials are specified. They are kept to a realistic level within the budgetary and technical capabilities to produce. The promotional budget that is recommended reflects what is required to undertake effective marketing, without being extravagant.

The promotional approach applied in the Uganda tourism plan is a comprehensive one. In addition to the considerations referred to in the plan, however, the country will also need to decide whether to establish overseas offices, an expensive type of operation, or some other form of overseas representation. Also a consideration is to what extent can the public and private sectors cooperate on joint promotion programmes, including joint funding of promotion, aimed at image-building and general marketing.

Chapter 30

Marketing strategy and promotion programme in the Sri Lanka tourism plan

The marketing strategy and promotion programme of Sri Lanka are specific and comprehensive. They particularly reflect the close relationship that must be maintained between product development and marketing.

BACKGROUND

Sri Lanka is located off the southeastern tip of India. The country's geography is varied. Central highlands of mountains and high plains are flanked by coastal flat and hilly lowlands. The climate is tropical with distinct dry and wet zones and seasonal distribution of rainfall. The southwest monsoon, which occurs between May and September, mainly affects the southwestern part of the country. The northeast monsoon, which takes place between November and February, affects the eastern areas. This results in the east and west coasts of the island having complementary tourist seasons.

Sri Lanka's population is estimated to be 17.2 million, of which more than 600,000 live in the main city and commercial centre of Colombo on the west coast. The majority of people live in villages and rural areas. Some 74 per cent of the population is Sinhalese, 19 per cent Tamil, and the remainder composed of various other groups. About 70 per cent of the population is Buddhist and 15 per cent is Hindu. The country has a long, interesting and varied history. There has been much indigenous cultural development, as well as many outside influences from India and various European colonial powers.

Sri Lanka possesses a great diversity of attractions for tourists. Natural features include many beaches and related marine areas, scenic beauty, abundant flora and wildlife, waterfalls and thermal springs. The country has 11 national parks, a marine sanctuary, and several nature and forest reserves. Archaeological and historic features include some major sites. Five of these places, termed the 'ancient cities', are located in the central part of the country. They comprise what is called the Cultural Triangle of Sri Lanka. These five places, another historic monument and an ecologically important rainforest have been designated by UNESCO as World Heritage Sites. There are several other significant attraction features – ancient irrigation works; tea plantations and processing plants; gem mines; botanical gardens; spice gardens; an elephant orphanage; traditional dance and music; major religious festivals; a wide range of handicrafts; and convention facilities in Colombo.

International tourism in Sri Lanka commenced in the 1960s and grew rapidly until the early 1980s. In 1968, a tourism plan was prepared for the country and partially implemented, particularly the development of an integrated resort on the southwest coast. From 1983, tourism suffered a major decline as a result of civil unrest within the country. Tourism operations greatly decreased and hotel occupancies and profitability were severely eroded. Proposed new investments were abandoned and only the most essential maintenance of facilities was carried out.

Tourism has recovered remarkably since 1990. There were almost 320,000 international tourist arrivals in 1991. With the resurgence of tourism, many hotels have been rehabilitated. By 1993, however, there had not been sufficient time for all the products to be brought up to full standard.

The access for virtually all international tourists to Sri Lanka is by air to the airport near Colombo. Most tourism development is based on beach-oriented accommodation on the west coast. There is some limited accommodation situated inland. However, many tourists staying in the coastal areas take tours to the Cultural Triangle, national parks, tea plantations and other places. Colombo has several high quality urban hotels.

TOURISM PLANNING APPROACH

In the early 1990s, a new tourism plan for Sri Lanka was prepared (UNDP and WTO. 1992. *Sri Lanka Tourism Master Plan*. Madrid: WTO). This plan is quite detailed and examines all aspects of tourism. It focuses on review of the current situation, a long-term strategic plan for 2001, a five-year development programme and pre-feasibility studies for selected priority projects. Both international and domestic tourism are considered in the plan. The planning analysis indicates that the country has considerable scope to expand its tourism industry, while still maintaining sustainable development. It states that Sri Lanka possesses major tourism resources which can be developed into a richer and more varied tourism product range attracting a broad spectrum of tourist markets.

The recommended strategy for tourism development is four-fold – diversify the market mix; increase tourist spending by developing and upgrading tourist facilities; increase the emphasis on cultural, natural and other tourist attractions; and create a positive image for Sri Lanka. The plan indicates that through this strategy, the economic benefits of tourism can be maximized, while environmental degradation and social problems will be minimized. The strategy calls for a carefully planned approach to developing tourism.

An optimum market target of 874,000 international tourist arrivals is established for 2001. A doubling in real terms of the average daily tourist expenditure is projected from 1991 to 2001. This increase of arrivals and expenditures will require a doubling of the present number of accommodation rooms. Emphasis will be on development of high and medium quality hotels. Foreign exchange receipts are projected to increase greatly by 2001. Some 70 per cent of these receipts will be retained in the country. Employment in tourism will also substantially increase.

The development strategy identifies 14 tourism zones throughout the country. Within these zones, the major product development proposals are as follows:

- New planned and integrated developments providing a range of facilities and services, catering to different international and domestic tourist markets and day visitors.
- Rehabilitation and upgrading of existing tourism areas in a comprehensive and coordinated way.
- Provision of a diversity of tourist attractions, including the major cultural, historic and wildlife attractions and related small-scale tourism development.
- Development of domestic tourist facilities, where they are not already covered in the other categories.
- Organization of new tour routes along with improvement of existing routes.

Two key elements of the strategy are encouraging planned developments in designated places and the opening up of new tourism areas. The plan strongly recommends that development incentives for the private sector be retained and extended to cover upgrading of existing facilities. Recommendations are made on several other elements – international air transportation; other transportation; economic enhancement; manpower training; organization and coordination; social aspects; community tourism; cultural heritage; environmental protection; and development guidelines. The plan states that implementation should be given priority, with establishment of a high level committee to oversee implementation.

MARKETING STRATEGY

The plan first examines the factors that determine the marketing strategy – the civil unrest that prevailed during most of the 1980s; the wide and not always accurate international media coverage of this unrest; the lack of awareness in source markets of the extensive range of attractions available; the seasonality of tourism; variable accommodation standards; the need to improve quality; the importance of achieving sustainable tourism; and the social effects of tourism.

Marketing objectives are set forth in the plan, as follows:

- Develop the perception in the major source market countries of Sri Lanka as a destination offering quality attractions, facilities and experiences.
- Design and execute marketing activities which build on Sri Lanka's distinctive features and advantages.
- Attract additional high spending tourists, taking account of various ways in which spending can be enhanced.
- Create destination awareness by the government, which facilitates the private sector in its own marketing efforts.
- Develop and penetrate further the traditional markets of Western Europe.
- Expand penetration in the regional Asian markets, particularly Japan, South Korea and India, as well as in Australia, North America and the Middle East.
- Conduct marketing and promotional activities targeted at market segments identified by ongoing market research.
- Promote the full range of tourist attractions and facilities developed throughout Sri Lanka.
- Achieve a more balanced distribution of tourist flows within the country in line with the development area strategy.
- Undertake seasonal and other types of promotion to improve the utilization of tourist operations to a profitable year-round level.

Based on these objectives, a three-point marketing strategy is recommended:

- Build up in the major tourist generating markets the perceptions of Sri Lanka as a destination offering a diverse range of quality attractions, facilities and experiences. All of these are readily accessible and exist in a vibrant and relaxing environment, without threat to personal safety.
- Differentiate Sri Lanka in terms of its tourist attractions, facilities and services from its neighbours, in particular India and the Maldives.
- Stress the high degree of emphasis being given to ensuring that the scale, pace and type of Sri Lanka's tourism development is sustainable, with respect to both the society and culture of the people and the country's outstanding natural resources.

The strategy elaborates on the specific attractions and other product improvements which should be undertaken to achieve a diversity of quality tourist attractions, facilities and experiences.

For domestic tourism, the plan specifies three promotion objectives – encourage travel for religious, cultural and recreational purposes among all parts of the community; promote youth travel; and encourage at least one annual holiday to be taken by employed people. The proposed strategy for promoting domestic tourism is set forth, as follows:

- Formulate and promote a 'Discover Sri Lanka' campaign.

- Promote one-week or weekend-inclusive packages.
- Promote holiday-taking through seminars and exhibits at various places.
- Publicize domestic tourism through newspaper holiday supplements and editorial coverage.
- Enlist the cooperation of the industry, trade unions and service organizations to develop and promote domestic tourism.
- Develop holiday guides for distribution.
- Evaluate the possibility of promoting the formulation and introduction of holiday schemes similar to those operated by *Comités d'Enterprise* (Works Councils) in France.

PROMOTION PROGRAMME

Based on the marketing objectives and strategy, the plan recommends a specific promotion programme. This is related to the target markets according to the timetable of the first five years of the plan. In determining the promotion programme, the plan first identifies the deficiencies related to present promotion activities. Among these are insufficient marketing staff and funding and the need for more market research. The plan recommends that consumer surveys in the five major market countries be undertaken in the immediate future.

On market positioning, the plan points out that the present image of Sri Lanka needs to be more focused on a single recognizable theme. On organization for marketing, the plan indicates that the respective roles of the government and private sector be clearly defined, with their promotional activities closely coordinated. Recommendations are made on the best approach to overseas representation – establishing overseas offices in the major market countries, contracting representation companies for other market countries, and making some use of individual representation and public relations agencies. The primary, secondary and opportunity market countries are identified. Priorities are set forth for the specific market segments to promote during the short-, medium- and long-term periods.

The plan describes the promotion techniques that should be used for the travel trade and potential tourists in the primary, secondary and opportunity markets. It emphasizes that because of its limited marketing budget, Sri Lanka should carefully direct its marketing efforts at well-defined targets, using the most effective techniques. Each type of promotion technique and activity is described and related to the relevant target markets.

A detailed promotion programme is recommended, and the estimated costs are specified. The plan points out that the total promotion budget, expressed as a percentage of gross tourism earnings, is within the range of similar budgets of many competing destinations – 3–5 per cent. A calculation is presented of the proposed marketing expenditure per target tourist arrival in the various market countries. Sources of funding for the promotion programme are proposed. The plan strongly emphasizes that a fully coordinated and collaborative approach to marketing is necessary. It recommends that the Tourism Marketing Committee, which has already been proposed, be organized in the near future.

CONCLUSIONS

Sri Lanka is an example of a country that has a great diversity of outstanding natural and cultural tourist attractions. However, it has in the past relied mostly on beach-oriented tourism and, in large part, attracted lower spending tourist markets. The development of tourism and the image of the country as a tourist destination do not reflect the tourism resources that are available. Compounding the image problem is the recent civil unrest which has been highly publicized in the international media. The development strategy is focused on improving and greatly expanding the tourism product of attractions, facilities and experiences. This will provide the basis for steady but substantial growth of tourism that has better balanced development throughout the country.

The marketing strategy for international tourism is derived directly from the development strategy and the need to project a focused and positive image. It is logically formulated based on identification of marketing problems and the marketing objectives. A key principle applied in formulating the marketing strategy is maintaining its close relationship to the development strategy, which emphasizes product improvements and diversification. The strategy approach also examines organizational and funding problems which need to be resolved in order to effectively implement marketing.

The marketing strategy for domestic tourism is interesting in that it considers the need to expose Sri Lankans to the concept of taking local holidays. This is a new type of activity for many residents of the country. The strategy also suggests ways in which holiday-taking can be made more feasible for Sri Lankans.

The promotion programme examines all the possible techniques of promotion. It justifiably recommends that the techniques applied be closely related to specific target markets, as the most efficient use of promotional resources. Overseas representation is always a major consideration in marketing because of the high cost involved. The Sri Lanka programme carefully examines the best approach to overseas representation. A fundamentally important type of recommendation made is the definition of the respective roles in marketing between the public and private sectors. Without this definition of respective roles and responsibilities, there can be contradictory images of the country projected and duplication of promotional efforts.

The promotion programme emphasizes the importance of maintaining close coordination between the public and private sectors on promotional activities. This type of coordination is needed in many countries. Finally, the programme makes a strong case for adequately funding promotion, as an essential element in achieving successful expansion of tourism.

Chapter 31

Development standards in the Philippines tourism plan

The tourism plan for the Philippines contains standards and guidelines for developing tourist facilities. These reflect a sound environmental approach to integrating facilities into their natural and man-made setting whilst, at the same time, fulfilling their functional purposes.

BACKGROUND

The background of the tourism development plan for the Philippines was described in a previous case study, and so is only summarized here. As a large multi-island country with various ethnic groups, the Philippines offer a diversity of natural and cultural attractions and activities for tourists. There has already been considerable development of tourism in the country, but tourism is experiencing some problems. Tourism is overly concentrated in the capital city region of Manila with limited development elsewhere in the country. Thus economic benefits from tourism are not well distributed throughout the country. Also the flow of tourist arrivals is erratic because of the influences of natural disasters and political events. The country has considerable potential to expand tourism, for this sector to make a greater contribution to the country's economy and society.

The tourism planning approach is a comprehensive one that examines and makes recommendations on all aspects of tourism (UNDP and WTO. 1991. *Tourism Master Plan for the Republic of the Philippines*. Madrid: WTO). The planning study is organized based on formulating a long-range plan, medium-term development programme, and detailed plans for priority destination areas. Time periods are established for recommending development objectives, strategies and policies, up to the plan's horizon year of 2010. The overall strategy is based on the concept of decentralization by developing three tourism clusters or regions, each focused on a major international gateway. Within each region are satellite tourism areas, many of which would be integrated resorts. From a marketing and product development standpoint, tourism would be based on a combination of a general interest 'mass' market and special interest 'niche' markets.

The development standards and guidelines in the plan are organized according to site planning, environmental protection, building development, and utilities. These were prepared particularly for the several tourism areas for which detailed plans were formulated.

SITE PLANNING CONSIDERATIONS

With respect to site planning considerations, the plan makes several recommendations. In coastal locations, the common use facilities, such as swimming pools and restaurants, are best located close to and facing the beach, but still maintaining the required minimum setbacks from the beach. Accommodation facilities, however, are often best situated on promontories or hills, further from the beach but offering good views. Service facilities, such as parking and utility areas, should be in convenient locations but not be obtrusive or block views.

The plan indicates that careful land clearing and grading should be done, making sure that special environmental features such as hills and other natural landforms are preserved and enhanced. Large trees and other important vegetation should not be removed or disturbed. In coastal sites, the beach area should be cleared of litter. Swimming areas may be improved with clearing of rocks, dead coral and other material, but only with strict controls applied so that marine disturbance is minimized.

Ten-metre buffer zones, where no development is allowed, are recommended along the entire perimeter of tourist facility areas including golf courses. These buffer zones should be mounded and landscaped.

The plan emphasizes that the coastline should be left undeveloped, in order to allow for natural coastal ecological processes to continue. A mandatory beach-front zone of 30 metres inland from the beach vegetation line should be maintained in its natural condition, except for careful landscaping. Any buildings and other structures should be set back 30 metres from the vegetation line. There may be exceptions made to this setback requirement in special circumstances, but only if an environmental impact assessment has been prepared. Piers, groins and breakwaters must be designed based on a detailed study of beach, water and underwater characteristics.

Various building setbacks are recommended. Buildings should be set back 5 metres from the edge of green areas. The recommended minimum distances between buildings vary from 7 to 10 metres, depending on the types of buildings.

The plan recommends that landscaping plans must be prepared for development sites. Landscaping should give preference to large shade trees along roads and footpaths, coconut and other palm trees along the beach-front, and flowering bushes and other plants in various places. 'Colour' landscaping can be achieved by the coordinated planting of flowering trees and bushes that bloom at different times of the year. Landscaping should consider not only beautification and enhancement of the natural character of the resort, but also the need to provide privacy, absorb noise and serve as wind barriers. Existing vegetation should be preserved as much as possible.

The plan recommends density requirements based on the concept of gross density – the maximum number of rooms allowed within a given hotel or resort site. The density recommendations are as follows:

- High density – 60–80 rooms per hectare
- Medium density – 30–45 rooms per hectare
- Low density – 10–15 rooms per hectare

The plan indicates that parking areas should be designed in a landscaped cluster manner including landscaping around the areas. Other parking design guidelines are recommended. All facilities, grounds, beach areas and the tourism zones generally should be well maintained.

For implementation of site planning standards, the plan recommends that preparation of a site development plan be required for each hotel or resort site. These plans must be submitted to the local development authority for review, evaluation and approval. Also, an environmental impact assessment must be conducted by a competent body for each proposed development before a construction permit can be issued.

ENVIRONMENTAL PROTECTION

The plan gives particular attention to protection of the marine habitat. It notes that there has already been serious damage of this habitat in many places. The plan recommends that the coral reef, seagrass bed and mangrove areas should be assessed and zoned for appropriate uses. Strict protection measures should be applied to the undamaged marine areas so that they can properly serve their important ecological functions.

The plan makes specific recommendations for marine habitat conservation. The commercial sale of corals, shells and mangrove wood should be prohibited, as should the manufacture of decorations from corals, shells and other marine products. The disposal of garbage at sea by boats and any other sea-going craft should be prohibited.

The plan points out that a serious threat to the marine environment in the country is dynamite fishing. This activity has destroyed or damaged many coral reefs. Dynamiting must be stopped; but the problem is that fishermen make their livelihood from this type of fishing. The plan indicates that an alternative source of income should be developed for the fishermen. It suggests a cooperative fishing approach that utilizes fish traps, which has been successfully developed in some places. Associated with the fish traps, fish storage cages could be installed in the water and restaurants developed, with tourists allowed to view the fish and select some for cooking in the restaurant. Tourism could provide the impetus for using more appropriate fishing techniques.

BUILDING STANDARDS

The plan recommends that maximum building heights for tourist facilities be established outside of urban areas. These would be four floors and 16 metres for high density developments, and two floors and 10 metres for medium and low density areas. Building height is measured from the natural grade to the top of the roof.

The plan indicates that the overall architectural design of tourist facilities should conform to the environment and indigenous styles of the development area. However, the point is made that new buildings should not be just replicas of traditional houses, but should be inspired by traditional styles and adapted to the environmental situation. In this manner a contemporary vernacular style can evolve. The plan recommends that local building materials be utilized to the extent possible. Building materials should not dominate the natural landscape but rather complement it.

The plan considers standards for the design of signs. They should fit well into the environment and be constructed of local building materials. Signs should be informative and express prohibitory activities in a tactful manner. All proposed signs should be approved by the local authority.

UTILITY FACILITIES AND SERVICES

The plan makes recommendations for environmentally appropriate utility facilities and services. These include solid waste disposal, sewage treatment, water and electric power supply, drainage, fire protection and communications.

For solid waste disposal in coastal tourism areas, the waste should be sorted, with biodegradable material deposited in a local sanitary landfill that is covered immediately after disposal. Non-biodegradable waste should be taken to an inland landfill. On the development sites, all wastes should be kept in covered receptacles and screened from view. Development of compost pits for the disposal of organic wastes should be encouraged. A centralized collection and disposal system should be organized for inorganic garbage. The sites for sanitary landfills should be carefully selected based on suitable criteria. Burning of waste should be regulated. The method of sewage treatment must be designed based on a thorough assessment of the site and soil characteristics.

The quality of water supply should adhere to the national water code. When water is pumped from the ground, pumping tests should be conducted periodically to ensure that there is not over-extraction of groundwater. Electric power generation facilities should be designed to reduce noise levels. Electrical installations should meet the national electrical code. Drainage systems for dirty and storm water should be properly designed. Storm water may be drained into the sea, but dirty water such as from laundry use should be filtered before being allowed to drain into the sea. Fire protection facilities and services must be developed, and fire water hydrants installed. All resorts, even in remote areas, must have at least one means of outside communication.

CONCLUSIONS

The development standards and guidelines for the Philippines are comprehensive. Virtually all the important types are considered. The site planning considerations include the important factors of maintaining the natural features and appearance of the development sites. Establishment of buffer zones around the sites helps give them a separate 'sense of place', protects them from any undesirable nearby land uses and, in turn, protects nearby land uses from any intrusiveness of the tourism development.

The setbacks required from coastlines and beaches are critically important in order to preserve the natural shoreline appearance and ecological processes, and protect buildings from possible erosion and wave damage. These setbacks also provide better public access along the shore. Setbacks between buildings provide for greater privacy of the building occupants, and allow for landscaping among the buildings which enhances the appearance of the site. Establishing maximum building densities is an essential standard to maintain the desired character of the development, whether it is designed to be at a higher or lower intensity of use.

The requirement for a landscape plan is very appropriate in order to give greater assurance that proper landscaping will be carried out. The landscaping approach of preserving existing trees and using trees and other plants for various functional, as well as aesthetic, purposes follows good landscaping practices. The requirement for environmental impact assessments of proposed projects is very important in any tourism area.

The concern expressed in the plan about damage to the marine environment, especially from fish dynamiting, identifies a common and serious problem in many tropical countries. Also, a common problem in many places is removal of coral from the reefs for use in construction. The marine habitat is a very vulnerable one, easily degraded by misuse. It is also a type of environment that, when damaged, cannot be restored in a short period of time. Besides its importance to tourism, the marine environment serves essential ecological functions. Reefs, for example, protect the shore from wave erosion and provide a habitat for many organisms. The proposal made in the plan for developing alternative means of fishing, in order to stop dynamiting, is a practical and humane one. It recognizes the need for fishermen to maintain their livelihood in an alternative manner.

The building design standards and architectural guidelines are reasonable ones. The valid point is made that contemporary building design need not exactly imitate traditional styles. Rather, the traditional design character, along with environmental considerations, can be incorporated into somewhat new styles that are still unique to the area. The emphasis on use of local building materials is very relevant because this helps integrate new buildings into the cultural and natural environment. Use of local materials also generates more economic benefits to the area through the production and sale of these materials for the construction of tourist facilities. The plan recognizes that signs in tourism areas should be suitably designed to reflect the local environment, and be informative to tourists.

The recommendations made on utility facilities and services are important. Infrastructure should be developed to standards that will prevent any environmental problems being generated by tourism development.

The standards and guidelines presented here are those which are appropriate for coastal resort type development in somewhat remote areas. Although the same types of standards and guidelines would be applied everywhere, the specific standards and guidelines might be somewhat different for other kinds of tourism development.

Chapter 32

Community tourism programme in the Sri Lanka tourism plan

The community tourism programme of the Sri Lanka plan represents an effective approach to involving local communities in the tourism development process. Through this involvement, communities can gain more benefits from tourism, and any adverse socio-cultural impacts can be lessened.

BACKGROUND

The background of the Sri Lanka tourism plan was described in a previous case study, and so is only summarized here. Sri Lanka is located off the southeastern tip of India. The country has varied mountain and coastal geography and a tropical climate. Sri Lanka has a population of 17.2 million, composed of Sinhalese, Tamils and other groups. There is a great diversity of attractions for tourists. These range from beaches and marine environments, national parks with forests and wildlife, outstanding archaeological and historic sites and interesting cultural patterns to tea plantations, spice gardens and gem mines. Tourism was substantially developed from the 1960s to the early 1980s. Then internal civil strife led to a marked decline of tourist arrivals and some deterioration of tourist facilities.

Since 1990, tourism has recovered rapidly and there were some 320,000 international tourist arrivals in 1991. Tourist facilities are being rehabilitated and new investments in tourism development are being proposed. Most tourism is based on beach-oriented accommodation, although some tourism development exists in the inland areas where most of the natural and cultural attractions are located.

The tourism plan of Sri Lanka was prepared in 1992 (UNDP and WTO. 1992. *Sri Lanka Tourism Master Plan.* Madrid: WTO). This is a comprehensive plan that examines all aspects of tourism. The tourism development strategy is four-fold – diversify the tourist market mix; increase tourist spending by developing and upgrading tourist facilities; diversify tourist attractions by emphasizing development and promotion of cultural, natural and other types of features; and create a positive image of the country. An optimum market target of 874,000 international tourist arrivals is established for 2001. A doubling of the average daily tourist expenditure is projected. The plan also makes recommendations on domestic tourism.

The development strategy identifies 14 tourism zones throughout the country. Within these zones, the plan proposes upgrading of existing development in a coordinated manner and initiation of major new planned integrated tourism developments. The strategy emphasizes providing a diversity of tourist attractions and related small-scale tourism development. New and expanded tour routes are recommended. Elements of the plan are focused on environmental and social issues and enhancing the economic benefits of tourism. Part of the consideration on social and economic issues is encouraging more involvement of communities in the tourism development of their local areas.

COMMUNITY TOURISM PROGRAMME

As stated in the plan, community tourism seeks to balance community aspirations with the type and pace of tourism development undertaken, in order to ensure that all community interests are represented. Several approaches are recommended to achieve community involvement in tourism. These are described in the following paragraphs.

In areas of tourist resorts or where substantial tourism activity exists or is proposed, tourism committees should be established. These committees would be composed of representatives of community interests, local police, tourism-related businesses, other business interests directly or indirectly affected by tourism, social and community liaison workers assigned to tourism projects and local government officials. The committees would receive technical and organizational support from Ceylon Tourist Board (CTB) – the national statutory tourism organization.

When setting up the committees, there should be a public relations campaign to inform local residents of what to expect in tourism development, and how to take advantage of the new business coming to their area. The local socio-cultural issues on tourism would also be addressed in this public information programme. After being established, the committees should first decide the objectives of tourism in the area and agree on a set of policies and principles that should be adhered to.

The main functions of the committees would be as follows:

- Solicit proposals for tourism projects from the community.
- Act as consultative bodies for tourism development proposals in the area.
- Identify and raise any issues relating to local tourism operations.
- Instigate arbitration of conflicts arising between the community and tourism industry within the area.
- Instigate initiatives benefiting tourism and the community.

In each area of high social vulnerability where major tourism projects are proposed, a tourism community liaison officer should be appointed by the tourism committee. The officer's salary would be borne by the developer of the tourism project. A liaison officer should also be appointed in areas of existing tourism activity where problems exist or are anticipated. Training of these officers will be required on community issues related to tourism. The CTB would provide this training. The officer should represent the interests of the community, including low income and socially vulnerable groups. The officer would coordinate with the CTB or other organizations to meet special training needs, for example on trade skills or small business management. Public health and AIDS awareness would also be addressed by the officer.

The local hotel associations should be committed to working with the local tourism committees, to their mutual advantage. Policies should be drafted to include ways in which the local communities can benefit directly from tourist spending, and indirectly through supplying the hotels and other tourism enterprises with goods and services. Hoteliers should also help communicate local codes of behaviour and social traditions to their guests.

Guest houses and informal accommodation units are the interface where many social problems arising from meeting of tourists and residents begin. The tourism liaison officers should work closely with the owners and managers of these establishments. These owners and managers should become involved in AIDS awareness programmes and be encouraged to participate in and circulate community information. They should also become involved with the activities of the tourism committees.

Tour operators (both national and local) should commit themselves to respect and promote local culture and small business in the areas in which they operate. Furthermore, they should establish guidelines on their own operations. These guidelines would cover various activities – taking tourists to designated handicraft centres where small businesses operate; passing on information about the socio-cultural policies of Sri Lanka; and informing and encouraging tourists to respect local cultural standards.

Community tourism centres should be set up in resorts, as places where both tourists and residents can obtain information and buy and sell local products. The centres should be centrally located in the resorts. They should include a tourist information office, the office of the tourism liaison officer and retail shops. Encouragement should be given to establishing a branch of the tourist police in each resort area.

CONCLUSIONS

In many tourism areas – especially in the past – local community involvement in tourism was neglected as being too troublesome and expensive for government or business to support. However, lack of community involvement has led to problems in some tourism areas. These problems have related both to adverse socio-cultural impacts on the communities and the local residents not having the opportunity to participate in and receive economic benefits from tourism development in their areas.

The proposals made in the Sri Lanka plan reflect a sound approach to achieving community involvement. Establishing local tourism committees composed of all the relevant parties will provide focal points for discussion and action. Appointing tourism liaison officers in critical tourism areas will provide the additional focus needed in those places to resolve problems and offer assistance. The financial support for these officers by the resorts is justified – the resorts receive benefits from having good community relations and they have a responsibility to assist their communities.

Especially important is the approach of giving responsibility to the local tourism enterprises – applying measures that will prevent social problems from arising and encouraging development, and use of other local businesses and community handicraft centres. A common problem in many tourism areas is tourists being guided to shops that may pay the guide a high commission, but do not greatly benefit the local business community. Without the support and initiative of tourism enterprises, the community tourism programme could not be successful.

Setting up community tourism centres is a well established technique to disseminate information and provide local entrepreneurs with a central place from which to sell their products. Making tourist police available in resorts is also a recognized technique, not only to enforce local regulations but also to give information and a sense of security to tourists.

After government adoption of these community tourism proposals, the next step is implementation. This will require organizational initiative, technical assistance and some funding – at least for training and perhaps also for making loans to establish local small tourism businesses. The funding could be provided jointly by the government (national or local) and the local private sector.

Often a successful implementation technique is to organize one or two demonstration projects. Such projects can provide the basis for refining techniques, and they serve as prototypes for other communities to organize their programmes. The CTB, along with the provincial or district governments, could serve as the catalyst for initiating these demonstration community tourism projects. The local communities, however, will need to be very supportive of and actively participate in the projects in order for them to be successful.

Chapter 33

Master plan for Ambergris Caye, Belize

The master plan for Ambergris Caye in Belize is an example of integrated planning for a tourism-based island community. Planning is directed toward preserving the community's distinctive informal character, while still allowing for the controlled growth of tourism.

BACKGROUND

The country of Belize is located in Central America fronting on the Caribbean Sea. It shares a boundary with Guatemala on the west and the Yucatan Peninsula of Mexico on the north. The population of about 180,000 is primarily English speaking with Spanish also widely used. Belize City, situated on the coast, is the main urban centre. The planned and relatively new town of Belmopan, located inland, is now the country's capital. Offshore, and part of Belize, is the Western Hemisphere's longest barrier reef. On this reef are several islands or cayes, of which the largest is Ambergris Caye in the north.

Tourism in Belize has grown rapidly in recent years – from 94,000 international arrivals in 1986 to 222,000 arrivals in 1990. However, many of these arrivals come on short-stay border crossings from the neighbouring countries. In 1990, some 80,000 tourists arrived by air. Most tourists are from the USA and Canada, with much lesser numbers from the UK and other countries in Europe.

Tourism in Belize has been – and still is – focused on beach and marine activities, combined with the pleasant sub-tropical climate. Sport fishing and diving are especially popular. The main tourism development is on Ambergris Caye, concentrated in and near the main town of San Pedro. Recently the country has also been developing nature tourism, based particularly on the scenic mountains and wildlife of the southern area of the country. Some land and marine conservation areas have been designated. Belize also possesses several Mayan archaeological sites, some of which are accessible and visited by tourists. *La Ruta Maya* (The Mayan Route) links several of the Mayan sites in Belize with those of the nearby countries of

Mexico, Guatemala, Honduras and El Salvador. This forms a 2,400-kilometre road network of accessible archaeological sites in Central America.

PLANNING APPROACH

Although the main tourism centre of Ambergris Caye was functioning reasonably well in the late 1980s, there was concern that continued uncontrolled development would be detrimental to the island's environmental and social character. At the same time, certain improvements were required to the existing development patterns, especially in San Pedro. Consequently, the master plan for Ambergris Caye was prepared to guide the island's future development (UNDP and WTO. 1989. *Ambergris Caye Master Development and Zoning Plan – Belize*. Madrid: WTO). This plan comprises three major components:

- The development strategy, which deals with the entire island.
- The San Pedro District plan, which is detailed land use planning of the San Pedro town area.
- The institutional framework, which outlines ways to facilitate implementation of the master plan.

The planning approach is quite comprehensive. It considers overall community as well as tourism development needs in an integrated manner. A planning appraisal was conducted of several elements – population and employment; physical and environmental characteristics; San Pedro town; communications (road, air and sea transport); public utilities (water supply, sewage and solid waste disposal, electric power and telecommunications); and a legislative and institutional overview. A summary was made of major problems and opportunities. Tourism on Ambergris Caye was reviewed with respect to several factors – the national context; general characteristics; specific tourism statistics; tourist attractions; and accommodation and other tourist facilities. Extensive field surveys were carried out and meetings held with government agencies, the private sector and community leaders. The plans were prepared to a time scale from 1988 to 2005, with intermediate periods established for 1990, 1995 and 2000.

The key development objectives are set forth in the plan as follows:

- Provide opportunities for the future natural expansion of tourism in keeping with the general character, environment and the unspoilt nature of the island.
- Generate jobs for the future natural increase of the resident population, as a minimum level of jobs needed.
- Maintain as far as possible the existing character of urban and rural environments.
- Protect sensitive ecologies from excessive human activity.

- Avoid levels of immigration that put an undue social strain on the community or its facilities.
- Plan for the ordered expansion of San Pedro town to meet existing and future population needs.
- Establish a context for the systematic planning and development of tourist accommodation and associated facilities.
- Inhibit speculation in and the high cost of land.

The plan states that, given these objectives, strategic options are limited. Development alternatives mainly revolve around the quantity of tourism development and its consequent impact, with a balancing of social and economic costs and benefits. Too little growth would not take advantage of the potential benefits to be gained from increases in employment and foreign currency earnings. Too much growth would involve excessive rates of immigration and impose intolerable burdens on the community, the environment and social infrastructure. The preferred option seeks to control the expansion of tourism to be at a similar rate and form to that experienced in the recent past. It continues the image of a relaxed, small-scale, informal tourism community that has been so successful, and which residents and visitors both prefer.

MASTER PLAN

The island-wide development strategy comprises several elements – the programme for tourist accommodation; employment and population; land use strategy; and infrastructure. The plan estimates that, by 1990, existing and committed accommodation development will be 500 hotel rooms and 100 apartments or houses for rent to tourists. The accommodation development rate is recommended to be controlled, producing a total of about 1,200 hotel rooms by 2005. The maximum size of hotels is recommended to be no more than 60 rooms – in keeping with the objective of maintaining the small to medium scale character of the resort community. The remaining new accommodation would be in the form of about 250 rental apartments and housing units. Also 500 retirement and vacation homes are projected for development by 2005 – retirement and vacation home development by expatriates was already commencing on Ambergris in the late 1980s.

The plan states that this is considered to be a modest programme, in relation to market expectations, but it should be regarded as the maximum level of acceptable development. Even this programme is conditional upon developing new sources of potable water supply. At this level of development, visitors to Ambergris are likely to increase from between 10,000 and 12,500 in 1988 to between 69,000 and 89,000 in 2005, depending on the average length of stay. Tourist expenditures are estimated to rise from an annual US$ 11 million in 1990 to US$ 37 million in 2005 (at constant prices). The plan indicates that, even with a substantial leakage out of Belize (for imported goods used in tourism), the recommended programme will still make a substantial net contribution to the economy and foreign exchange.

The plan projects that the 2005 level of development will generate an additional 4,000 jobs, for a total of 5,000 persons employed in tourism by that year. Slightly over 80 per cent of these jobs can be filled by Belizeans. This is in keeping with the objective of minimizing immigration. However, reaching that level of Belizean employment will require special efforts – tighter immigration controls; training citizens to properly assume tourism positions; and establishing the right conditions, such as good housing and schools, to attract some Belizeans from the mainland to live and work on Ambergris.

Based on the growth of employment, the plan projects the population of the island to increase at a rate of nearly 10 per cent per year – from 2,600 in 1988 to 12,700 in 2005. After allowing for the natural growth of the present population, there will be a need for about 7,400 Belizean and 1,350 non-Belizean migrants to the island. The plan emphasizes that assimilating these migrants will be a major task, including providing more school facilities.

The land use development strategy set forth in the plan is shown in Figure 33.1. This strategy consists of five key elements, as follows:

- Reservation of the whole of the northern part of the island to be kept in its natural condition.
- Definition of three specific conservation areas (in addition to an existing marine reserve).
- Restriction of development on the east coast to a specific area.
- Expansion and consolidation of San Pedro within a specific area.
- Establishment, in the medium to longer term, of a new settlement in the centre of the island.

The strategy includes development on the east coast of three low density resorts consisting of several beach-front hotels of about 60 rooms each. These would be associated with an equivalent area of residential tourism subdivisions. Each resort should be comprehensively planned in partnership between the owners and planning authorities. Each resort would have a small commercial and entertainment centre, and provide lots for housing of employees. Each hotel would be allowed to develop one pier that should be open to the public and nearby residential tourists. Public access would be provided to the beach at intervals of no more than 300 metres. A similar nuclear resort would be developed on the west coast.

The plan specifies various types of land use zones – suburban hotels (150 beds per hectare); rural hotels (50 beds per hectare); residential tourism outside of San Pedro (two densities of 5 and 10 houses per hectare); nature reserves; conservation zones; and Special Coordinated Development Areas

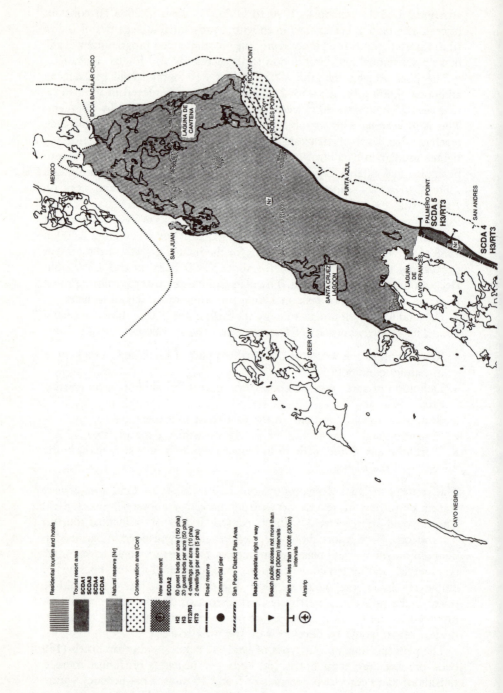

Residential tourism and hotels

Tourist resort area
SCDA1
SCDA3
SCDA4
SCDA5

Natural reserve [Nr]

Conservation area [Con]

New settlement
SCDA2

60 guest beds per acre (150 pha)
H2
20 guest beds per acre (50 pha)
H3
4 dwellings per acre (10 pha)
RT2/R3
2 dwellings per acre (5 pha)
RT3

Road reserve

Commercial pier

San Pedro District Plan Area

Beach pedestrian right of way

Beach public access not more than
100ft (300m) intervals

Piers not less than 1000ft (300m)
intervals

Airstrip

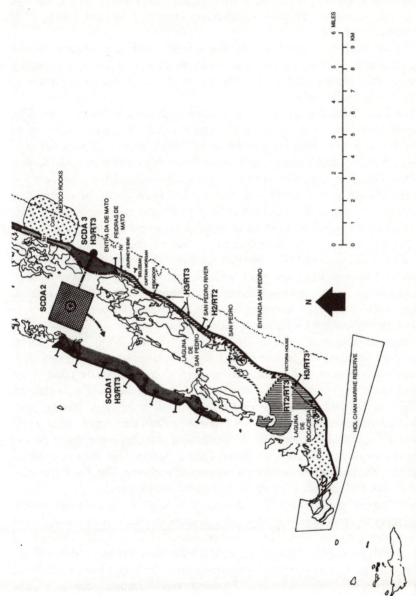

Figure 33.1 Ambergris Caye master plan

(SCDAs). The SCDAs are places which are required to be planned comprehensively and the development closely coordinated. There are five such areas shown on the plan – four resort areas and the new settlement in the centre of the island.

Recommendations are made on the infrastructure development of the airport, roads, water supply and other utility services. The plan states that, if a new potable groundwater supply cannot be found, it will be necessary to install a desalination plant.

The San Pedro district plan is a detailed land use and zoning plan. The present town area is expanded north and south of the traditional core to provide for a total resident population of 8,000, as well as sites for new hotels, holiday condominiums and subdivisions for retirement and vacation homes. The plan states that San Pedro will increasingly perform the function of the island's urban centre – it will be the main focus of commercial activities, services to tourists, high density hotels and guest houses, and self-catering apartments. This consolidation will be effected by changes in the use of existing buildings, the development of vacant sites and the renewal of outworn buildings. Specific recommendations are made for the different types of land use areas, the road network and dredging of the river, with development of a storm-sheltered commercial harbour and marina. Improvements are recommended to social and public facilities.

In order to maintain the present small-scale and pedestrian-oriented urban quality and character of San Pedro, the plan sets forth urban design guidelines. Building heights are restricted to two storeys, except in two areas where three storeys will be allowed if there is commensurate open space allocated on the building sites. Building form will be confined to traditional designs – finished in timber cladding, painted white, and having open balustraded verandahs and low-pitched roofs. Different types of land use zones are specified for the town. More detailed planning is presented for the central area of San Pedro – the Town Centre Action Area Plan and, within that area, the town plaza development proposals scheme. The San Pedro plan makes recommendations on all the infrastructure elements.

The report states that, 'The master plan will be of little use unless machinery is established for, and the resources devoted to its management and implementation.' It makes several recommendations on the institutional framework for implementing the island development strategy and San Pedro land use plan. The master plan is expressed in the form of a Planning Scheme for Ambergris Caye under the Housing and Planning ordinance. The adoption of this scheme, along with its accompanying maps (the island-wide Development Strategy Map and the San Pedro District Plan Map), will provide the statutory basis for enforcing the master plan. The responsible ministry will then be in a position to set up an Ambergris Caye Planning Authority to oversee implementation of the plan. The Authority would be composed of representatives of the concerned agencies, and a member nominated by the San Pedro Town Board.

The planning authority will need to establish a technical staff to advise on its actions. The technical staff will have three primary responsibilities – receiving and evaluating development proposals; monitoring development and residential subdivisions; and modifying the plan in the face of changing circumstances.

The plan examines the serious problem of land speculation on Ambergris. It attributes this problem to the lack of development controls and adequate restrictions on the sale of land to foreigners. Adoption and implementation of the plan will establish the appropriate development controls. On sale of land to foreigners, the plan recommends that any foreign land sale must be approved by the appropriate Ministry, and that no more than 50 per cent of any residential subdivision be allowed to be sold to foreigners. In this way, an assured number of land plots would become available for the use of citizens at a price which reflects the local market value among citizens. An appendix of the plan report sets forth the detailed legal regulations for the Ambergris Caye Planning Scheme. After review and any necessary modifications are made, the regulations can be adopted by the government.

The plan recommends on several other specific needs – deep drilling to try to locate a new potable water source; conducting a feasibility study for improvement of the airfield; designs for liquid waste stabilization ponds and a solid waste disposal site; purchase of land and design for a new primary school; and reservation of a new road alignment.

CONCLUSIONS

The Ambergris Caye planning study takes a comprehensive approach to planning for a resort island community. Emphasis is placed on maintaining the small-scale and informal character of the community, while still allowing for substantial increases in tourism and the resident population. The plan rightfully does not try to emulate more structured resort development elsewhere. Ambergris offers a distinctive environment for residents, that also satisfies particular market segments, and it would be a mistake to try to change this special ambience. This approach, however, implies highly controlled development in the face of rapidly growing market demand.

Controlled development can be achieved in Ambergris because Belize has ample opportunity to develop other tourism areas elsewhere in the country, based on beach, marine, nature and archaeological tourism resources. Development of tourism elsewhere has several advantages – diversifying the tourism product and tourist markets; spreading economic benefits more widely; and providing incentives for conservation of natural areas and archaeological sites.

In the planning process, the plan examines all the necessary influencing factors – the natural environment; urban and tourism land use patterns; the society and economy; and the infrastructure. Utmost consideration is given to conservation needs in the plan. This is important for both the success of tourism and benefit of residents. Sound planning principles are applied of concentrating accommodation and other tourist facilities in certain areas, as well as consolidating town development. Eventual development of a new settlement in the centre of the island will help absorb the additional population, while maintaining the tightly-knit character of San Pedro. Establishing controls on the maximum size of new hotels and on development character, such as height limits, are appropriate techniques. These controls can help retain the desired small-scale character of both community and tourism development.

The plan establishes the specific implementation mechanisms and procedures that need to be followed. By setting forth, in the appendix, the legal regulations for the Ambergris Caye Planning Scheme, the government is given precise legislation which it can adopt directly from the report, if it wishes. Continuous control and management of development will be essential to achieve the plan's concepts and recommendations.

Chapter 34

Travel facilitation recommendations in the Ethiopia tourism plan

The recommendations made in the national tourism plan of Ethiopia for improving travel facilitation requirements and procedures for tourists represent those that are applicable to many countries. Efficient travel facilitation is essential for the substantial development of tourism.

BACKGROUND

Ethiopia is situated in East Africa, north of Kenya, south of Eritrea and between Sudan on the west and Somalia and Djibouti on the east. The country has a wide range of environmental zones and associated wildlife and vegetation. Highlands with elevations of more than 2,000 metres extend over much of the central parts of the country. There are still some coniferous forests above the 3,000-metre level but most of the highlands have been cleared for agriculture. Lowland regions surround the highlands with semi-arid and arid climatic and vegetation patterns. The rift valley and its several lakes lie in the south-central part of the country – this valley extends through several eastern and southern African countries. Lake Tana, in the northwest, is the source of the Blue Nile.

Ethiopia has a long history extending through thousands of years. It is referred to in ancient Egyptian texts and was an early centre of Christianity in Africa. The country was never colonized except for a brief period from 1936–41. The present population of about 50 million is composed mostly of farmers and herders. The capital of Addis Ababa, with some 1.5 million inhabitants, is an attractive city located in the central highlands. Addis is the seat of the Organization of African Unity and the United Nations Economic Commission for Africa, and is the regional headquarters for other international organizations. In recent years, the country has been troubled by internal political disturbances and famine. These have been a serious deterrent to both tourism and general development.

The country possesses substantial resources for tourism. There is a diversity of scenic areas and wildlife (including many types of large animals and abundant birdlife) related to the different environmental zones. Some wildlife species are unique to the country. Several national parks and nature reserves have been designated and conservation programmes are underway. However, certain animal species require further conservation efforts to be fully rejuvenated. The largest concentrations of wildlife exist in the southwestern corner of the country near the border with Kenya and Sudan. The second major type of attraction is the many archaeological and historical sites, notably the rock-hewn churches at Lalibela, remains of the 2,000 year-old Auxmite Empire and medieval monasteries at Lake Tana, found particularly in the northern areas of the country. Because of the extensive tropical highland environment, the climate is generally pleasant throughout the year.

During the late 1980s to 1990, Ethiopia received somewhat more than 70,000 tourist arrivals annually. Only about 20 per cent of these were holiday tourists and the remainder were business travellers or in transit. Several thousand of the arrivals are coming to attend international association meetings being held in Addis. Controlled hunting tourism is allowed. Although not attracting a large number of tourists, hunting is a very high value form of tourism that generates considerable revenue. Foreigners living in the country provide an important source of 'domestic' tourists visiting the national parks and historic sites. There have been several constraints on developing tourism – the limited supply and quality of tourist facilities and services; attractions that are spread over large areas and, in some places, poorly linked by transportation services; and the negative international image of the country because of political disturbances and famine.

TOURISM PLANNING APPROACH

The national tourism plan was prepared for Ethiopia in 1990 (UNDP and WTO. 1990. *National Tourism Development Plan of Ethiopia. Vols. I, II and III.* Madrid: WTO). This was a comprehensive planning programme. However, because of security problems prevailing in some parts of the country at the time of plan preparation, the planning programme focused primarily on the southern region. It includes the structure plan, a five-year action programme, master planning of three tourism priority areas and detailed plans and prefeasibility analyses of priority tourism development sites. The national plan is prepared for 1989–2005 and encompasses several elements – designation of tourism development regions; tour patterns and programmes; economic cost and benefit analysis; environmental impact with recommended conservation measures and development and design standards; socio-cultural impact evaluation; manpower planning and training programmes; recommendations on organizational structures and legislation; and an implementation strategy and need for monitoring implementation. The action programme includes physical development projects, other actions needed and a marketing strategy to implement the first stage of the tourism plan.

A three-step methodological approach is applied in formulating the plan. The first step is a review of the country's characteristics and the overall national development policy including existing policies for developing tourism. Then the tourism supply is surveyed and evaluated. This includes several elements – existing and potential natural and cultural tourist attractions and activities; access to the country, internal transportation facilities and services and other infrastructure; accommodation, catering and entertainment; and technical resources such as organization, commercial, training and financial factors. Lastly, the tourism demand is analysed. This involves a detailed analysis of each of the domestic and international tourist flows. Demand forecasts are made on the basis of quantitative and qualitative considerations, and include tourist arrivals and their characteristics and the future need for accommodation by location and type. The tourism image of the country is considered, and possible competitive destinations are reviewed. Substantial increases in the numbers of tourist arrivals are targeted for the future.

In planning the priority tourism areas, calculation of their carrying capacities was an important consideration in determining the type and level of development.

The planning analysis concludes that the country's strong points for tourism are its impressive natural and cultural attractions which can be related to sight-seeing, educational, special interest and adventure tour groups. The plan designates Addis Ababa as the tourism gateway and staging area and ten tourism development zones. Seven of these zones are shown as priority development areas. One of the priority zones is identified as weekend areas for trips from Addis. The action programme recommends that, in addition to some existing historical tour routes, new areas should be opened soon which include circuits of game parks. These are located in the southern part of the country.

The number and type of accommodation rooms are allocated to each of the zones. Some of these units are recommended to be in the form of 'ecological habitations (ecohabs)'. These are detached units built from local materials in the regional architectural styles. They could be located within national parks and reserves because they do not interfere with the natural environment. Other types of accommodation – 'bungalow parks' – would be constructed outside the parks. Accommodation would also be substantially expanded, in Addis, with new hotels developed. As the country's tourism gateway and conference and commercial centre, the capital will continue attracting large numbers of holiday and business tourists.

TRAVEL FACILITATION RECOMMENDATIONS

The Ethiopia plan makes specific recommendations on measures to facilitate tourists travelling to and within the country. It first identifies the obstacles affecting individual tourists visiting the country, including the following:

- Currency restrictions imposed upon visitors.
- Entry visas, identity documents and limitation on duration of stay.
- Formalities concerning entry of motor vehicles.
- Formalities concerning applicability of drivers' licences, car insurance, etc.

The plan explains that the requirement that entry visas of all visitors (except from Kenya and Djibouti) be obtained before arrival is a deterrent to encouraging tourism. However, the plan recognizes that there was the need to control entry carefully in the past. It recommends that, in the future, visas be issued on the arrival of tourists, and that visas be valid for multiple entries. Within the country, the plan recommends that internal travel be liberalized to the extent possible. The plan also describes the complications entailed in tourists completing the currency forms and maintaining records of currency transactions. It points out that this requirement should be investigated.

On entry procedures at the international airport, the plan indicates that the procedures are confusing and time-consuming. It recommends several ways to improve entry facilitation at the airport, as follows:

- Clear entry instructions should be printed in several languages informing arrivals that they must go through 1) immigration, including passport examination, 2) currency control and 3) customs.
- Explicit instructions should be given to tourists concerning the necessity to produce a record of currency transactions on departure.

The plan states that the airport terminal still has enough space to handle a moderate increase in traffic, but the efficiency of handling tourists could be improved. It recommends several approaches:

- A system of directional signs should be installed to ensure a smoother flow of arrivals and departures.
- Customs and immigration procedures should be adapted to the potential importance of tourism to Ethiopia's economy (that is, efficient and courteous).
- The language barrier for tourists is a serious one. This applies to both officials and the staff on duty at the airport building. As a first step, the installation of multi-lingual signs listing vital information would do much to alleviate this situation.
- There are no posters or photographs to acquaint the tourist or in-transit passenger with the attractions of Addis Ababa and Ethiopia. A simple information pamphlet in one or two colours would be informative for the arriving tourist or in-transit passenger.

The plan indicates that Ethiopia has no airport departure tax as do most other countries. It recommends that, as tourism expands in the future, the introduction of a departure tax would provide revenue that could help finance the promotional budget of the country in its marketing of tourism.

On internal travel facilitation and transportation improvements, the plan makes several recommendations. It indicates that automobile tourism could be expanded in the future. Maximum advantage should be taken of using the existing road system, which is quite good in some areas, for tourist travel. Car rental services should be competitively priced to encourage individual auto travel. The plan makes recommendations on ways to improve domestic air travel for tourists, bus services throughout the country and taxicab services in the urban areas. To encourage tourist use of the railway system, the plan recommends that first class coaches be introduced in the future for tourist use to specific places.

Recommendations are also made on improving the number and quality of local tour guides. This should include training of the guides in more foreign languages.

The plan notes that credit cards are widely used by tourists everywhere, and that facilitating use of credit cards in Ethiopia would provide an important convenience to tourists and they would increase their spending. It recommends that the tourism office encourage the acceptance and use of credit cards by operators of hotels and other tourist services and, if necessary, make the appropriate arrangements with monetary control authorities.

The plan states that directives on improving various aspects of travel facilitation should be decided at government level. The tourism office should have the responsibility of coordinating with the appropriate agencies in implementing the improvements.

CONCLUSIONS

The Ethiopia tourism planning programme is a comprehensive one that uses a systematic methodological approach. It examines the overall characteristics of the country, including the institutional elements, as the basis for planning; it analyses the tourism supply of existing tourist facilities, services and infrastructure, existing and potential tourist attractions and activities and the technical resources for development; and it analyses the tourist demand in detail. Particular attention is given to inventory and evaluation of tourism resources. The principle of establishing tourism development zones and prioritizing development of these zones is applied. The action programme sets forth the requirements for implementing the first stage of development.

Among other considerations, the plan emphasizes the importance of improving travel facilitation requirements and procedures for tourists. On a global basis, encouraging travel facilitation improvements has been a significant programme of the World Tourism Organization for several years. These improvements are essential for facilitating international travel among different countries – they are especially needed in countries which are commencing to develop tourism. At the same time, it is recognized that all countries must maintain some controls on entry of visitors and goods.

In the Ethiopia plan, the importance of providing visas on arrival, at least from the major tourist market countries, is emphasized as a basic facilitation improvement. Also the plan makes the valid point that the overall entry procedures at the international airport should be efficient and courteous, and the necessary information provided. Providing efficient entry procedures is also, of course, applicable to any international entry point including land border crossings and seaports. The convenience experienced by tourists when they enter a country forms their first, and often lasting, impression of the destination. In many countries needing entry improvements, an approach commonly used is to organize sensitivity training courses for airport officials, especially those in immigration and customs, so that they better understand how to handle arriving tourists.

The recommendation for establishing an airport departure tax is a valid one. Departure taxes are required in many countries. This tax can provide an important source of revenue for the government, especially if it is used to improve and promote tourism in some manner. However, the departure tax should not be so high as to irritate tourists.

To facilitate travel within the country, the recommendation to make it easier for tourists to rent cars will encourage more individual automobile travel. This will broaden the tourist markets, extend their average length of stay and bring some benefits of tourism to places that otherwise might not be visited by tourists. Facilitating use of credit cards by tourists is now a major consideration in any tourism area.

The plan justifiably identifies the tourism office as being the logical responsible agency for coordinating facilitation improvements. However, many of the actual improvements must be undertaken by the various other agencies involved. Because of the complexity of entry procedures, it is common practice in many countries to establish a permanent travel facilitation committee. This committee is composed of representatives of all the concerned government agencies and autonomous boards or authorities. It has the responsibility to recommend improvements needed to facilitation requirements and procedures, and to monitor the effectiveness of facilitation activities.

Chapter 35

Implementation manual in the Uganda tourism plan

The implementation manual in the Uganda tourism plan sets forth a systematic and specific procedure for adopting and maintaining the tourism plan and development programme.

BACKGROUND

The background of Uganda was described in a previous case study, and so is only summarized here. Uganda is located in east-central Africa, inland from Kenya. The country has a population of about 17 million and includes several cultural groups. The capital city of Kampala has about half a million inhabitants. The primary attractions for tourists are outstanding scenic areas, including lakes, rivers, mountains, rainforests and savanna, and a variety of wildlife. Important specific features include Murchison Falls, the Ruwenzori Mountains and mountain gorilla reserves. Ten national parks have been designated in the country although most of these still have limited tourist facilities. The upland climate is very pleasant for tourists.

Tourism was relatively well developed in Uganda in the late 1960s and early 1970s. Then, because of political turmoil and changes in government policy, tourism became virtually non-existent. Much of the tourist facility development and infrastructure was damaged or deteriorated from lack of maintenance. Since the mid-1980s, rehabilitation of the country's economy has been taking place, including of tourism development. Major conservation programmes are being implemented to rejuvenate the wildlife. Substantial progress has been made on rehabilitation, and game populations are recovering, but these programmes are still underway.

The government policy is now for revitalization of the tourism sector as an important source of economic development. Tourism is also seen as a means to achieve conservation objectives. In 1991, Uganda received 68,000 international tourist arrivals. Only about 10,000 of these arrivals were holiday tourists, with the remainder coming for business, official mission and other purposes. Most of the holiday arrivals were budget types of tourists.

The large international aid community in Uganda provides many of the present visitors to the national parks.

In the early 1990s, a tourism plan was prepared for Uganda (UNDP and WTO. 1993. *Integrated Tourism Master Plan – Republic of Uganda. Vols. I, II and III*. Madrid: WTO). The planning approach is comprehensive, and examines all aspects of tourism. The development strategy emphasizes that tourist market development must take place slowly because tourist facilities and the wildlife will remain rather limited for the next few years. The spatial development concept is based on establishment of tourism zones – three primary, two secondary and three tertiary zones. Several possible tourist circuits are identified which link the tourism zones. The plan recommends that tourist service centres be developed to provide tourist information, nature interpretation exhibits, tourism services, medical clinics and commercial facilities.

IMPLEMENTATION MANUAL

As part of the implementation section of the Uganda tourism plan, an implementation manual was set forth. This manual focuses on the procedures for adopting and maintaining the development plan and programme. The diagram in Figure 35.1 depicts the implementation procedure. Under the purpose section of the manual, it states that the National Structure Plan establishes the planning and policy strategy for the development of the tourism sector over the period of 1993 to 2002. This is translated into an Action and Development Programme of priority projects for the first five years. This programme is the foundation of the implementation process – it expresses the principles and phasing of the plan in terms of actual projects. These projects can then be allocated to an implementing body and budgeted for accordingly.

The manual makes recommendations on how to establish the authority and status of the tourism structure plan. It states that the plan must be given an authoritative status which can only come from Cabinet approval. This will involve a two-stage process. First, there should be approval in principle. An Inter-Ministry Coordination Committee should be established – this would be composed of senior representatives of all the ministries and agencies which are affected by the plan. The committee would review the proposed plan in detail, make any recommendations for modifications, and submit it to the cabinet for approval. This approval would be confined to basic planning and policy issues and would not extend to detail.

The second stage is general public and private sector participation. Following Cabinet approval, the structure plan should be published and made available for sale and inspection in libraries and schools, with press releases describing the plan. In districts that are particularly affected by the plan, public meetings could be organized. Dialogue would also be organized

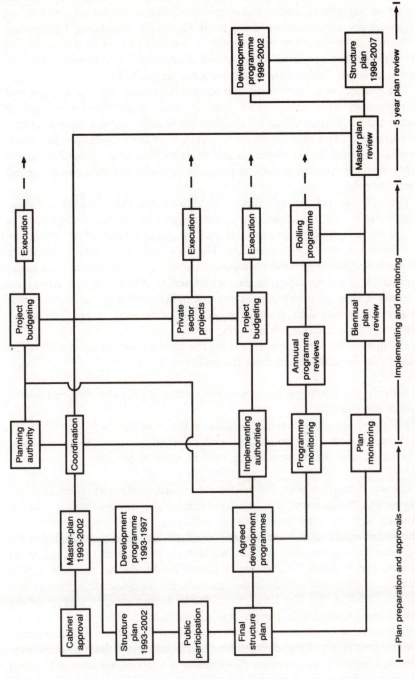

Figure 35.1 Implementation diagram for the Uganda tourism plan

with the private sector interests in tourism. All serious comments on the plan would be assembled, and a report prepared that identifies any matters of substance for consideration of the Inter-Ministry Coordination Committee. Following deliberations by this committee, it would present its conclusions to the Cabinet for approval. Any agreed changes of importance could be published as an Addendum to the National Structure Plan.

The manual next sets forth the approval process for the Action and Development Programme. The manual states that this programme is composed of projects which are considered desirable and reasonably realistic to implement. The manual states, however, that the programme has wide-ranging implications on resources and budgets. Reaching agreement on the public sector commitments of the programme could be time-consuming and controversial.

The manual recommends that a small Development Programme Sub-Committee of the Inter-Ministry Coordination Committee be organized to review the proposed programme. It lists the organizations which should be represented on this Sub-Committee. The Sub-Committee would review the programme from a general standpoint, balancing the economic and social advantages of taking different courses of action. Then it would arrive at a mutually agreed programme. The manual indicates that any changes to the programme would likely relate to scheduling of projects, rather than to the specific projects included in the programme.

The manual then indicates that, using the agreed programme as a basis, the Ministry of Tourism would have the following tasks:

- Identify the executive implementing authorities for the different public sector projects.
- Inform them of their responsibilities in this regard.
- Prepare briefs on the specific policy action or project development required, and the proposed time of the action or project.

Following discussion with the respective implementing authorities on their programme obligations, any changes that might be required would be mutually agreed. The implementing authorities would then prepare the requisite budgets and submit these through the normal procedures for approval. They would then inform the Ministry of Tourism of the approved projects and budgets, and any amendments made. At the same time, they would identify potential aid-funded projects and relevant aid agencies. The Ministry would collate the results of all the budgetary process, and refine the Action and Development Programme accordingly.

Private sector projects are also identified in the Development Programme. The projects selected are all considered financially viable based on the pre-feasibility analyses conducted in the planning study. The Ministry of Tourism would coordinate development of the private sector projects. It would specify the projects and prepare planning and design briefs for them. These briefs would specify the following:

- Nature of the project, and its general or specific location.
- Scale and maximum size of the project, and its space, equipment and facility standards.
- Design and landscaping guidelines.
- Access requirements and utility service standards.
- Programme for development.
- Any other matter of relevance.

When prepared, this list should be submitted to the Uganda Investment Authority. The Ministry would recommend to the Authority that all private sector proposals for implementing the projects in accordance with the briefs should be given favourable consideration for approval. A condition of this approval would be that preliminary sketch designs and plans should be submitted to and approved by the Ministry, before work is allowed to commence. The manual also specifies procedures to be followed for projects proposed in or near national parks. These projects would involve the consideration of the National Park Service. The manual recommends that the Ministry should open discussion with the Uganda Hotels Ltd – owner and manager of several older hotels – about renovating their properties.

The manual recommends that the Ministry of Tourism should develop a programme for promoting private sector investment in tourism. A high quality investment promotional brochure should be prepared. This brochure would identify all the development opportunities for accommodation projects. The manual specifies the type of information that should be contained in this brochure. The brochure should be made available to investors involved in tourism – both domestic and foreign.

The manual emphasizes the importance of plan monitoring and review. These activities would focus on three tasks – continuous monitoring of progress and performance; regularly refining data and adjusting the plan and programme as necessary; and periodically making a formal plan review. The point is made that a critical aspect of plan monitoring is the collection and analysis of sufficient, reliable data. These data would confirm or refute the market projections, tourist characteristics and patterns of behaviour. The planning study contains guidelines for establishing a comprehensive tourism information base.

For monitoring the development programme, quarterly reports on the progress of projects would be made to the Inter-Ministry Coordination Committee. These reports would identify any reasons for project implementation delays, deferments or cancellations. Based on these records, the Ministry would prepare an annual review of the development programme, updating it as necessary and advancing it by a further year. Thus, a 'rolling' five-year programme will be established. Private sector project implementation could be monitored from various sources which are described in the manual.

Biannual reviews of the plan are recommended to be undertaken. Matters to be updated or revised in this review could include the following:

- Projection of tourist arrivals and characteristics over five to 10 years.
- Inventory of tourist accommodation and facilities.
- Programme of tourist accommodation assessed in the light of the revised projections.
- Any revealed necessity to change the emphasis or priorities related to the tourism zones.
- Reassessment of gross and net foreign exchange earning.

The manual recommends that, after a period of about five years, a major plan review should be undertaken. By then, the tourism sector should be sufficiently developed, and accumulated data adequate enough, to provide a sound basis for assessing the progress of tourism and the direction that it is taking. This review should address all the matters dealt with in the planning study. It should be seen, however, as an updating process and not preparing a new plan. The manual states that the principal purpose of the review would be to test the validity of the application of the plan's principles in detail, not overall. Based on the review, any necessary amendments would be made to the plan, and it would be projected forward for a further five years.

CONCLUSIONS

The implementation manual in the Uganda plan represents a more detailed approach to recommending implementation procedures than is usually included in tourism plans. Preparation of a manual such as this is becoming increasingly common. It is very appropriate because of the difficulty experienced by many countries in implementing their tourism plans. The manual is comprehensive – it focuses on procedures which should be followed to implement both the National Structure Plan and the Action and Development Programme, and both public and private sector projects. Other implementation techniques, such as applying development standards and guidelines, are implied in the process set forth in the manual for reviewing development proposals.

The manual justifiably makes a strong point that the National Structure Plan should be adopted by the Cabinet. This gives the plan a legal basis for implementation. Whether the procedure is a two-stage one, as is proposed in the Uganda manual, or one stage – with public review taking place before the initial adoption – depends on the particular circumstances of the country.

The proposed review of the Action and Development Programme is a detailed one, as it should be. This ensures that all concerned parties have the opportunity to be involved in the review, so that the final programme balances all the considerations that need to be made. Identification of the responsible authorities for carrying out specific projects – and the incorporation of these projects into their respective programmes – is an essential aspect of the procedural process, if implementation is to be well coordinated. Specification of the projects by the Ministry of Tourism will encourage that they are included in other agencies' programmes in a proper format.

The approach to development of the private sector projects is a good one, to achieve coordination of these private projects with related public projects. It also gives greater assurance that the private sector projects conform to the plan and programme and meet acceptable development and design standards. To promote private sector investment, the approach recommended of preparing and distributing an investment brochure is a standard one that is commonly applied. The government will need some guidance on where to distribute the brochure internationally, and how to follow up on enquiries.

The manual's recommendations on plan and programme monitoring and review are important. Too often, there is not this type of follow-through on planning. As indicated in the manual, establishing a reliable and comprehensive tourism information system is essential for monitoring. Viewing the development programme as a 'rolling' programme, that is updated every year, is an approach that is increasingly being used. This keeps development programmes viable and current. The proposed biannual and five-year reviews of the basic plan are also very appropriate, in order to maintain a continuously usable plan. Minor adjustments can be made, but the plan's long-term objectives, policies and structure are expected to remain valid. These provide the framework for achieving sustainable tourism development, while still bringing substantial socio-economic benefits to the country.

Chapter 36

Conclusions from the case studies

The case studies represent several different types of countries and regions, and various kinds of tourism situations. The kinds of tourism development – both existing and recommended – also range widely. However, all the case studies reflect an integrated and sustainable development approach to developing tourism. They all reflect tourism being developed based on coherent policy, a logical physical structure plan and progressive institutional elements. The case studies all give great consideration to balancing environmental, socio-cultural and economic objectives. At the same time, they are realistic in recognizing the importance of developing tourism that will meet certain market demands. However, they recognize that imaginative new products may also create their own tourist markets, even though specialized ones.

On implementation, the case studies reflect the need to establish firm controls, but within the framework of cooperation between the public and private sectors. Often, divergent development interests must be reconciled. Implementation approaches must often be innovative and tailored to the local circumstances.

Several more specific conclusions can be drawn from the case studies. These can be summarized as follows:

- Carefully planned and managed tourist destinations are much more likely to be successful on a long-term basis than unplanned areas. Planning maintains the viability of tourism resources, with development meeting community and market expectations.
- Tourism planning can be effective for both less and more developed tourist destinations. Planning provides guidelines to less developed countries and regions for commencing tourism on the right track. It helps already developed places to improve and expand tourism, and often redirects this sector to be more beneficial.
- Effective planning must be based on sound methodological approaches, with application of a sequential planning process. A basic technique in planning sustainable tourism is carrying capacity analysis which, although

far from being a perfect analytical tool, provides invaluable guidelines in establishing appropriate types and levels of development for an area.

- Much emphasis is now being given to development of quality tourism. This concept implies protecting the environment, maintaining cultural identity and integrity and achieving a high level of tourist satisfaction, while still generating substantial economic benefits.
- Many possible forms of tourism exist, and they are increasing. A tourism area should consider all these forms of tourism, and select the combination that is most suitable for the environment, society and economy. The most appropriate forms of tourism may also change through time for a particular area.
- Some basic planning principles are applicable in all tourism areas. These principles include establishing tourist gateways, staging areas and tourism zones, clustering attractions and staging development. Adequate transportation facilities are essential to provide proper access to the country or region and convenient travel within the tourism areas.
- Other infrastructure for tourism – water supply, electric power, sewage and solid waste disposal, and telecommunications – must be properly developed in order to provide adequate facilities and services for tourists and prevent environmental problems arising.
- Marketing and product development go hand-in-hand, and must be carefully coordinated to achieve successful tourism development. Tourist markets are becoming increasingly fragmented, and a diversity of imaginative tourism products is being developed.
- Community involvement in tourism is now being recognized as essential. Various successful techniques have evolved to achieve local participation in tourism, and bring direct benefits of tourism to communities.
- Emphasis is now being given to integrating tourism into national, regional and local economies. Techniques for enhancing the economic benefits of tourism, without creating environmental or social problems, are now better understood and being refined.
- Environmental and socio-cultural considerations in tourism can be analysed and programmed in a systematic manner. Much attention is now being given to integrating tourism into the local environment and society.
- Effective approaches for implementation must be emphasized in the planning and development process. Implementation requires not only procedures and techniques, but also political commitment and strong leadership. Adequate financial resources are essential, but many approaches can be applied to secure the necessary funding.
- Carefully coordinated short- and medium-term development programming, that includes both actions to be taken and projects to be developed, is one of the fundamental ways to implement plans.
- Demonstration or pilot projects can be an excellent means of showing

how new forms of tourism and development approaches can work. Such projects also provide the opportunities to refine approaches and techniques.

- Organizational structures for tourism must be carefully established, with emphasis on coordination among government agencies and between the public and private sectors. Public–private sector coordination is an essential ingredient in successful implementation.
- Investment incentives – and disincentives – can be a very useful technique to implement development strategies. However, incentives should be applied on a selective basis and modified through time based on changing circumstances.
- All types of education and training are essential for successful tourism, and must be carefully planned and programmed. Persons working in the many aspects of tourism must be properly trained. The general public and people living in tourism areas must be educated about tourism. Tourists must be informed about their destination – its geography, history, cultural patterns and society – and be encouraged to respect it.
- The national and regional governments must often take the initiative in setting development and quality standards for tourism development, in order to ensure that the actual development is implemented properly. However, the local tourism area governments should also be involved in setting and applying appropriate standards.
- Continuous monitoring and management of tourism are essential. Monitoring techniques and procedures should be established early in the development process, and applied to both plan implementation and the on-going progress of tourism. Problems and changing circumstances inevitably arise in tourism development, and monitoring can detect these at an early stage so that appropriate action can be taken. Effective management of tourism is a continuing function and the responsibility of both the public and private sectors.

Tourism planning follows fairly definite procedures and principles, but it is also a continuous process. It involves some experimentation to determine the best specific approaches to be applied in each area. Also, as demonstrated in these case studies, much can be learned from what is being done elsewhere in the world. Although kept reasonably flexible, approaches must still reflect such basic principles as achieving sustainable development, respecting cultural values and spreading economic benefits.

Selected references

This list of references includes the few books which are available specifically on tourism planning, as well as other publications which have sections on planning and development or relate to certain aspects of tourism planning. Some books on tourism marketing are also listed, as are a few basic references on the environmental planning approach. Most of these references are currently in print and others are available in libraries. This list is not intended to be a comprehensive one which covers the entire field of tourism.

Ashworth, Gregory and Goodall, Brian (eds) (1990) *Marketing Tourism Places*. London: Routledge

Ashworth, G. J. and Turnbridge, J. (1990) *The Tourist-Historic City*. London: Pinter Publishers.

Boniface, Priscilla and Fowler, Peter J. (1993) *Heritage and Tourism*. London: Routledge.

Bosselman, Fred P. (ed.) (1978) *In the Wake of the Tourist: Managing Special Places in Eight Countries*. Washington, DC: The Conservation Foundation.

Coltman, Michael M. (1989) *Introduction to Travel and Tourism: An International Approach*. New York: Van Nostrand Reinhold.

————— (1989) *Tourism Marketing*. New York: Van Nostrand Reinhold.

Cooper, Chris, Fletcher, John, Gilbert, David and Wanhill, Stephen (1993) *Tourism: Principles and Practices*. London: Pitman Publishing.

De Kadt, Emanuel (ed) (1979) *Tourism: Passport to Development?* New York: Oxford University Press.

Edgell, David L., Jr. (1990) *International Tourism Policy*. New York: Van Nostrand Reinhold.

Edington, John M. and Edington, M. Ann (1986) *Ecology, Recreation and Tourism*. Cambridge: University of Cambridge Press.

Gee, Chuck Y., Makens, James C. and Choy, Dexter J. L. (1989) *The Travel Industry*. (2nd edn) New York: Van Nostrand Reinhold.

Getz, Donald (1991) *Festivals, Special Events and Tourism*. New York: Van Nostrand Reinhold.

Gunn, Clare A. (1988) *Tourism Planning*. (2nd edn) New York: Taylor & Francis.

————— (1988) *Vacationscape: Design of Tourist Regions*. (2nd edn) New York: Van Nostrand Reinhold.

Hudman, Lloyd E. and Hawkins, Donald (1989) *Tourism in Contemporary Society: An Introductory Text*. Englewood Cliffs, New Jersey: Prentice Hall.

Inskeep, Edward (1991) *Tourism Planning: An Integrated and Sustainable Development Approach*. New York: Van Nostrand Reinhold.

Krippendorf, Jost (1987). *The Holiday Makers: Understanding the Impact of Leisure and Travel.* Oxford: Heinemann.

Kuss, Fred R., Graefe, Alan R. and Vaske, Jerry J. *Visitor Impact Management. Vols 1 and 2.* Washington, DC: National Parks and Conservation Association.

Lawson, Fred and Baud-Bovy, Manuel (1977) *Tourism and Recreation: A Handbook of Physical Planning.* Boston: CBI.

Lea, John (1988) *Tourism and Development in the Third World.* London: Routledge.

Lickorish, Leonard, Bodlender, J., Jefferson, A. and Jenkins, C. L. (1991) *Developing Tourism Destinations: Policies and Perspectives.* Harlow: Longman.

Lindberg, Kreg (1991) *Policies for Maximizing Nature Tourism's Ecological and Economic Benefits.* Washington, DC: World Resources Institute.

Lindberg, Kreg and Hawkins, Donald E. (1993) *Ecotourism: A Guide for Planners and Managers.* North Bennington, Vermont: The Ecotourism Society.

McHarg, Ian L. (1991) *Design with Nature.* New York: John Wiley & Sons.

McIntosh, Robert W. and Goeldner, Charles R. (1990) *Tourism: Principles, Practices, Philosophies.* (6th edn) New York: John Wiley & Sons.

Mathieson, Alister and Wall, Geoffrey (1982) *Tourism: Economic, Physical and Social Impacts.* Harlow: Longman.

Middleton, Victor T. C. (1988) *Marketing in Travel and Tourism.* Oxford: Heinemann.

Mill, Robert Christie and Morrison, Alastair M. (1985) *The Tourism System: An Introductory Text.* Englewood Cliffs, New Jersey: Prentice Hall.

Morrison, Alastair M. (1989) *Hospitality and Travel Marketing.* London: Chapman & Hall.

Murphy, Peter E. (1985) *Tourism: A Community Approach.* New York: Metheun.

Pearce, Douglas (1989) *Tourist Development* (2nd edn) Harlow: Longman.

Ritchie, J. R. B. and Goeldner, C. R. (eds) (1987) *Travel, Tourism and Hospitality Research: A Handbook for Managers and Researchers.* New York: John Wiley & Sons.

Simonds, John Ormsbee (1978) *Earthscape: A Manual of Environmental Planning and Design.* New York: Van Nostrand Reinhold.

Singh, Tej Vir, Theuns, H. Leo and Go, Frank M. (eds) (1989) *Toward Appropriate Tourism: The Case of Developing Countries.* Frankfurt am Mein: Peter Lang.

Smith, Stephen L. J. (1989) *Tourism Analysis: A Handbook.* Harlow: Longman.

Smith, Valene L. (ed.) (1989) *Hosts and Guests: The Anthropology of Tourism.* Philadelphia: University of Pennsylvania Press.

Smith, Valene L. and Eadington, William R. (eds) (1992) *Tourism Alternatives: Potentials and Problems in the Development of Tourism.* Philadelphia: University of Pennsylvania Press.

Weiler, Betty and Hall, Colin Michael (eds) (1992) *Special Interest Tourism.* New York: Halsted Press.

Whelan, Tensie (ed) (1991) *Nature Tourism.* Washington, DC: Island Press.

Witt, Stephen F. and Moutinho, Luiz (eds) (1989) *Tourism Marketing and Management Handbook.* London: Prentice Hall.

World Tourism Organization (1983) *Risks of Saturation or Tourist Carrying Capacity Overload in Holiday Destinations.* Madrid: WTO.

——— (1983) *Study of Tourism's Contribution to the Environment.* Madrid: WTO.

——— (1985) *Methodology for the Establishment and Implementation of Tourism Master Plans at Both the Domestic and Regional Levels.* Madrid: WTO.

——— (1985) *The State's Role in Encouraging the Development of New Destinations and Ensuring Balanced Distribution of Tourist Flows.* Madrid: WTO.

——— (1988) *Quality Control of Tourism Products and Services.* Madrid: WTO.

——— (1992) *An Integrated Approach to Resort Development.* Madrid: WTO.

——— (1993) *Sustainable Tourism Development: Guide for Local Planners.* Madrid: WTO.

World Tourism Organization and United Nations Environment Programme (1983) *Workshop on Environmental Aspects of Tourism*. Madrid: WTO.

———— (1990) *Carrying Capacity in Mountain and Alpine Regions*. Madrid: WTO.

———— (1992) *Tourism Carrying Capacity*. Madrid: WTO.

———— (1992) *Guidelines: Development of National Parks and Protected Areas for Tourism*. Madrid: WTO.

Various tourism journals contain articles related to tourism planning. These include: *Annals of Tourism Research, Journal of Tourism Studies, Journal of Travel Research, Journal of Sustainable Tourism, Tourism Management, Tourism Recreation Research* and *The Tourist Review*.

Index